THE
TRANSFORMED
LIFE

DISCOVER HOW TO LIVE
FROM THE INSIDE OUT

John R. Carter

THE
TRANSFORMED
LIFE

DISCOVER HOW TO LIVE
FROM THE INSIDE OUT

John R. Carter

5 Fold Media
Visit us at www.5foldmedia.com

ISBN: 978-1-936578-40-5

Library of Congress Control Number: 2012948786

Printed in the U.S.A.

DEDICATION

For Robert and Mary Carter,

For living transformed lives before me.

For teaching me that loving Jesus means loving His church.

For leaving an example of Christian integrity I will

spend the rest of my life aspiring to attain.

You will always be my heroes.

ENDORSEMENTS

"One of the greatest challenges people face in today's culture is *how to connect*. In a distracted, disrupted, and rapidly transforming world, how do we meaningfully engage with others, ourselves, and God? That's why *The Transformed Life* by John Carter is so important. It's a road map for experiencing what the Bible teaches about personal transformation. We'll never transform our culture if our lives are not changed first, and this is an owner's manual for biblical change. *The Transformed Life* will help you understand God's priorities for living and have a powerful impact on your future."

Phil Cooke, Ph.D.
Filmmaker, Media Consultant, and Author of *One Big Thing: Discovering
What You Were Born to Do

"John Carter has taken a fresh look at the foundations of the believer's life and developed a tool for guiding a person through true biblical transformation. This book is a great tool for self-development or for use in a class format to guide a person into the transformed life that Christ offers. No life can rise above the potential of its foundation. This book enables a person to lay a foundation that can support an outstanding life."

Mike Cavanaugh
President of Elim Bible Institute, and Vice-President of Elim Fellowship

"In his book, *The Transformed Life*, John Carter has simply, but profoundly, captured the essence of the secrets of walking with God. This book is a must read! The rich treasures found within his writings can be summed up in one sentence contained in the book's introduction: "It is knowing what you can change, and having the skills and courage to manage the direction of change, that determines whether you will overcome your circumstances or become a victim of them!"

Reverend Tim O'Leary

"A disciple-making masterpiece! Through his book, *The Transformed Life*, Pastor John Carter shows us how to practically and intentionally make Jesus' last command our first priority. This powerful tool is biblical, inspirational and thankfully transferable. Leaders, this course will add tremendous value to your ministry culture."

Pastor Joshua Finley
Lead Pastor of Elim Gospel Church, Lima, NY

"In his book, *The Transformed Life*, John Carter offers so much. This book is a study guide on doctrine, an aid to help you know how to recognize a good church, and a map to help you discover, identify, and develop your gifts with insights on how to utilize them effectively—all this and so much more. Honestly, I've never seen such a well-written or more fully developed book of this type before. John Carter has combined his theological knowledge and spiritual gifting to produce a book so comprehensive in scope that it will prove helpful both to new believers and to long-time church members as well. Amazing!"

Rick Renner
Teacher, Author, and Senior Pastor of Moscow Good News Church, Moscow, Russia

"It was a great joy reviewing Pastor John Carter's work, *The Transformed Life*. Three words came to mind as I reviewed this work: intelligent, spiritual, and practical. As John walks readers through biblical truths and insights, he does so in a very intelligent way. He helps readers think through the Scriptures. Second, the work is spiritual. His work honors the integrity of Scripture and the dignity of God. He acknowledges the supernatural aspects of Christian life and God's work in our lives. Third, this work is practical. While John covers theological issues very well, he always brings the reader to a solid, practical application in one's life. I believe pastors will be very eager to put this great tool into the hands of believers to help educate and establish them in the things of God. I believe it will find wide usage among churches that value the authority of Scripture and the development of believers."

Tony Cooke
Bible Teacher and Author of *Grace: The DNA of God* and *Qualified: Serving God with Integrity and Finishing Your Course with Honor*

"In *The Transformed Life*, John Carter becomes an interlocutor—a guide—both challenging and encouraging the reader to go deeper into the truths of God and living life in God. I believe as you read it, you will find answers to questions you may have never asked, and recognition of truths sought after but never expressed. *The Transformed Life* is a book I highly recommend."

Reverend Sharon Stromley
Christian Musical Artist of Sounds from Heaven

"In his book, *The Transformed Life*, John Carter answers the age-old question, what now? Within its pages, every believer, whether new in Christ or a seasoned leader, will find their purpose in the body of Christ! No more wondering! This book is a big deal—scholarly in its approach, yet relatable in its application. Thank you, John. This is long overdue!"

Garylee Syphard
Lead Pastor of The Country Church, Molalla, OR

"For over twenty years, John Carter has been our pastor. Over those two decades, the truths and the principles that he taught us from God's Word, have become this book, *The Transformed Life*. We have both taught from the principles that inspired it and are now seeing lives transformed, as ours were, as a result of it. Believe us when we say that you can build a church on it; we are!"

Joe and Dawn Coudriet
Pastors of Southern Tier Family Life Church, Binghamton, New York

"Since I first met John over twenty years ago, I have been impressed with his passion for, and giftedness in, helping Christ followers grow in faith and everyday living. I personally do not know anyone better at creating resources for systematically empowering believers for service in the church. *The Transformed Life* is proof of that. Whether you use it for personal or group study, I heartily recommend this valuable resource."

Kirby Andersen
Director of Dry Gulch USA, Tulsa, OK

"*The Transformed Life* is not just a great read, but also a spiritual playbook for the believer. If you are eager to grow in your relationship with God, then I seriously recommend that you utilize *The Transformed Life* to navigate you on your journey. Whether you are new in Christ or a seasoned Christian, you will benefit from this book for the rest of your life."

Lee Wilson
Student Ministries Director for Abundant Life Christian Center, Syracuse, NY

CONTENTS

FOREWORD

In a world of instant coffee and everything microwaved, the desire for "instant spiritual growth" has infected the church of Jesus Christ. Many Christians are misdirected by various teachings that promise instant power, success, and prosperity without the process of spiritual formation that leads to spiritual maturity.

They look for supernatural experiences, miraculous turning points, and instant solutions to their problems, but true joy and lasting victory doesn't come that way.

Launching his ministry from our church, The Christian Cultural Center, New York, in 1990, I have watched John and his wife, Lisa, build their church, in levels and stages, learning to adapt and adjust to the many changes and demands of growth. Today they have not only a successful ministry, but a healthy church—built to last.

In *The Transformed Life*, John Carter lays out a systematic approach to spiritual growth and development from a Protestant/Evangelical perspective. This much-needed perspective emphasizes the building blocks for a truly Christian spiritual life.

He begins by establishing the Holy Bible as the sole source of our Christian faith and rule of conduct. It calls for a personal conversionary experience expressed in a lifestyle befitting the honor of a relationship with Christ.

John Carter goes on to emphasize the transforming work of Christ in His incarnation, life, death and resurrection, which afford to the believer the same transforming power in daily life.

Finally, he leads you to your God-given design for service and purpose. The information John shares in this book is not from theory, but from experience.

The result is a well-grounded ambassador for Christ, living a balanced Christian life and spreading the good news of God's grace, ultimately discovering your own personal mission in Christ.

Prepare for a major "life change" through the pages of this book!

Dr. A. R. Bernard
Pastor of Christian Cultural Center, New York City, NY

PREFACE

Before building a house, it is essential that those who are involved in the construction process, along with the family that will occupy the home, agree on several things. First, the builders and the owners typically sit down and discuss what the home will look like, where it will be located, and perhaps most importantly, how it will be constructed. If the owners are expecting a two-story brick colonial with hardwood floors and central air conditioning, but the builders are planning a one-story ranch with inexpensive carpet and ceiling fans, chances are everyone is headed for an unpleasant experience. To successfully build anything, there must be agreement on the end result. Thus, an architect is employed.

The role of the architect is to develop detailed plans that reflect the vision of the owners, while simultaneously directing the actions of the builders. The blueprints specify measurements, materials, and methods. Once an agreement is reached, the architect's plan binds both the owner's vision and the builder's actions to a visible, objective standard. If there is a question, disagreement, or confusion, the blueprints are consulted.

In much the same way, in order to successfully build a vibrant Christian life, we have to establish a standard of authority. What is the source of information upon which we may build our Christian lives? If we claim to be followers of Jesus Christ, what will be our source to understanding His life and teaching? Without establishing a standard of authority, each person is left to create their own path, ignoring the uncomfortable parts of Jesus' teaching, and ultimately building their own faith (which will likely be very different than the faith of their neighbors).

Is this what Jesus intended when He left the earth with the final words in Matthew 28:19-20a, "Go therefore and make disciples of all the nations, baptizing them in the name of the Father and of the Son and of the Holy Spirit, teaching them to observe all things that I have commanded you"? These words do not describe a "do-it-yourself" religion of personal preference, but a prescribed and organized process of carefully instilling the correct and authentic truths that Jesus taught systematically into each believer. He commissioned the disciples to be thorough, exact, and consistent. The only way to accomplish this is by preserving, in some objective way, the truths He intended for the disciples to pass along to believers of every generation.

The Transformed Life is a book about the process God uses to transform hurting, lost, and broken people (like you and I) into His very own children. The book has been crafted for use as an interactive tool for personal growth. Each of the ten chapters are divided into four days of reading, followed by questions and exercises that are designed to help the reader integrate and digest what they are learning. The readings are written consecutively so that individual learners can use the book devotionally to begin a forty-day experience of personal transformation.

This book was also designed for use by small groups, classroom study, and for use as a primary discipleship tool for local churches. When used in this way, it is recommended that each learner/ group member receive a copy of *The Transformed Life* and study one chapter a week for ten weeks. Readings, questions, and exercises should be done by each learner weekly. Then, group leaders, teachers, or facilitators should host a weekly gathering so the learners may discuss the readings, receive instruction, and share their responses to the exercises and questions. This is an outstanding way to build community and encourage systematic learning.

However the book is used, *The Transformed Life* is primarily designed to take the reader on a journey. It has been my passion in writing to create a tool that will enable individuals, groups, and churches alike to experience the genuine transformation that Jesus promised to those who follow Him.

If you are not currently a follower of Jesus Christ, this book will help you to understand the Christian story and to consider the journey of transformation that Jesus promised. If you are a seasoned believer, this book will help you develop a logical understanding of your faith and challenge you to live the life you were designed to live. If you are new to exploring spiritual truths and want to learn how the Bible, the teachings of Jesus, can help you experience positive personal change, *The Transformed Life* is an excellent place to start.

INTRODUCTION

Everything changes. Change is the only aspect of life that happens to everyone. Over time this fact is evident in all that we see. The earth itself is constantly changing, reacting to the forces of energy that move constantly upon it. Our bodies are imperceptibly changing every day. We may not see the changes over a few days or weeks, but over time the changes mount until one day we look into the mirror and realize that we appear very different now from how we were just a year ago. It has been said that the only thing you can count on in this world is that nothing stays the same. The real question is: How does one navigate through all the changes to become a better person, to truly be transformed into the person God has designed you to be?

The process of transformation requires our participation. In fact, many things in life will not change for the better unless we take willful action. It is knowing what you can change, and having the skills and courage to manage the direction of change that determines whether you will overcome your circumstances or become a victim of them.

Positive change is very difficult to achieve. We tend to be set in the way we think, behave, and relate to others, and are often resistant to the kinds of challenges that bring genuine change. To bring about real change in our lives, our habits, our relationships, our finances, our health, and/or our character, we require a force that is equal to or greater than the forces of doubt, fear, skepticism, and mediocrity that constantly erode the edges of our spiritual ambitions and personal desires for excellence. Our flesh and our environment can work against us. We need an inner power that is greater than every excuse, opponent, and external force at work against our transformation.

The Frog Prince

There is a classic children's fable that has been loved for centuries throughout the world. It is the story of a "frog prince." While different versions of the fable exist, the story involves a mysterious frog that has been cursed to live its life in a pond that borders the palace of a great king. One day, the king's daughter discovers and befriends the frog. In the story, a simple kiss from the king's child breaks the curse, transforming the frog into a handsome prince who then lives happily ever after as a member of the king's family.

This story has resonated with generations of readers because it is essentially a story of hope and transformation. It teaches that things are not always as they appear, curses can be broken, and even the dirtiest of creatures can achieve a rich and meaningful life through the transforming power of love.

The Christian story is essentially the same. It also involves a King, His children, and a terrible curse. Deceived by a lying serpent, the children of a Great King fall under a terrible curse that transforms them into weak, broken, and corrupted versions of their former selves. Running from the presence of their Father-King, they make their new home in the swamplands. The curse changes them into fearful, selfish, and hurtful creatures that live under the dominion of the lying serpent who infuses them with his own twisted nature. The serpent teaches them hate for their former King and one another. Having forgotten their true identities, they go on to bear generations of twisted and cursed children—frogs just like themselves.

This King, however, is not content to leave His children under the lying dominion of the wicked serpent. He loves them—in spite of what they have become. One day the King sends His only Son down into the swamplands disguised as a cursed creature. The Son teaches them about their true Father, their rightful home in the palace, and offers them the opportunity to be transformed back into sons and daughters of the King. Enraged, the wicked serpent kills the King's Son, unwittingly releasing a deeper power that breaks the curse and opens the door of escape. When the King's Son returns from death, He offers this door to all who are willing to receive it. The Son's love breaks the curse and transforms the willing frogs instantly into elegant and beautiful children—restoring them to their original design.

The Christian story, however, does not end exactly like the old fable. Lasting transformation, it seems, requires a bit more than a kiss. Generations under the serpent's control, living in mud and croaking at night, had powerfully changed the children's image of themselves. Their hearts had been changed by the Father's love, but they still thought like frogs, acted like frogs, and had an appetite for swamp life.

At night, when the other frogs were carrying on in the swamps, the King's new children would sneak out of the palace window, run down to the pond, and fall back into the behaviors they had known. It turned out that genuine change had occurred in their lives, but changing their thoughts and behavior would only occur over time. It would take a process of transformation.

Thankfully, our King is committed to this process.

CHAPTER ONE

THE WORD OF GOD

CHAPTER ONE
The Word of God

DAY 1: GOD WROTE A BOOK!

The Bible: Our Starting Place

Everything in life has a beginning—a starting place. In this book we are going to study spiritual truths. We are going to learn that God is real and that He has a wonderful plan for our lives. But first we have to find a starting point. When learning about something as important as God, it's important that we choose the right place to begin our journey.

Where can we go to get correct information about God and His purposes? If we assume there is a God who created us, then wouldn't it make sense that He would want us to know about Him? Is there a place where anyone can go to get this knowledge? If there is such a place, then it must be accessible, dependable, consistent, and unchanging. It would have to contain truth that would work for anyone, living anywhere, and not become irrelevant over time.

In Christianity, we believe that everything we need to know about God and His plan for us is found in the pages of the Bible. In fact, we call the Bible, "God's Word." A *word* is a container of thoughts, ideas, hopes, instructions, and expectations. Each of us conveys our desires and feelings through our words. In the same way, God's Word—the Bible—is God's message to us. The Bible contains God's thoughts, plans, and of course, His expectations. That's why the Bible is the starting point in our study of spiritual truth.

> *The Bible contains God's thoughts, plans, and of course, His expectations. That's why the Bible is the starting point in our study of spiritual truth.*

God Chose a Book

When God decided to reveal Himself to the human race, He might have chosen any number of ways to tell us about Himself and His intentions for us. He might have chosen to send His mighty angels in flaming chariots to proclaim His love in a supernatural display. God could have thought of some very impressive and spectacular methods of making Himself known to the men and woman He had created and decided to love. *But God chose a book.*

Of all the ways He might have expressed Himself to the human race, He chose to do so in the form of the written word. Since God decided to use a book to communicate to us, it is vital for us to learn about this book so we can receive its message! In this chapter, we are going to learn about the Bible and why it is the source of our faith and guide to Christian living. We are going to see how God gave us the Bible, why we believe it to be reliable, and most importantly, how we may profit from its message—each and every day.

Why a Book?

- The Lord desired to reveal Himself in a way that was tangible. The Bible is a physical book that we can physically examine to understand spiritual truth.

- To guard us against wrong concepts of God, God placed His message to the world in writing so that it could be clearly understood and translated into many languages. When someone claims something about God that is new, His book may be consulted to make sure it is correct. The Bible keeps us from wandering into wrong thinking.

- The Bible says that God has books in heaven (Psalm 40:7; Daniel 7:10; Revelation 20:12). This means that God Himself is an author; the Bible is the result of God telling us about Himself.

Terms for the Bible:

The Bible
Comes from *ta biblia* and means "the books."[1]

Scripture(s)
Comes from Greek *graphe* and means "that which is written" or "the holy writings."

The Word, God's Word
How Christians often refer to the Bible, because we believe it is God's voice in written form.

How God Gave Us the Bible

> *"Knowing this first, that no prophecy of Scripture is of any private interpretation,* for prophecy [of Scripture] *never came by the will of man,* but holy men of God spoke as they were moved by the Holy Spirit" (2 Peter 1:20-21).

> *"All* Scripture is given by inspiration of God, and is profitable for doctrine, for reproof, for correction, for instruction in righteousness, that the man of God may be complete, thoroughly equipped for every good work" (2 Timothy 3:16-17).

The Bible tells us very clearly how God brought His book into existence. The Bible says that men wrote as they were moved by the Holy Spirit. Sometimes people ridicule the Bible by saying the Bible is just a book written by men. While it is true that God used people to record His words, God was working in a special way in their hearts and minds to record His thoughts without error. We call this process the *verbal* (spoken) *plenary* (every word) *inspiration* of Scripture. *Verbal plenary inspiration*—this means that the words in the Bible contain the complete message spoken by God written down through the people He had chosen.

---

1. *Webster's Collegiate Dictionary*, s.v. "Bible."

> *Because the source of the Scriptures is God Himself, the Bible speaks with divine authority that is binding upon the hearts of all true followers of Jesus.*

God called men, one by one, to the tops of mountains, into lonely deserts, by the rivers of great cities, as they slept upon their beds. He spoke to them, and told them to write down what He said. And they did (Exodus 17:14; Deuteronomy 27:8; Isaiah 8:1; Jeremiah 30:2).

Together, the writings of these holy people became the Bible: the greatest book on earth. Since the Bible is a book that addresses all the basic questions and challenges of life on earth, Christians consider its teachings to be the only authoritative source for faith, and a reliable guide to daily living. Because the source of the Scriptures is God Himself, the Bible speaks with divine authority that is binding upon the hearts of all true followers of Jesus.

ORIGINS AND ACCURACY

The Bible Testifies of Its Own Divine Origin and Accuracy

The thirty-nine books of the Old Testament were used by Jesus and the apostles as their Scriptures. Jesus quoted from the Old Testament many times and often acknowledged the human authors while simultaneously attributing their words to God Himself (Matthew 12:40). Because the Old Testament spoke of a coming Messiah who would be the Son of God, the early followers of Jesus recognized Him as the fulfillment of Old Testament prophecy.

> "Philip found Nathanael and said to him, 'We have *found Him of whom Moses in the law, and also the prophets, wrote*—Jesus of Nazareth, the son of Joseph'"
> (John 1:45).

Jesus taught that the Old Testament contained much information about Him and that if the people would study it, they would recognize Him as the promised Messiah. At some point in your walk with Jesus, you can look these prophecies up.

> "For if you believed Moses, you would believe Me*; for he wrote about Me.* But if you do not believe his writings, how will you believe My words?" (John 5:46-47).

Jesus plainly stated that the Bible was actual history written about real events and places. Today, it is popular to think that because the Bible is an ancient book with amazing stories of supernatural events, the things recorded in it are not literally true. Some people, for example, claim that Adam and Eve never existed, that Moses did not write the Law, that Jericho never existed, or that Jonah was only a "fish story" and cannot be taken literally. However, the Jews of Jesus' day never thought of them as anything other than real history. Jesus attributed all of the first five books of the Bible, also referred to as the Pentateuch, to Moses (Matthew 8:4). He said that Isaiah wrote the entire book of Isaiah, that David and Solomon were real people, and that Jonah really did spend three days and nights in the belly of a great fish! In fact, Jesus declared that not one pen stroke of the Old Testament would pass away or be lost, even into eternity (Matthew 5:18). That is a pretty strong case for taking the Bible seriously.

Peter called Paul's letters Scripture (2 Peter 3:15-16), indicating that all early Christians recognized that the letters of the New Testament contained the same anointing and authority as those in the Old Testament. This means that the first century believers viewed those letters, Gospels, and the rest of the New Testament as it was written, the same way they viewed the Old Testament body of Scripture.

The final book of the New Testament was written by the last surviving apostle chosen by Jesus—the Apostle John. At nearly one hundred years of age, Jesus appeared to John while he was in exile on the island of Patmos. His vision of Jesus and of the events that would occur at the end of time finished the revelation of God's Word. By the end of the first century, the New Testament Scriptures were completed.

The Miracle of the Bible

Between 1946 and 1956, the Dead Sea Scrolls were discovered in a series of twelve caves on the West Bank of the Dead Sea near Jerusalem. These scrolls contained hundreds of ancient copies of the Scriptures and commentaries on the Bible from before the time of Jesus. One of the most important documents discovered was an intact scroll of the book of Isaiah. At that time, many Bible critics claimed that Isaiah could not have been written hundreds of years before Christ since it prophesied many things about Jesus with such accuracy. They claimed that Isaiah had to have been changed over the years since it had been copied so many times. However when the copy of Isaiah from the Dead Sea was laid next to the copies of Isaiah we had, it was virtually identical! Word for word, the copy of Isaiah from the Dead Sea Scrolls said the same thing as the copies from years later. God is faithful to keep His Word!

One of the most remarkable facts about the Bible is its accuracy. Today we have thousands of ancient copies of the Scriptures in many languages that have been preserved in various places all over the world. When all these copies are placed together, they are virtually identical. Ninety-five percent of the manuscripts of the Bible are identical in every way. The five percent that vary are the result of minor differences in word order, omissions, and easily identified variations made during the tedious process of hand copying. However, because we have so many ancient copies, we are able to discover and correct these slight changes. Most importantly, the small percentage of variation we have in the manuscripts has no impact on the understanding of the text and does not change its meaning. There is no other ancient book with such a remarkable record of accuracy and consistency.

THE TWO NATURES OF GOD'S WORD

In order for communication to occur between two people, there must be both a message and a means to communicate it. The message is the *content*; the means is the *container*. God's Word follows this pattern. There are two distinct aspects of the Bible that must be considered if we are going to fully appreciate it. The first is the physical—the container—and the second is the spiritual—the content.

The physical aspect of the word is the written book. As already mentioned, God spoke His Word to real men who then transcribed His message. Today we have that message in the form of a written book that we can read and reread as we please.

The spiritual aspect of the Word is the message intended by its Speaker. This living and powerful message contains the heart, will, and intention of the speaker. Jesus told us His words were spirit and life (John 6:63); His very heart toward all mankind is revealed through these marks on paper.

We need the physical so that we can receive the spiritual. It is only when we think and reflect on the message that we actually connect with the Author. This is why *we begin studying God's Word by looking at the physical nature of the Bible*. We need to examine the book so that we can break open the container and receive the message that God placed inside it. By understanding the book itself—the characters which form words, sentences, chapters, and forms of literature—we can discover the message that God has placed within it. Over the next few days we will examine the physical and spiritual dimensions of God's Word.

DAY 1 EXERCISES

1. Imagine you have a child from whom you are going to be separated. The only thing you can leave is letters. As a human parent, what kind of letters would you want to write? What important ideas would you want to leave behind for your offspring? Write a note in the space provided below.

_____

_____

_____

_____

_____

_____

2. Through verbal plenary inspiration, God is the author of the Bible via the pens of men. It takes faith to accept the Bible's words as a record of God's thoughts toward us—a record without error. What is the definition of *verbal plenary inspiration*?

_____

_____

_____

_____

3. In the mid-1800s, people considered many stories as myths or fairy tales that really happened. This included Homer's account of the city of Troy as well as the biblical cities of Ur and Jericho. In the 1870s a man named Heinrich Schliemann decided to look for Troy, according to the clues in Homer's book, *The Iliad*. People thought him a fool to use a child's story book as a map. But over time he found it! This encouraged others to do the same using the Bible. Since then, several fabled cities have been discovered—Ur and Jericho among them. Knowing that the Bible is real history, what Bible stories are so amazing that most unbelievers would think they are fairy tales?

_____

_____

4. According to the reading, from what source does the Bible's authority come?

_____

_____

5. What are the two natures of God's Word?

1. _____

2. _____

DAY 2: THE PHYSICAL NATURE OF THE WORD

peech occurs through a physical process. Air moves over vocal cords, generating sound waves that are released through our mouths. The sounds are carried to the human ear, which captures the vibrations that the brain deciphers. This physical process describes the *means* by which the message of the speaker is transmitted.

However, the most important aspect of the communication process is the *message itself.* Many people study the Bible from a natural standpoint alone, and never receive the power of the message that God has placed inside it. They treat the Bible just like any other book, but they do not submit their own hearts to the power of God Himself. They read the Bible according to their natural reasoning abilities, so their conclusions are not based on revelation or faith. In doing this, they miss the messages God is speaking through its pages.

> *The Bible is a collection of sixty-six writings, composed by forty-four different authors, over a period of roughly 1,600 years. Each of these writings is called a "book."*

The Bible is a book and therefore we should study the nature of the book that holds God's thoughts. The Bible is a collection of sixty-six writings, composed by forty-four different authors, over a period of roughly 1,600 years. Each of these writings is called a "book." Many of the books in the Bible are lengthy, and contain histories covering long periods of time. Others are collections of poetry or prophecy. Still others are individual letters written to instruct God's people on how to live the Christian life. One of the keys to learning the Bible is to correctly understand its divisions. God instructs us to "rightly divide the Word of truth" (2 Timothy 2:15). The Bible is divided into two main sections: the Old Testament, consisting of thirty-nine books, and the New Testament, consisting of twenty-seven books.

> "Study to shew thyself approved unto God, a workman that needeth not to be ashamed, *rightly dividing the word of truth*" (2 Timothy 2:15 KJV).

The Old Testament

The first section of the Bible is the Old Testament. *Testament* means "covenant" or "promise." The Old Testament is a record of God's work in creation, the entrance of sin into the world, and God's plan to redeem His creation once they had fallen. The Old Testament contains God's promise to save the world from sin by sending a Savior. It covers the period of time from the creation of the world to the time of Israel's return from captivity in Babylon.

> *"Then Joshua wrote these words in the Book of the Law of God. And he took a large stone, and set it up there under the oak that was by the sanctuary of the Lord"* (Joshua 24:26).

> "Then Queen Esther, the daughter of Abihail, with Mordecai the Jew, *wrote with full authority* to confirm this second letter about Purim....So the decree of Esther confirmed these matters of Purim, *and it was written in the book*" (Esther 9:29, 32).

The Old Testament primarily tells the story of God's dealings with His chosen people, Israel. God raised up this special nation to demonstrate His love for sinful humans, to receive and teach His holy law, and to create a human family through which His Son could be born. These books were written in Hebrew, the ancient language of the Jewish people, with small portions written in Aramaic.

The New Testament

The New Testament is the historical record of how God Himself came into this world in the person of His own Son, Jesus Christ. He is the central figure of human history, and the single greatest revelation that God has ever given to us. Jesus Christ is the *living* Word of God and is the human embodiment of the *written* Word, the Bible. The gospel of John proclaims this when it says in John 1:1, "In the beginning was the Word," or *logos,* which is Greek for "word." Later in verse 14 it says, "the Word became flesh and dwelt among us," in reference to Jesus.

> "God, who at various times and in various ways spoke in time past to the *fathers by the prophets,* has in these last days *spoken to us by His Son,* whom He has appointed heir of all things, through whom also He made the worlds" (Hebrews 1:1-2).

> "We proclaim to you the one who existed from the beginning, whom we have heard and seen. We saw him with our own eyes and touched him with our own hands. He is the *Word of life*. This one who is life itself was revealed to us, and we have seen him. And now we testify and proclaim to you that he is the one who is eternal life. He was with the Father, and then he was revealed to us" (1 John 1:1-2 NLT).

The New Testament tells the story of Jesus' life, teachings, miracles, death, and resurrection. It further gives the history of the church He founded, and how it brought His message into the entire world. The New Testament ends with a book of prophecy that reveals what will happen on the earth at the end of time, and how God will ultimately confront and defeat every form of evil and restore peace to the universe.

The New Testament consists of twenty-seven books written by eight authors over a period of roughly fifty years. The majority of the New Testament is written by eyewitnesses of Jesus, either during His life or after His resurrection, who tell of Christ's impact on the world and the founding of His church.

It begins with the stories of God's Son, Jesus Christ, coming into our world, and a record of His teachings, death, and resurrection. These are called the Gospels. The Gospels are followed by the book of Acts, a history of the church Jesus founded, and how it grew. The other half of the New Testament is a series of letters written to followers of Jesus who were active members in local churches throughout the Roman Empire during the first century. These letters are crucial writings in the Bible because they help us apply the meaning of Christ's teachings in the Gospels. They also bring more depth of understanding to the promises God made in the Old Testament to send a Savior. The final book in the New Testament, Revelation, is a book of prophecy and contains powerful messages to the Christian churches throughout the ages, as well as predictions and warnings about the events that will bring Jesus Christ back to the earth in the last days.

The New Testament was originally written in Greek because it was the primary language spoken throughout the world. The Greek language was an invaluable tool used to spread the message of Jesus quickly and effectively.

The earliest followers of Jesus taught the gospel by using the Old Testament. This is important because it shows us that the teaching of Jesus is found throughout the Old Testament. The first Christians successfully preached about Jesus Christ using the Old Testament alone. This is possible because the Old Testament is the New Testament *concealed*, where the New Testament is the Old Testament *revealed*. It was only after several decades that the New Testament letters and Gospels were recorded and available for Christians to use.

The first book of the New Testament written was the letter of James. Afterward, Paul wrote many letters to the churches he had established. These letters were written between 48 AD and 62 AD. Paul taught the churches to receive his letters not as the word of man, but as the Word of God. Later, Paul specifically said that God had given him the special assignment to complete, or fulfill, the Word of God. In other words, he knew that what he was writing was specially anointed by the Holy Spirit as divine Scripture.

> "For this reason we also thank God without ceasing, because when you received the word of God which you heard from us, you welcomed it *not as the word of men, but as it is in truth, the word of God,* which also effectively works in you who believe" (1 Thessalonians 2:13).

> "Whereof I am made a minister, according to the dispensation of God which is given to me for you, *to fulfil the word of God"* (Colossians 1:25 KJV).

Along with these apostolic letters, considered to be Scripture, the first eyewitness biographies of Jesus' life were recorded as early as 60 AD. These Gospels were the written firsthand accounts of those who had walked with Jesus (Luke 1:1-2).

> "And consider that the longsuffering of our Lord is salvation—as also our beloved *brother Paul, according to the wisdom given to him, has written to you,* as also in all his epistles, speaking in them of these things, in which are some things hard to understand, which untaught and unstable people twist to their own destruction, as they do *also the rest of the Scriptures"* (2 Peter 3:15-16).

> "And truly Jesus did many other signs in the presence of His disciples, which are not written in this book; but *these are written that you may believe that Jesus is the Christ*, the Son of God, and that believing you may have life in His name" (John 20:30-31).

"Many people have set out to write accounts about the events that have been fulfilled among us. They used the eyewitness reports circulating among us from the early disciples. Having carefully investigated everything from the beginning, I also have decided to write a careful account for you, most honorable Theophilus, so you can be certain of the truth of everything you were taught" (Luke 1:1-4 NLT).

Learning the Books of the Bible

When memorizing the books of the Bible, it is helpful to learn them by working on each section one at a time. Many people become overwhelmed at first by the idea of memorizing such unfamiliar names. But actually the vast majority of students discover it is much easier than they imagined, especially when they do it one section at a time. The benefit of this discipline will last your whole life, and will greatly help you in locating passages of Scripture when they are referenced in church or when ministering to others. Remember, the more you know about the natural aspects of the Bible, the easier it will be to discover the spiritual message it contains! The books of the Bible have been listed on pages 30-31 for your convenience.

DAY 2 EXERCISES

1. There are many methods to learn the books of the Bible. Here are a few:

   • Write them down and read through them. Erase one every time you finish the list until there are none left. Keep at it until you know them all.

   • Flip through your Bible daily, reading the names of the books as you go.

   • See how fast you can locate a Scripture. Get a varied list, mix it up, and go!

   • Memorize the books in sections (refer to pages 30-31).

2. One of the keys to learning the Bible is to:

   _____

   _____

3. The "minor" prophets weren't minor at all! We think of "minor" as lesser, but that's not what they mean when they talk about the minor prophets. They are named that only because their books are shorter; they are not less important. Since there are twelve of them, they are also known as the "Book of the Twelve." Make a list of the Book of the Twelve here. (Writing is remembering!)

   1. _____   7. _____
   2. _____   8. _____
   3. _____   9. _____
   4. _____   10. _____
   5. _____   11. _____
   6. _____   12. _____

4. How many books are in the Bible? _____ How many are in the Old Testament? _____ How many are in the New Testament? _____

5. What is the primary story of the Old Testament?

   _____

   _____

6. What is the primary story of the New Testament?

   _____

   _____

Old Testament

1. Five Books of the Law

(Creation – 1800 BC)
> Genesis
> Exodus
> Leviticus
> Numbers
> Deuteronomy

2. Twelve Books of History

(1800 – 412 BC)
> Joshua
> Judges
> Ruth
> 1 & 2 Samuel
> 1 & 2 Kings
> 1 & 2 Chronicles
> Ezra
> Nehemiah
> Esther

3. Five Books of Wisdom

(Written between 1010–930 BC, except Job, which was written before Moses' time, around 2000 BC)
> Job
> Psalms
> Proverbs
> Ecclesiastes
> Song of Solomon

4. Five Major Prophets

(Written between 740-545 BC)
> Isaiah
> Jeremiah
> Lamentations
> Ezekiel
> Daniel

5. Twelve Minor Prophets

(Written between 840-410 BC)
> Hosea
> Joel
> Amos
> Obadiah
> Jonah
> Micah
> Nahum
> Habakkuk
> Zephaniah
> Haggai
> Zechariah
> Malachi

New Testament

1. Gospels
(Eyewitness Biographies of Jesus Christ)
    Matthew
    Mark
    Luke
    John

2. History
(How God Established His Church)
    Acts of the Apostles

3. Paul's Epistles
(Paul's Messages—Letters—to Local Churches)
    Romans
    1 & 2 Corinthians
    Galatians
    Ephesians
    Philippians
    Colossians
    1 & 2 Thessalonians
    1 & 2 Timothy
    Titus
    Philemon

4. General Epistles
(Messages to Christians by Various Apostles)
    Hebrews
    James
    1 & 2 Peter
    1, 2, & 3 John
    Jude

5. Prophecy
(The End-Time Prophecy of John)
    The Revelation of Jesus Christ

DAY 3: THE SPIRITUAL NATURE OF GOD'S WORD

Living and Powerful

I t is helpful to know how the Bible was compiled. We must remember God's Word is so much more than a book full of words like any other book. It is alive with God's Spirit and full of His power. When we approach the Bible with faith, God speaks through its words to give us instruction, direction, and encouragement for our daily lives. The Bible says that the whole Bible was given by the direct inspiration of God and is profitable for teaching, correction, spiritual training, and instruction on how to live rightly.

> "For the word of God is living and powerful, and sharper than any two-edged sword, piercing even to the division of soul and spirit, and of joints and marrow, and is a discerner of the thoughts and intents of the heart" (Hebrews 4:12).

God's Word is *anointed by the Holy Spirit*
The words of the Bible were inspired by the Holy Spirit, and therefore carry His anointing. Jesus declared that His words were spirit and life (John 6:63).

God's Word is *filled with power*
The Lord's words carry the full authority and power of the One who spoke them. God used His words to create the world (John 1:1-3), and continues to sustain all of creation by the power of His Word. This means that when we believe God's Word, it has the power to transform our lives and our circumstances (Hebrews 11:1; 1:3).

Eternal

Because it came from God Himself, the Bible has an eternal nature to it. It is both permanent and unchanging. Jesus taught that the Scriptures will never pass away (Matthew 5:18; 24:35).

God's Word is *Permanent*
It cannot be altered nor can anyone add to it.

> "My covenant I will not break, nor alter the word that has gone out of My lips" (Psalm 89:34).

God's Word is *Relevant*
Though it is an ancient book, its truths are always fresh and meaningful to every generation. While many of the cultural and historical references in the Bible require further study to fully appreciate, the truths contained in the Bible apply to all humans across time.

> "For the Lord is good; His mercy is everlasting, and His truth endures to all generations" (Psalm 100:5).

> "*For ever*, O Lord, *thy word is settled* in heaven. Thy faithfulness *is unto all generations*: thou hast established the earth, and it abideth" (Psalm 119:89-90 KJV).

> *We must remember God's Word is so much more than a book full of words like any other book. It is alive with God's Spirit and full of His power.*

God's Word is *Complete*

We do not need any additional holy books or writings to understand everything we need to know about God. He has given us a full revelation of Himself and His plan of salvation. There are no other writings outside of the Bible that are equal to its authority or add to its content. There are books that help us in our walk with the Lord, but none of them carry the authority of Scripture or could ever take its place.

> "But you must continue in the things which you have learned and been assured of, knowing from whom you have learned them, and that from childhood you have known the Holy Scriptures, which are able to make you wise for salvation through faith which is in Christ Jesus. All Scripture is given by inspiration of God, and is profitable for doctrine, for reproof, for correction, for instruction in righteousness, that the man of God may be complete, thoroughly equipped for every good work" (2 Timothy 3:14-17).

God's Word is *Reliable*

We may count on its accuracy and expect God to act on His promises every time.

> "'All flesh is as grass, and all the glory of man as the flower of the grass. The grass withers, and its flower falls away, but the word of the Lord endures forever.' Now this is the word which by the gospel was preached to you" (1 Peter 1:24-25).

Effective

With God Himself standing behind His Word, it always produces the effect it was sent to accomplish. The prophet Isaiah said that God's Word always produces what He intends.

> "It is the same with my word. I send it out, and it always produces fruit. It will accomplish all I want it to, and it will prosper everywhere I send it" (Isaiah 55:11 NLT).

Wherever the Bible is taught, preached, prayed, and spoken, it has an effect.

The Immediate Effects of God's Word

The Word always has an immediate effect on those who hear it. It produces comfort, conviction, encouragement, faith, and strength in the hearts of those who receive it. It also has an effect on those who do not receive it. The Word can harden, anger, judge, and repel those who resist its truth. We must understand that no one is unchanged by hearing the Word. They will respond with either faith or rejection. This is why God's Word causes so much controversy on the earth. It stirs immediate responses wherever it is sent.

The Long-Term Effects of God's Word

Because God's Word is alive, it has a sustained impact on the people and places it touches. The Word of God grows in its effects over time. The more we apply the Word to our lives, the greater it grows in power and influence. When Paul went to the city of Ephesus, he began teaching the Word day and night to just a few spiritually hungry men (Acts 19:1-6). Soon the Holy Spirit began to perform outstanding miracles of healing, and deliverance from demon power. So many people were impacted over the course of two years that the whole city and surrounding region became filled with new Christians. And so many lives were changed that the primary industry of idol making in Ephesus was impacted because people stopped worshipping other gods! Acts 19:20 tells us why this happened: "So the word of the Lord grew mightily and prevailed." Never underestimate the long term effects of the Word of God.

God Watches Over His Word

One of the most important truths we can know about the Bible is that God Himself stands behind every word (Jeremiah 1:12). The Prophet Jeremiah said that God is watching over His Word to perform it. This means that God has obligated Himself to do what He said in the Bible. This truth alone should give every believer a strong motivation to learn the Bible and claim its promises. He has not obligated Himself to act on anything but His written Word. The Lord strongly desires to do what He promised and is waiting for people who will put His Word to work in their lives.

DAY 3 EXERCISES

1. What are the four eternal attributes of God's Word?

    1. _____

    2. _____

    3. _____

    4. _____

2. What are the immediate effects of God's Word?

    _____

    _____

3. What are some long-term effects of God's Word?

    _____

    _____

4. The longest chapter in the Bible is Psalm 119 (176 verses). Each verse celebrates the benefits of God's Word. Select three verses from this chapter and list the benefit each one highlights.

    1. _____

    2. _____

    3. _____

5. Our problems find their help in the Word of God. Within its pages, God provides words of help and encouragement that have the capacity to be planted and grow in our hearts. Write down the verses below that are God's answers to the following problems we face.

    • Anxiety or worry (Philippians 4:6-7)

    _____

    _____

    • Fear (Psalm 57:1-3)

    _____

    _____

    • Financial need (Philippians 4:19)

    _____

    _____

    • Insecurity (Colossians 3:1-3)

    _____

    _____

    • Disease (Isaiah 53:5 or Psalm 103:3)

    _____

    _____

DAY 4: HOW TO BENEFIT FROM THE WORD

Understand the Unity of God and His Word.

Everything God does in the earth and in our lives, He does through the agent of His Word (Hebrews 1:1-4).

God is One with His Word

Because the Bible comes from the heart of God, God and His Word are one. The attitude and respect we show to God's Word is a reflection of our attitude towards God Himself. You cannot have a casual attitude towards the Word of God and claim to respect God. How you treat the Word of God is how you treat God.

> *"He who rejects Me, and does not receive My words,* has that which judges him—the word that I have spoken will judge him in the last day. For I have not spoken on My own authority; but the Father who sent Me gave Me a command, what I should say and what I should speak. And I know that His command is everlasting life. Therefore, whatever I speak, just as the Father has told Me, so I speak" (John 12:48-50).

> "He who does not love Me does not keep My words; and the word which you hear is not Mine but the Father's who sent Me" (John 14:24).

> "For whoever is ashamed of Me and My words, of him the Son of Man will be ashamed when He comes in His own glory, and in His Father's, and in the holy angels" (Luke 9:26).

We Must Pass the Test Adam Failed in the Garden

When God created Adam and Eve, He established His relationship with them on the basis of His Word (Genesis 3:1-5). He gave them promises and blessed them with all that was good. He also warned them about what would happen if they touched the tree that He had forbidden. He gave them His word on that. When Satan entered the garden, he immediately endeavored to get Eve to doubt God's Word. "Did God say that you would die? You will not die," he said. It was Eve and Adam's choice to disregard the Word of God, which separated them from God.

Our test each and every day is whether or not we will believe and act upon His Word. If we desire to please and honor God, we must obey and honor His Word.

> *The Word is spiritual food. Just as our natural bodies require food to live and grow, so our spiritual being requires the Word of God to grow and reach its potential.*

Plant the Seed of the Word in Your Life

Jesus taught that the Word of God is sown as a seed (Mark 4:14). Seeds must be planted in the right soil and given time to germinate and grow. Each time we receive the Word of God, we are planting it as a seed in our hearts. Everything God does begins as a seed, and grows into an experience.

> "[God's kingdom] is like a mustard seed which, when it is sown on the ground, is smaller than all the seeds on earth; but when it is sown, it grows up and becomes greater than all herbs, and shoots out large branches, so that the birds of the air may nest under its shade" (Mark 4:31-32).

The Full Harvest is Present in the Seed
A seed contains within itself the full DNA blueprint of its future potential. The full grown oak tree is present in the acorn before it's ever planted.

The Seed is Dormant until It is Sown
It has been discovered that seeds nearly two thousand years old have been able to produce life when properly planted in today's modern soil. This proves that a seed cannot reproduce until it is properly planted.

As long as the Bible sits on our shelves or coffee tables, it will produce nothing in our lives. Often, when we first hear the Word, it may seem as if its promises are distant and impossible. Our natural circumstances and feelings do not give any evidence that what the Bible says about us is true. However, as we meditate upon the Word and confess it with our mouths, the seed begins to change. They take root inside our hearts and, over time, produce results.

The Word Must be Mixed with Faith
Just reading and listening to the Word alone will not benefit us if we do not believe and act upon it. The Bible says that the Word that was preached to Israel in the wilderness did not profit them because they did not mix it with faith (Hebrews 4:1-3).

The Seed Reproduces after Its Own Kind
God set in motion in Genesis the law of seedtime and harvest. He ordained that all living things—human, plant, and animal—contain seed within itself that reproduces after its own kind. Within each seed is not only the power to reproduce a copy of itself, but the force of multiplication. Within a grain of corn are hundreds of grains of corn. Within Adam was the seed for reproducing not just one human, but the entire human race. So it is with God's Word. It contains God's seed and has the power to reproduce God's promises and blessings in our lives, our families, and our world.

> "And the earth brought forth grass, the herb that yields seed according to its kind, and the tree that yields fruit, whose seed is in itself according to its kind. And God saw that it was good" (Genesis 1:12).

> "While the earth remains, seedtime and harvest, cold and heat, winter and summer, and day and night shall not cease" (Genesis 8:22).

We Become God's Children by Receiving the Seed of God's Word
When we hear and believe the good news of Jesus Christ, God's own seed is planted in us by the Holy Spirit. This seed begins a change that will free us from the power of sin and bring forth God's own nature in us.

> "Having been born again, not of corruptible *seed but incorruptible, through the word of God* which lives and abides forever" (1 Peter 1:23).

> "By his divine power, God has given us everything we need for living a godly life. We have received all of this by coming to know him, the one who called us to himself by means of his marvelous glory and excellence. And because of his glory and excellence, he has given us great and precious promises. These are the promises that enable you to share his divine nature and escape the world's corruption caused by human desires" (2 Peter 1:3-4 NLT).

Seven Ways to Benefit from God's Word

The Word is spiritual food. Just as our natural bodies require food to live and grow, so our spiritual being requires the Word of God to grow and reach its potential. Jesus said that man does not live by bread alone (natural food), but by every word that proceeds out of the mouth of God (Matthew 4:4). The only way to grow into maturity is by feeding on the Word of God and acting upon it in your life.

> "As newborn babes, desire the pure milk of the word, *that you may grow thereby*" (1 Peter 2:2).

Here are seven ways to make God's Word a part of your life:

1. Read the Bible Daily

Find a daily Bible reading plan that will help guide you through the various sections of Scripture so that you may read the entire Bible in one year. The readings should include both Old and New Testaments passages so that you learn from the entire Bible. When you begin to read, start by praying and asking the Holy Spirit to teach you the truths God has for you that day. Select a time and a place where you can devote at least twenty minutes to uninterrupted and thoughtful reading. Put your phones, devices, and all natural distractions on hold and do your best to create a peaceful and quiet place to learn. Underline the words and passages in the Bible that speak to your heart. Keep a notebook with you to mark down your thoughts and inspirations from your reading, as well as the impressions you receive from the Holy Spirit. This simple daily ritual will do a lot to build the Word of God in your heart.

2. Become a Committed Member of a Bible-Teaching Local Church

Early Christians did not have access to their own Bibles. They gathered multiple times each week with other believers and heard the teaching and preaching of the Word from the pastors, prophets, and evangelists God had placed over them in the local church. The book of Hebrews tells us to regularly assemble together and receive the teaching of the Word. Paul taught that God set ministers in local churches in order to cause believers to grow up into maturity. God designed every Christian to attend a local church where they can receive regular instruction in the Word of God. Believers who ignore this Scriptural teaching leave themselves open to personal deception and the spiritual assault of the Devil.

> "And He Himself gave some to be apostles, some prophets, some evangelists, and some pastors and teachers, for the equipping of the saints for the work of ministry, for the edifying of the body of Christ…that we should no longer be children, tossed to and fro and carried about with every wind of doctrine,

CHAPTER ONE: THE WORD OF GOD | 39

by the trickery of men, in the cunning craftiness of deceitful plotting"
(Ephesians 4:11-12, 14).

A good local church will not just deliver inspiring practical messages or read a few passages of Scripture each week. Find a church that puts the Bible and its teaching as the highest priority. You cannot reach your potential in Christ by reading the Bible on your own. Every believer needs to gather weekly to receive the spoken Word in a great local church.

> "But we request of you, brethren, that you appreciate those who diligently labor among you, and have charge over you in the Lord and give you instruction, and that you esteem them very highly in love because of their work" (1 Thessalonians 5:12-13a NASB).

> "Appreciate your pastoral leaders who gave you the Word of God. Take a good look at the way they live, and let their faithfulness instruct you, as well as their truthfulness. There should be a consistency that runs through us all" (Hebrews 13:7 MSG).

3. Meditate on the Word of God and Commit it to Your Heart

All through the Bible we are encouraged to put the Word of God in our minds, and to meditate upon its truths. When we do this, God's Word gets into our hearts and produces powerful results.

It strengthens our faith. As we feed on the Word, our faith grows in whatever area we are studying. If we study the Word on grace, our faith in God's grace will increase. If we study the Bible on the subject of forgiveness, our faith will grow to forgive others. The same is true for any Bible subject, including salvation, healing, deliverance, guidance, marriage, prosperity, etc. (Romans 10:17).

God lights our path and guides us through the Word. When we put the Word in our heart, the Holy Spirit has something to work with when He speaks to us. Most of the time, God guides His children by speaking through passages of the Bible. The more of the Bible you have in your heart, the more "heavenly vocabulary" God has available to speak to your mind (Psalm 119:105).

The Word that is in our hearts enables us to minister to others. If we do not know the Bible, we are powerless to bring lasting help to other people's lives. Every day God gives us opportunities to help others in prayer or counsel. If we learn the promises of the Bible, we can share them with others and see the power of God operate to change their lives.

> "The only letter of recommendation we need is you yourselves. Your lives are a letter written in our hearts; everyone can read it and recognize our good work among you. Clearly, you are a letter from Christ showing the result of our ministry among you. This 'letter' is written not with pen and ink, but with the Spirit of the living God. It is carved not on tablets of stone, but on human hearts" (2 Corinthians 3:2-3 NLT).

4. Confess the Word of God

There is something powerful about speaking the Word out loud. When we declare the Word, we are releasing its power into our atmosphere and circumstances. God created the universe by speaking. He did not throw a book at the emptiness in order to bring forth light, the earth, the sun and the planets, animals, or man. He spoke them into existence. We have been made in His image and we are the only creatures who have been given the power of speech. God gave humanity the same power that He used to create all things, and then told us to speak His Word. When we face a problem or need our circumstances to change, we must find Bible promises that apply to our need and then declare the Word out of our mouths to the very things that need to change. There are many examples of this in the Bible. Speaking the Word of God releases the power of the written word and creates new realities in our world.

> "Let this book of the law *be ever on your lips* and in your thoughts day and night, so that you may keep with care everything in it; then a blessing will be on all your way, and you will do well" (Joshua 1:8 BBE).

5. Act on the Word to Receive Its Benefits

James 1:22 says that we must be doers of the Word and not hearers only. When we only take in the Scripture, but never act upon it, we become like people who always eat, but never exercise. We become stuffed with spiritual food and soon become complacent and lazy. God wants us to be more than "Word hogs." He wants us to be "Word warriors"—spiritually fit athletes who always endeavor to apply what they are learning. A good rule of thumb is this: always act immediately to apply the Word that you are learning. When you act on the Word, you release its power and God begins to move in your life (Joshua 1:8; Matthew 7:26).

6. Give the Word First Place in Our Lives

The Word must become your highest priority. You cannot claim to have a great relationship with God, but have a casual relationship with His Word. We have to let it take the highest position of honor in our hearts and homes. Since God and His Word are one, the place you give to the Word is the place you give to God. How you treat one is how you treat the other. By giving the Word first place in your life, you give God first place and He will bless you (Psalm 119:1; 112:1). Make Bible reading a part of your home and marriage. Make a habit of reading Scripture to your children when explaining your discipline. The Bible should be in the very center of your life and home.

7. Ask God to Open the Scriptures to Your Heart

The Holy Spirit has anointed the Bible so that every time we read it, God speaks through it to our hearts. While you may not understand everything you read when studying Scripture, look for the parts that do make sense to you. Ask the Lord to enlighten you to see what He is saying in each passage. Then apply those truths to your life. God is always present when His Word is read, spoken, or acted upon. He is watching over His Word to perform it (Jeremiah 1:12). This book is designed to help you understand the Lord by learning what He has said about Himself in His Book—the Holy Word of God. Open up your Bible and release the mighty power of God in your life!

Strong Body, Strong Mind, Weak Spirit

It is possible to develop your mind and body and ignore your spirit! Many people spend a lot of time and attention feeding their minds on television, entertainment, video games, secular music, surfing the web, social networking, and secular media. But they give very little time or attention to feeding their spirit on the Word of God.

Others spend long hours on strict eating plans and exercise routines. They build their bodies and develop their physiques. However, their spiritual bodies are weak and emaciated. They can run many miles, but cannot pray more than five minutes at a time.

Many people spend long hours developing their minds academically. They attend college, read books, and increase their understanding on many subjects, but often ignore their own spirits. They may have a robust knowledge of politics or world events, but know very little of God or His plan for their lives. We must feed on the Word consistently if we desire to grow strong spiritually.

The Study of God's Word is the Responsibility of Every Christian!

The first Christians gathered weekly to worship, receive baptisms and the Lord's Supper, and hear the Scriptures read and taught (1 Timothy 4:13). The pastors and elders of these churches treasured these copies of God's Word, and the only way to receive God's Word was to come to fellowship to hear it. What a blessing it is today to have the complete and accurate record of these holy words in various translations in almost every home. We need to treasure our Bibles and make every effort to study and read them with the help of the Holy Spirit.

> "You have been taught the holy Scriptures from childhood, and they have given you the wisdom to receive the salvation that comes by trusting in Christ Jesus. All Scripture is inspired by God and is useful to teach us what is true and to make us realize what is wrong in our lives. It corrects us when we are wrong and teaches us to do what is right. God uses it to prepare and equip his people to do every good work" (2 Timothy 3:15-17 NLT).

> "For whatever things were written before were written for our learning, that we through the patience and comfort of the *Scriptures* might have hope" (Romans 15:4).

> "Study to shew thyself approved unto God, a workman that needeth not to be ashamed, rightly dividing the word of truth" (2 Timothy 2:15 KJV).

KEYS TO UNDERSTANDING THE WORD

When studying the Bible, there are a few simple principles that we can follow. These principles will help us open our hearts and minds to the Bible.

The Bible is Progressive Revelation

The Bible was written in levels of truth. Just as a child moving through grade school progressively gains more knowledge that builds upon the information previously learned, the Bible gradually builds upon itself from Old to New Testaments. The deepest and most precise knowledge of God is found in the New Testament letters written to the church. These letters shed light back upon the message of Jesus in the four Gospels. The entire New Testament sheds light back upon the Old Testament. We call this progressive revelation.

> *The Old Testament is the New Testament concealed, where the New Testament is the Old Testament revealed.*

Jesus told His disciples at the end of His life that even after three-and-a-half years of teaching, the deeper truths were yet to be revealed when the Holy Spirit would be poured out. This meant that the truths in the Bible would be further illuminated through the light and revelation of the Holy Spirit. Jesus said that the promised Holy Spirit would lead us into all the truth (John 16:13). He would bring deeper revelation to the teachings of Jesus in the Gospels, and the Epistles of the New Testament would reflect that understanding.

Consider the Audience

When reading the Bible we need to ask ourselves, "Who is being addressed?" *While all of the Scripture is written for you, not all of it is written to you.* There are three primary audiences Scripture speaks to (1 Corinthians 10:32):

1. The Jews

2. The Gentiles (or the world)

3. The church of God

The third group is made up of members of the first and second groups who have come to believe on Jesus Christ for their salvation. When approaching the Bible, we need to begin with the parts that are written directly *to* the church—the New Testament and the Epistles to the churches.

Develop a Reading Plan

When trying to learn the Bible, many people begin with a method similar to playing a game of darts with a blindfold. They close their eyes, let the Bible fall open and point to something, hoping that God will speak to them. While God is good and will still speak to those people, the best way to learn the Bible is to begin with a Bible reading plan. Another excellent way to learn the Bible is to take one book at a time and study it by reading it through several times in a good study Bible. A study Bible will introduce each book of the Bible and teach you about the historical setting in which it was first written. This information gives you a background to understand the various stories and teachings you will find in each book, and insight into the people the book was originally written to. (Visit www.heartlight.org for a free Bible reading plan.)

Join a Local Church that Emphasizes Strong Bible Teaching

Every believer needs a pastor and a spiritual family where they can be taught the Word of God and discover its truths. A good church will also offer Bible studies so that you can go deeper in your knowledge of God and His Word. The local church is God's gift to each of us and is designed to help us learn Scripture and discover how to apply it to our lives. Once we have established that the Bible is the place where God has chosen to reveal His truth to us, we can begin our journey of discovery.

Beginning Daily Devotions

Set aside half-an-hour daily to read your Bible. This may require you to get up earlier or stay up later, but whenever and however you can, plan it. Begin with the gospel of John and Psalms.

Read a section of John and the Psalms. Put bookmarks in your Bible so you can easily find your place again tomorrow.

Begin this habit with prayer. Take a few minutes to glorify God and ask for His guidance and understanding as you read His Word.

As you are reading, jot down any short prayers you say or any verses that jump out at you in a journal. Journals are available very inexpensively in discount stores or you could use a simple spiral notebook or filler paper in a binder. You could put it on your laptop or blog it! Use whatever means works best for you. Also include any thoughts you have on what you are reading. Continue to use your journal every day.

Take a few minutes after reading Psalm 1 to allow the Lord to fill your mind with a picture of that psalm. Creatively think about what a "tree planted by streams of water" looks like.

DAY 4 EXERCISES

1. Your attitude toward the Word of God is indicative of what?

_____

_____

2. Read Hebrews 4:1-3. What does the Word need to be mixed with in order for it to benefit you?

_____

_____

_____

3. Finish this sentence: This was possible because the _____ _____ is the
New Testament _____, where the _____ _____ is
the Old Testament _____.

4. What three primary audiences does the Scripture speak to?
   1. _____
   2. _____
   3. _____

5. Every believer needs a _____ and a _____ _____
where they can be taught the Word of God and discover its truths.

CHAPTER TWO

THE NATURE OF GOD

CHAPTER TWO
The Nature of God

DAY 1: WHAT WE THINK ABOUT GOD IS IMPORTANT

God is not hiding from you. In fact, He wants you to know Him (John 17:3). He does not just want you to know *about* Him, He wants you to know *Him personally.* God desires to have a personal, intimate relationship with you. Stop and think about that last sentence. What does it mean to you to know that the Creator of the universe wants to share His heart with you? What does that say about God? Maybe even more significantly, what does that say about you?

Perhaps the most astounding and unique teaching of the Christian faith is not the supremacy of God, but rather the love that drives Him to be known by His creation. Numerous religions teach that there is a supreme and all-powerful deity or force that is the source of all things. But only in the Christian faith do we see that this all-powerful being is also a loving, relational, and knowable person.

In His Word, the Lord has spoken about His own nature. The Scripture is often like a diary in which God has recorded His innermost thoughts, desires, purposes, and feelings. Of all the things we could learn by studying the Bible, nothing is more important than learning about the One who authored it.

> *One of the most remarkable characteristics of the Bible is how much God says about Himself in a way that leaves no uncertainty about His nature, personality, attributes, and purposes for our lives.*

Common Ideas about God

It is a common belief today that while all religions appear to be different, they actually are teaching the same truths, and that each of these paths lead to the same God. This statement may sound appealing, but in reality nothing could be further from the truth. On the surface, many religions appear to teach the same things, but in reality they are very different. Actually, while most religions have cosmetic similarities, a close examination will quickly reveal that they are significantly different in their view of reality, God, and the right path to know Him.

While most religions have common truths that are shared by all, it is totally incorrect to say that all religions teach basically the same thing. We are living in a world that has many conflicting ideas about God. While some people see God as an impersonal force that fills the universe,[2] others worship multiple gods—each one with specific abilities and limitations.[3]

---

2. Pantheism, Pan-en-theism, Platonism, Buddhism, Taoism.
3. Poly-theism, Paganism, Hinduism, Wicca, Voo Doo.

In many parts of the world, people believe that god(s) lives in the trees, rocks, and animals, and worship nature as divine.[4] Some faiths teach that each of us is a god in the making,[5] while others say that we once were gods who have somehow become lost in this world and forgotten our true identity.[6] Some people believe that God automatically lives inside of everyone and hell does not exist.[7] Others teach that very few people will ever make it to heaven.[8] A growing number of people today claim that God does not exist at all.[9]

As you can see, these ideas about God cannot all be correct, because these ideas are fundamentally *contradictory*. God either exists, or He does not. He is either the only true God, or He is one of many gods. One of the fundamental laws of the universe is the law of noncontradiction. In other words, two opposite things cannot be true about the same thing at the same time. For example, while it may be both day and night at the same time in different parts of the world, it cannot be both day and night at the same time in the same place in the world.

So then, *we must make a decision* about which claims are true. As Christians, we make our decisions about God's nature and plan for our lives by studying what He has revealed about Himself in the Bible.

> *The way you think about God makes all the difference in the world as to how you will live your life.*

Why We Need to Know the God of the Bible

The Bible, in both the Old and New Testaments, presents a consistent and clear understanding of God. One of the most remarkable characteristics of the Bible is how much God says about Himself in a way that leaves no uncertainty about His nature, personality, attributes, and purposes for our lives.

It is vitally important for us to know what the Bible says about God, so that we do not become deceived by the many popular errors and false doctrines that can cause us to fall into spiritual deception.

1. We Must Guard against Error

Jesus and the apostles warned us to be on guard against false ideas about God. In fact, much of the New Testament was written to correct false concepts of God that were being taught in the churches.

> "Beware of false prophets, who come to you in sheep's clothing, but inwardly they are ravenous wolves....Not everyone who says to Me, 'Lord, Lord,' shall enter the kingdom of heaven, but he who does the will of My Father in heaven"
> (Matthew 7:15, 21).

---

4. Animism, native tribalistic religions.
5. Mormonism, Satanism.
6. Scientology.
7. Universalism, Unitarianism.
8. Jehovah's Witnesses and extreme fundamentalism.
9. Atheism.

"For false christs and false prophets will rise and show great signs and wonders to deceive, if possible, even the elect" (Matthew 24:24).

"Beloved, do not believe every spirit, but test the spirits, whether they are of God; because many false prophets have gone out into the world" (1 John 4:1).

2. All Roads Do Not Lead to the Same God

Jesus never presented Himself or His teachings as a spiritual option that sits as one among many. He never indicated that those who did not believe His message were in anything other than imminent mortal danger of being eternally lost (Luke 13:5; John 3:36; 8:24). He never spoke as if those in other faiths were following an equally valid path. He never gave comfort to those who followed Him saying that their unbelieving relatives would find eternal life apart from accepting Him. He said powerful and radical things about Himself and God that stand in stark contrast to the views of God that are taught by every other world religion—both in His day and our own. He said:

"Jesus said to him, 'I am the way, the truth, and the life. *No one* comes to the Father *except through Me*'" (John 14:6).

"He who believes in the Son has everlasting life; and *he who does not believe* the Son *shall not see life, but the wrath of God abides on him*" (John 3:36).

"He who believes in Him is not condemned; but *he who does not believe is condemned already,* because he has not believed in the name of the only begotten Son of God" (John 3:18).

Therefore, what you believe about God has eternal consequences.

3. Who You Worship Will Determine How You Live

It has been said many times that your thoughts toward God reflect who you really are. We cannot rise above the God we worship. We tend to become like the people we admire and respect. This is especially true when it comes to the things we "idolize"—whether they are movie stars, basketball players, or musicians. Wrong thinking about God can lead us to either a casual, unholy lifestyle, or a rigid, fearful, religious bondage. How you and I see God will determine how we will relate to Him. It will affect how we pray, impact how we live, and determine whether we spend eternity with or without Him. Nothing could be more important for us to learn.

THE CREATOR AND HIS CREATION

The Bible teaches that God created two distinct realms and creatures to populate them: the spiritual realm, and the physical realm. Understanding these two realms is essential because the Bible tells us that as humans, we were designed to occupy both the physical and spiritual realms.

> *We are the only creatures that God has made who have both material and spiritual dimensions at the same time.*

> For through him God created everything in the heavenly realms and on earth. He made the things we can see and the things we can't see—such as thrones, kingdoms, rulers, and authorities in the unseen world. Everything was created through him and for him" (Colossians 1:16 NLT).

THE SPIRITUAL WORLD

Heaven

The Bible teaches that the spiritual world is an invisible dimension that existed before our material world. The spiritual world currently exists alongside our physical world and is very much like the canvas upon which our material world is painted. The first place God created was heaven. It is the dwelling place of God, and all spirits who are in harmony with Him.

Heaven is a real place, and was the pattern God used in making the material world. This means that the things in earth are very similar to the things in heaven. The Bible says there are cities, homes, streets, trees, rivers, seas, creatures, angels, and humans in heaven. There is also a great temple and a throne upon which God sits as King of all things (Psalm 11:4; 103:19; Isaiah 6:1; Hebrews 8:1-5; 11:7, 10, 16; Revelation 21:2).

> "That at the name of Jesus every knee should bow, of those in heaven, and of those on earth, and of those under the earth" (Philippians 2:10).

The Spiritual Realm on Earth

There is also a spiritual dimension on the earth that exists and observes our visible world. This realm is teeming with invisible beings, who are in harmony with God as well as those who are in rebellion against Him. God's enemy, Satan, is an angel who led a great rebellion against God in the ancient past and has been confined to the spiritual dimension on earth for the time being. He has multitudes of spiritual beings called "demons" that followed him in his rebellion and are under his power today. Together, these spirits seek to corrupt the earth and influence humans to resist God and His authority (Ephesians 2:2; Daniel 10:11-21). Yet Satan himself is a created being. This means that he is in no way equal to God. As a created being he is a finite—or limited—creature who is ultimately subject to the authority of God Himself (Ezekiel 28:13-25).

It is important to know that the spiritual realm on earth is also filled with good beings, angels, who are God's servants. These beings were created to serve God and the human race by influencing humans to obey and follow God. They are in a constant state of conflict with the demonic kingdom, but are greater in power and number than the forces of darkness (2 Kings 6:15-17; Hebrews 12:22).

The Spiritual Realm under the Earth

Finally the Bible speaks of a spiritual dimension "under the earth" called hades or "hell." This awful place is a prison for the spirits of humans who have died without receiving

God's saving grace in their lifetimes. Hell is a real place from which God wants to save us. Originally, God created hell as a prison for the rebellious angels and their leader, Satan.

> *Heaven is a real place, and was the pattern God used in making the material world. This means that the things in earth are very similar to the things in heaven.*

THE PHYSICAL WORLD

By now we have seen clearly that God created a spiritual world first, then a physical universe. The visible universe is a wonder to behold and demonstrates the immense variety and creativity of our God.

The Bible says that what may be known about God can be learned by studying what He has made. Creation itself is a signature of the Creator. It tells us that we have a Maker who is astoundingly detailed, imaginative, and a lover of beauty (Psalm 19:1-6; Romans 1:19-20).

Science and Creation

Science is the study of God's creation. The first modern scientists were people who believed in God and sought to study His creation in order to understand Him. In fact, the scientific method itself was developed as a way to properly discover the laws that God created to govern His universe. Today, modern science has largely divorced itself from the Creator by placing the processes of the physical universe over the One who invented them.

It would be the equivalent of studying a beautiful painting in order to understand the artist, but somehow getting lost in the paint. Those examining the painting become so enamored with the paint that they begin to imagine that painting came about of its own accord. Eventually the art students exclude the artist and treat the created piece of art as if it itself was the creator.

Paul said, "Claiming to be wise, they instead became utter fools. And instead of worshiping the glorious, ever-living God, they worshiped idols made to look like mere people and birds and animals and reptiles....They traded the truth about God for a lie. So they worshiped and served the things God created instead of the Creator himself, who is worthy of eternal praise! Amen" (Romans 1:22-23, 25 NLT).

Materialism and Creation

We must never forget that God is the Author and Owner of everything. Materialism is the result of confusing the things God created with God Himself. We often live as if we own our homes, cars, clothes, and careers. People jealously and competitively seek to gain money and things in order to impress others (Psalm 50:10; Haggai 2:8).

Such behavior is a form of idolatry and is deeply offensive to God. He made us, put us on His earth, permits us to breath His air, build homes with His things, and drive in vehicles made from the materials of His creation. Even our bodies belong to God (1 Corinthians

6:20). In reality we don't own anything, but are the temporary "stewards" of everything in life. Someday we will give an account for what we have done with His creation.

THE CREATOR IS SEPARATE FROM THE CREATION

God is Transcendent

When we say that God is *transcendent* it means that He is completely *separate from* and *above* everything He has created. This is an important truth for us to understand because many concepts of God have crept into our culture that have their roots in pagan philosophy. To say that God is transcendent simply means that the artist is not the artwork. The builder is not the building. The writer is not the book. The driver is not the car.

Pagan Concepts of God and Creation

There are several non-Christian and unbiblical ideas about God that should never be confused with the Bible's teaching of God's transcendence.

Pantheism

Pan is the Latin word for "all." Pantheists believe that God IS the universe. Pantheists tend to see God as an all-encompassing force that connects the physical universe. Like the atoms that make up all material things, God is the "life-force" that runs through and connects everything. This view is akin to the concept of "the force" in a popular film—having both a "light" and "dark" side. Pantheism also incorporates the idea that all religions are different ways of following the same God, and all life is in a continuous process of birth, death, and rebirth. Buddhism and Hinduism incorporate this non-Christian philosophy.

Animism

There are different forms of this belief ranging from Native American folklore, to African and Hindu concepts of nature. In this view, God is nature, or inside of nature, in such a way that what you do to nature, you do to God. If you cut down a tree, you cut into God Himself. God is in the rocks, the animals, the flowers, etc. This concept is popularized in many modern movies in which nature is elevated to a divine status. The Egyptians worshipped the sun. The ancient Chaldeans worshipped the moon. While God teaches us to respect His creation, He is never to be confused with His creation. If the whole world were to be destroyed, not one aspect of God Himself would be reduced or lost.

Deism

Many of the founding fathers of the United States shared this non-Christian philosophy. Deists believe that God is a distant and disconnected Creator. In this view, a Supreme Being formed the universe, set it in motion, and then left it alone to evolve or disintegrate on its own. While Deists ascribe correctly to an all-powerful divine being, they incorrectly assume that He has chosen to disengage from what He created, leaving us to fend for ourselves.

Polytheism

This ancient view holds that there are many gods, with varying degrees of power and different personalities, who are primarily self-interested. These deities interact with one another and with humans much like a soap opera—some being benevolent, others being evil. Ancient polytheists used the tales of the gods to explain the phenomenon of the material world, and sought to appease the gods through various forms of worship, and by making sacrifices. Modern polytheists, such as Mormons, teach that the God of our earth was once a man who became God by following the laws of Mormonism. They teach that through strict adherence to Mormon laws, every person may someday become a god themselves and rule their own world.[10] Hinduism holds that there are over three million different gods and goddesses that live in the spirit world and control events on earth. Both of these views are incompatible with the biblical concept of God.

God Cares Personally for Creation

God is present within, and intimately involved with, His creation. While God is not to be confused with the creation He has made, He is not disinterested or distant from it. On the contrary, God is intimately involved with His creation, and loves the universe and the creatures He has made. The psalmist said, "When I consider Your heavens, the work of Your fingers, the moon and the stars, which You have ordained, what is man that You are mindful of him, and… visit him?" (Psalm 8:3-4).

Creation Has Temporarily Fallen into Bondage

It is important, as we study God as Creator, that we also acknowledge that He created earth and delegated its care to mankind. In Genesis 1:26, God said, "Let Us make man in Our image... [and] let them have dominion over...all the earth." By giving humans dominion over the earth, He did not abdicate His ownership or right to rule over all things, but rather He made mankind to rule under His authority as stewards and caretakers. In this way, man was given a lease to live on earth, develop its potential, and enjoy its beauty.

Man, however, broke his dependent relationship with God and submitted to God's enemy, Satan (Romans 8:20). In committing this act of treason, Satan gained dominion over the human race and access to the world. The Scripture says that this event brought creation into bondage, and it became corrupted by sin and death. The earth became a dangerous place when the law of sin and death spread to the rest of creation.

It is important to remember that as beautiful as this world appears to be, it is a shadow of its former state. With Satan's entrance into the human experience, men and women opened the door to every form of evil: Famine, poverty, disease, natural disasters, war, hatred, greed, and injustice are all manifestations of the evil that entered creation as a result of human irresponsibility. We cannot blame God for these things. He created all things good. Yet He also created mankind with the freedom to use or abuse His creation. The problems of this world cannot be placed upon God: It is man who is ultimately responsible before God for the fallen condition of this world.

---

10. See Joseph Smith's *Doctrine and Covenants* 132:20 from the 1976 version.

DAY 1 EXERCISES

1. On the surface, many religions appear to teach the _____ things, but in reality they are very _____.

2. What is materialism? _____

_____

_____

3. What does *transcendent* mean? _____

_____

_____

4. Name a pagan concept of God and why it is different from the Christian worldview.

_____

_____

_____

_____

5. What Scripture reference supports that God gave man ownership of the Earth?

_____

_____

_____

6. Ideas have consequences. One of the ideas prevalent today is that we must all be "open" to everything. We are not allowed to say anything is wrong or sinful; if we do, we are being judgmental and intolerant of others. Jesus was not open to everything; instead, He had clear ideas and absolute standards. He created and loved all people, but came to bring healthy change to their lives. Take a moment to consider how you have changed as a result of knowing Jesus. List some of those changes here.

_____

_____

_____

_____

DAY 2: THE UNIVERSAL ATTRIBUTES OF GOD

God's attributes are the personal qualities He possesses. These are aspects of His being that are essential for us to know. We could call them the features that make God who He is. If we were describing the attributes of a horse, we would use words like solid-hooved, four-footed mammal, vegetarian, strong, fast, etc. These characteristics help us identify the horse from other animals by describing its physical attributes. There are three dimensions that describe God's attributes: universal, primary, and personal.

GOD IS A TRIUNE BEING

Christians believe in one all-powerful God who is manifested in three distinct persons—Father, Son, and Holy Spirit. We call this community of persons the *Holy Trinity* and refer to them collectively as the *Godhead*. This is perhaps the most wonderful mystery that God reveals about Himself. God is one being comprised of three persons. These three persons are distinct individuals who are inseparably connected to each other as one complete being. The right understanding of this revelation is absolutely essential to the Christian life (Matthew 3:16-17; 28:18-19; 1 John 5:7; 1 Peter 1:2).

The Oneness of God

It is important to remember that although we may know, address, and worship each person of the Godhead distinctly, we are never to think that we worship three different "gods." The Father, Son, and Holy Spirit share equally every divine quality and work in perfect union with one another. We serve One God who within Himself is a community of three persons.

The Trinity of God

There are several illustrations that can help us to understand the triune nature of God. A human body is comprised of many distinct parts. Each part has a purpose and place in the body that no other part may occupy. However we do not say that there are many "humans" in the one body, even though each part is fully "human."

The heart pumps blood and is located in the chest; the brain, located in the head, controls thought and every other system of the body. The stomach digests and distributes nutrition throughout the body and is located beneath the rib cage. Each part has a unique function and is interdependent upon the other. Yet, if one were to take a cell from each organ and examine its DNA, at the cellular level its DNA contains the chemical blueprints for the entire body. In other words, the DNA blueprint for the brain is present in the heart. The total composition of the heart is written into each cell of the brain. The blueprint for the entire body is present within *each cell* of the body. So complete is this blueprint that if we had the technology to do so, a complete copy of your body could be cloned from the information encoded in one cell taken from the bottom of your foot or a hair on your pillow.

An egg has three distinct parts—shell, white, and yolk. Each part is still called "egg." Yet when separated, we do not say that there are three eggs. Water has three states—solid, liquid, and gas. Each state looks different than the other and functions uniquely.

On a spring day, one part of a lake may remain frozen from winter, the center may splash with the jumping of fish, and the morning sun may reveal steam slowly rising from the surface. It is not three lakes that we are observing, but three distinct aspects of one single lake. Each part of the lake—water, steam, and ice—are comprised of the same thing, H_2O, even though they each have unique attributes. In much the same way, the three persons of the Godhead share all the qualities and characteristics of God equally, while still possessing distinct roles and functions. These roles distinguish the three persons of the One True God. Following are some of the things that the Bible says about each member of the Trinity.

The Nature of God the Father
When the Bible speaks of God, it is typically referring to the Father. He is the One who planned, ordered, and established all things in creation. As Father, He is the One who sent the Son and the Spirit to redeem mankind, and is the one Source of all things and the One to whom all glory and honor is given (1 Corinthians 8:6 NLT). He once walked upon the earth with the first human parents, Adam and Eve (Genesis 3:8). Since their fall into sin, the Father is seated on the throne of His majesty in heaven. He will someday place His throne on earth and live visibly once again with His people (Revelation 21:3), but only after Satan and sin have been thoroughly removed and His plan of salvation is fully carried out.

The Nature of God the Son
> In the beginning [before all time] was the Word (Christ), and the Word was with God, and the Word was God Himself. He was present originally with God. All things were made and came into existence through Him; and without Him was not even one thing made that has come into being (John 1:1-3 AMP).

The second Person of the Trinity is the central figure of the Christian faith and the Lord of all creation. His name is Jesus. He was known in eternity past as the Living Word (John 1:1; 1 John 1:1-2). The Bible teaches that through Him, the Father made the universe and all that is in it. He is the One who accomplishes and executes what the Father has planned. He was chosen to take a human nature and redeem us from the curse of sin. He carries out the work of salvation that the Father has planned, and is the only way that we may come into a relationship with the Father. The Son appeared on the earth in various ways in the Old Testament, but walked visibly upon the earth when He was made man. Today, Jesus is seated at the right hand of the Father upon a throne in heaven, until He is sent once again by the Father to return to the earth for His church.

> "In these last days spoken to us by His Son, whom He has appointed heir of all things, through whom also He made the worlds; who being the brightness of His glory and the express image of His person, and upholding all things by the word of His power, when He had by Himself purged our sins, sat down at the right hand of the Majesty on high" (Hebrews 1:2-3).

The Nature of God the Holy Spirit
The third person of God reveals and manifests what the Father has planned, and the Son has accomplished and purchased, on our behalf. He is the member of the Trinity who is active

upon the earth today, having been sent by the Father and the Son after Jesus' resurrection (John 15:26). He draws sinners to Jesus through the preaching of the gospel, and changes the hearts of those who believe in Jesus. He gives new life to believers in Christ (Titus 3:5), then empowers, guides, and connects believers together through the local church. The Holy Spirit distributes spiritual gifts and power to each member of the body of Christ so they might serve God through the work of the church (1 Corinthians 12:4-9; Hebrews 2:4). His presence also restrains the forces of darkness at work in the world so that the church may fulfill its mission until Jesus returns (2 Corinthians 13:14; 1 Corinthians 3:16-17).

GOD IS SOVEREIGN

The term *sovereignty* means supreme power and right to rule. When we say that God is sovereign we are saying that He has absolute power and control over everything in heaven and earth. This means that nothing escapes His knowledge or happens outside His will. Not a single molecule in all of creation is able to rebel against God, except with His permission. He is the absolute King of heaven and earth and His sovereign rule is made possible by three distinct characteristics He possesses:

God Can Do Anything

God has the power to do anything He chooses. There is no force, energy, or being, that is greater than God. This is known as *omnipotence*. It comes from two Latin words: *omnius*, which means "in every thing, in every place, in every way"; and the word *potent*, which means "having power." The Bible teaches that God has both the *authority* to do anything He desires and the *ability* to carry it out. Nothing can resist His power and no one can challenge or diminish His authority. All the power in the universe comes from God in some way. God is able to exercise His power without losing any of it. He never becomes depleted, tired, or in need of recharging (Isaiah 40:28).

This is an attribute that belongs exclusively to God as the Sovereign King of all things. His power is what created and upholds everything in the universe (Hebrews 1:3). Scripture says nothing is too difficult for Him (Genesis 18:14; Job 42:2). He has the power to do whatever He has planned and nothing is impossible for Him (Luke 1:37; Isaiah 46:10-11).

> "Ah, Lord God! Behold, You have made the heavens and the earth by Your great power and outstretched arm. There is nothing too hard for You"
> (Jeremiah 32:17).

The Bible does indicate that there are some things God cannot do. His limitations are based on His character—not a deficiency in ability. For example, the Word says it is impossible for God to lie (Titus 1:2). This means that what God has said in His Word is true and He is obligated to perform it. To do otherwise would be to lie—something He is incapable of doing. In addition, He cannot deny Himself. In 2 Timothy 2:13, it says, "If we are faithless, He remains faithful; He cannot deny Himself." This means that once He has saved someone, He joins them to His family permanently. To later deny them salvation would be to deny Himself, regardless of the strength or weakness of their faith. It should bless us to know how committed He is to His Word and His people! The Bible often refers to God as the Almighty for this very reason.

God is Everywhere

You cannot hide from God. There is no place that escapes His watchful eye or powerful hand. This truth is known as God's *omnipresence* (*omni*, meaning "all or everywhere"). When we say that God is omnipresent, it means that there is no place in time and space where God is not personally present and aware. This characteristic of God flows from His all-powerful nature. His omnipotence *enables* His omnipresence. Because God can do anything, He is able to be everywhere.

> "'Am I a God who is near,' declares the Lord, 'and not a God far off? Can a man hide himself in hiding places so I do not see him?' declares the Lord. 'Do I not fill the heavens and the earth?' declares the Lord" (Jeremiah 23:23-24 NASB).

The ancients sometimes referred to God as the "all seeing eye." The Scriptures say, "Nothing in all creation is hidden from God. Everything is naked and exposed before his eyes, and he is the one to whom we are accountable" (Hebrews 4:13 NLT). In Psalm 139:7-10, King David said, "Where can I go from Your Spirit? Or where can I flee from Your presence? If I ascend into heaven, You are there; If I make my bed in hell, behold, You are there. If I take the wings of the morning, and dwell in the uttermost parts of the sea, even there Your hand shall lead me, and Your right hand shall hold me." Yes, God is even present in hell itself.

God's omnipresence not only means that He is present everywhere in physical space, but in time as well. Since God dwells in eternity, He is present in both at once. He is present with Adam in the garden of Eden, Jesus on the cross, each of us right now, and with us in our future 10,000 years from now—all at the same moment (Psalm 90:1-2; Jude 1:25; Isaiah 44:6). How amazing is that?

God Knows Everything

This is also called *omniscience* (*omni*, meaning "all," and *science*, meaning "knowledge"). Because God is everywhere observing everything—past, present, and future—He is all knowing. This is one of the attributes that belong exclusively to God. Satan is limited in power, and can only be in one place at one time. Satan cannot see or know the future, except where God has already foretold it. This knowledge of God covers details that are trivial, as well as matters of the greatest importance.

Scripture says that not one sparrow falls from the sky without His knowledge. He knows each person by name and the number of hairs on our heads (Matthew 10:29-30). He knows not only facts about our past, present, and future, but He knows our hearts and souls as well. He sees every motive, observes every thought, and is aware of the darkest secrets of our hearts.

HOW CAN AN ALL-KNOWING GOD ALLOW EVIL?

The fact that God knows the future as well as we know our own past is sometimes overwhelming to think about. Many people stumble at this truth about God because they conclude that if God knows everything that will happen, including every evil deed, He is cruel in not using His power to prevent them from happening. Others feel that if God knows what they will choose, then they cannot be truly free and conclude that life is nothing more than a puppet show put on by a master puppeteer who controls everything that happens on the stage.

While our limited minds cannot possibly grasp the full implications of omniscience, it is wrong to conclude that because God knows everything and has the power to do anything, He is then responsible for occurrences of evil in the world. God has chosen to allow true freedom for His creatures. This means that even though God knows what we will do, He is not the cause of the acts we freely choose of our own accord. Most people would deeply defend the fact that they possess a free will. In the United States, liberty and freedom to act are rights that are celebrated and defended.

> *When God decided to create His children free, he gave them the ability to love Him or to reject Him. While the gift of freedom comes from God, the choice to do evil is the responsibility of those that choose it.*

We cannot have it both ways. God could either create real free beings, or He could create preprogrammed robots or puppets. Freedom is the ability to choose between opposites. If one is given the choice between having two apples, then the choice is really controlled by the lack of options. But if one is given a choice between an apple and a poisonous spider, then the decision and its results are the responsibility of the one who makes the choice.

In the same way, in order for God to make beings that are truly free, they would have to possess genuine moral freedom. And moral freedom requires that His children had to be free to either choose or reject Him. Therefore when God decided to create His children free, he gave them the ability to love Him or to reject Him. While the gift of freedom comes from God, the choice to do evil is the responsibility of those that choose it.

We need to find comfort in the fact that our God is sovereign and has control of the universe and its direction. Though He has chosen to create a universe where His creatures experience real freedom to choose and act, nothing can happen that will surprise Him, confound Him, or ultimately fail to flow into His overall plans and purposes.

DAY 2 EXERCISES

1. What are the terms "God's attributes" referring to?

_____

_____

2. What is the definition of the Godhead?

_____

_____

_____

3. What does the word *sovereignty* mean? _____

_____

_____

4. God has both the _____ to do anything He desires and the _____ to carry it out.

5. Omnipotence means: _____

   Omnipresence means: _____

   Omniscience means: _____

6. Name the two major universal attributes of God from your reading and briefly describe what each means.

   1. _____

   2. _____

DAY 3: THE PRIMARY ATTRIBUTES OF GOD

od is a being who is in a class all by Himself. By identifying the primary attributes of God, we are given a selective list of the qualities that enable us to know Him.

GOD IS A PERSON

While this truth about God may seem obvious, it is important to remember that several of the major world religions, including many in the New Age movement today, describe God as a cosmic energy, an impersonal intelligence, or the "great life force" that connects all things. These views of "God" are centered in ancient Eastern pagan philosophy. These philosophies portray the divine as a universal power that contains within itself good and evil, light and dark, joy and pain. In popular fiction it is the "force" that fills the universe, the "mother energy" that flows through all living things equally, or the "great mind" that we must be absorbed into.

The true God, however, is a living Person. He thinks, feels, and experiences emotion in its truest form (Psalm 37:13; Isaiah 62:5; John 11:35). He rejoices, weeps, laughs, comforts, corrects, punishes, and plans. As an infinite Being, He is the ultimate reality holding the universe in the palm of His hand. As a personal Being, He knows each of us individually, and cares about each person intimately (Psalm 139:14-18). The Christian faith is unique in that it reveals a God who not only knows us, but also invites us to know Him (Jeremiah 29:11-13; 24:7; John 16:27). It is one thing to know about God; it is quite another to have a personal relationship with Him. No other world religion makes this unique claim.[11]

> "I am the good shepherd; and I know My sheep, and am known by My own. As the Father knows Me, even so I know the Father; and I lay down My life for the sheep" (John 10:14-15).

GOD IS UNIQUE

There is No One like God (Incomparable)

God is unique in that He is the one Supreme Being in all the universe. We must believe first that the God of the Bible is the one true God.

> "I am the Lord, and there is no other; there is no God besides Me. I will gird you, though you have not known Me, that they may know from the rising of the sun to its setting that there is none besides Me. I am the Lord, and there is no other" (Isaiah 45:5-6).

---

11. Islam teaches a single, all-powerful, creative deity that is personably unknowable. In this understanding, the deity desires submission, but not personal relationship.

> "And there is no other God besides Me, a just God and a Savior; there is none besides Me. Look to Me, and be saved, all you ends of the earth! For I am God, and there is no other" (Isaiah 45:21b-22).

There Are No Other Gods (Exceptional)

The very first words that were written in the Bible were *written by God Himself* in tablets of stone. These were the Ten Commandments given to Moses. Even though they appear in the second book of the Bible, they were written before anything else. And the first words that God wrote on that tablet were about Himself. He said:

> "You must not have any other god but me" (Exodus 20:3 NLT).

God is unique in that He is not only the greatest of all gods, He is the *only* God. There may be many different deities worshipped by the people of earth, but there is only one *genuine* God. The Lord requires us to believe not only in His existence and His supremacy, but also that every other god is false. It is not enough to believe in the God of the Bible while allowing that other people have equally legitimate non-biblical gods. God commands us to admit that He alone is God and that all other conceptions of god are false. It is completely fair and right for the Lord to require this, especially since He made us and has revealed His true identity to us. It is right for Him to demand our undivided attention in worshipping Him.

> "Truly, Lord, the kings of Assyria have laid waste all the nations and their lands, and have cast their gods into the fire; for they were not gods, but the work of men's hands—wood and stone. Therefore they destroyed them. Now therefore, O Lord our God, save us from his hand, that all the kingdoms of the earth may know that You are the Lord, You alone" (Isaiah 37:18-20).

GOD IS ETERNAL

Outside of Time

When we think of God as being eternal, we often think of a timeline. We imagine that God stretches all the way back and forward in time. Because we live inside of time, we imagine both that God is very old, and that He will live forever. These ideas do not properly describe God. Eternity is not a period of time, but a place. It is the place where God lives—completely outside of time as we know it. The Bible says,

> "For thus says the High and Lofty One *who inhabits eternity*, whose name is Holy: 'I dwell in the high and holy place'" (Isaiah 57:15a).

> "Known to God *from eternity* are all His works" (Acts 15:18).

Eternity is a state of being that God alone fully occupies. Every other creature in heaven and earth experiences time as a *sequence of events*. But God exists outside of time and therefore is above it. In fact, the Bible says that God created time (Titus 1:2; 2 Timothy 1:9), which means that there is a place that exists outside of time. The Bible says that time had a beginning, and will have an ending. But before time began, and after time ends, God exists in what could be called the "eternal now." God, then, is not an aging being, but an ageless being who is the Creator of time and everything that experiences time in the material universe.

"In hope of eternal life which God, who cannot lie, promised *before time began*" (Titus 1:2).

"Who has saved us and called us with a holy calling, not according to our works, but according to His own purpose and grace which was given to us in Christ Jesus *before time began*" (2 Timothy 1:9).

"And the angel…lifted up his hand to heaven, and sware by him that liveth for ever and ever, who created heaven, and the things that therein are, and the earth, and the things that therein are…that *there should be time no longer*" (Revelation 10:5-6 KJV).

Without Beginning or End

It goes without saying that if God is eternal, then He had no beginning. This concept is particularly mind-boggling to think about. As creatures of time, we know of nothing that doesn't have a start and an end. All that we see had a beginning, experiences aging, and eventually dies, decays, or is destroyed and disappears. But not God. There was never a time when He was not. No one created God. He did not accidentally become God. He has always been.

In the same way, God will always be. He will never stop being. Long after this material creation and time have been absorbed into eternity, God will remain. The Apostle John had a vision of heaven and saw angels who surround God's throne, "And they do not rest day or night, saying: 'Holy, holy, holy, Lord God Almighty, who was and is and is to come!'" (Revelation 4:8). This wonderful truth should give great comfort to us. He is the only constant, the only reality. Everything else starts, grows, changes, dies, and passes into memory. But our God is permanent and the "rock of the ages" upon which all else is built, and from whom all things are held together.

"Lord, You have been our dwelling place in all generations. Before the mountains were brought forth, or ever You had formed the earth and the world, even from everlasting to everlasting, You are God" (Psalm 90:1-2).

"All glory to him who alone is God, our Savior through Jesus Christ our Lord. All glory, majesty, power, and authority are his before all time, and in the present, and beyond all time! Amen" (Jude 1:25 NLT).

"I am the Alpha and the Omega, the Beginning and the End, the First and the Last" (Revelation 22:13).

Unchanging

"Of old You laid the foundation of the earth, and the heavens are the work of Your hands. They will perish, but You will endure; yes, they will all grow old like a garment; like a cloak You will change them, and they will be changed. But *You are the same, and Your years will have no end*" (Psalm 102:25-27).

Another very important aspect of God's eternal nature is that He does not change. God is always the same. He does not become more intelligent, nor grow in knowledge. He does not become more powerful or gain strength. He isn't turning into something that He hasn't always been. This simple truth is extremely important. We can be confident in the Word of God because it does not change. Most of the religions of the world evolve as culture changes. The gods of Greece, Rome, Babylon, and Egypt constantly changed their minds and even their personalities. People today want Christians to change their view of God. They want certain aspects of His personality to "evolve" along with human culture.

But the God of the Bible is always the same. He may change the way He deals with humans, and He has a wonderful variety of ways that He interacts with us, but *He does not change.* What He loves, He has always loved. What He despises and calls evil, will always be evil. As humans, we are constantly trying to reinvent God into someone who will approve of whatever we want to do at the time. We try to make God into our image. But the Bible declares that we are to be conformed to His image.

"I am the Lord, and I do not change" (Malachi 3:6a NLT).

"Whatever is good and perfect comes down to us from God our Father, who created all the lights in the heavens. He never changes or casts a shifting shadow" (James 1:17 NLT).

"Jesus Christ is the same yesterday, today, and forever" (Hebrews 13:8).

Because God does not evolve and change, we can know that He is reliable and dependable. His unchanging nature does not mean that God is rigid and insensitive to the constant shifts and changes in our lives. He is not a distant and emotionally unresponsive observer, like a statue standing over our world. In fact, the opposite is true. He is always working and acting in our world to draw our unreliable hearts and shifting affections back to His always dependable love and eternal values.

GOD IS CREATIVE

While God is eternal and unchanging, He is at the same time infinitely creative and personal. One of the most wonderful attributes of God is His creativity. The first thing we learn about God in Genesis is that He is a creative being. The immense variety of creation can be observed in the universe above, on the earth around us, and in the tiniest of creatures beneath our feet. While He does not change personally, He is continually working creatively. This keeps both God and our world from being anything but boring!

Maker of All Things

The Bible tells us that God made everything that exists in time and space—from the farthest stars and galaxies, to the earth and everything in it. He created everything out of nothing. There was no pre-existing material that God used in His creation. When we think of an artist or builder creating something, we understand that their "creation" was formed from materials that already existed. Actually, what we do is closer to "assembly" than creation. Everything man makes, he makes from things that already exist.

By faith we understand that the entire universe was formed at God's command, that what we now see did not come from anything that can be seen" (Hebrews 11:3 NLT).

"Praise Him, sun and moon; praise Him, all you stars of light! Praise Him, you heavens of heavens, and you waters above the heavens! Let them praise the name of the Lord, for He commanded and they were created" (Psalm 148:3-5).

By using His voice and His imagination, God called everything into existence. As Maker of everything, He is also Owner of all things. While many of His creations do not acknowledge Him as their Creator, nor follow His ways, there is coming a day in which everything in creation will recognize and submit to its Creator (Ephesians 1:10; Colossians 1:16).

"And by Him to reconcile all things to Himself, by Him, whether things on earth or things in heaven, having made peace through the blood of His cross" (Colossians 1:20).

"You are worthy, O Lord our God, to receive glory and honor and power. For you created all things, and they exist because you created what you pleased" (Revelation 4:11 NLT).

DAY 3 EXERCISES

1. The Lord requires us to believe not only in His _____ and His _____, but also that every other god is _____.

2. When we think of God as being eternal, we often think of a timeline. Describe what eternity is according to today's reading.

_____

_____

_____

_____

3. Because God does not evolve and change, we can know that He is _____ and _____.

4. What is the first thing we learn about God in Genesis?

_____

_____

5. "For since the creation of the world His invisible attributes, His eternal power and divine nature, have been clearly seen, being understood through what has been made, so that they are without excuse" (Romans 1:20 NASB). Think about this verse. What kinds of things that you can see in the creation around you remind you of God's power and divine nature? Write them down here.

_____

_____

_____

_____

DAY 4: THE PERSONAL ATTRIBUTES OF GOD

God's *primary* attributes deal with the characteristics that define Him. His *personal* attributes are the qualities of His personality and the way in which He interacts with us as His children. It is like the difference between describing the characteristics of a human being, and defining the personality and character of a particular person.

God's Character

Knowing God means knowing God's personality and character. Prophetic Bible teacher Tim O'Leary has taught about the character of God all over the United States and in many parts of the world for over forty years. One thing Tim O'Leary repeats nearly every time he teaches is: "If you know who He is, you will know what He does. And if you know what He does, you will know who He is." What Tim is communicating is that God's actions are a manifestation of His nature. If you want to know who God is, you must study His actions in the Word of God. Conversely, if you really know Him and have embraced His character, you will understand why He does what He does and why He acts as He does in various ways in the earth.

> *Because God is a person, He has a personality. He may be known and loved. God desires relationship, intimacy, and loving connection with His creation, particularly the men and women He has formed in His own image.*

GOD IS LOVE

Of all the statements the Bible makes about God, the one that is most precious to consider is that He is love. God does not merely possess love; He actually is the very essence of pure love. Some people believe that God created the human race because He was lonely and needed someone to whom He could express His love. But this idea is incomplete. Love requires a connection of the heart and should occur between two distinct persons. Does this mean that God was without love prior to His creating the angels and the human race? If that were the case, then God could not be eternal or complete within Himself. But the Scripture reveals that the Lord is self-sufficient and has need of nothing—including love.

Because God is a community of persons in the Holy Trinity, He has perfect love within His own being. The Bible says that the Father loves the Son and the Son loves the Father. This is one of the strongest arguments for the Trinity. True love requires relationship. In the Trinity there is perfect relationship and, therefore, perfect love. God did not create man because He needed anything. He created man because He desired to share His love in an expanding circle of relationship with His creation. God didn't need to love us; rather, He chose to share His love with us. This love is what moved the Father to create His family, the church, from the foundation of the world. It was love that moved Jesus to go to the cross for our sins. It is love that motivates the Holy Spirit to abide within us, securing us for eternity unto the Father, and working every day to sanctify and purify our lives for the glory of the Father and Jesus.

GOD IS RELATIONAL AND KNOWABLE

Because God is a person, He has a personality. He may be known and loved. God desires relationship, intimacy, and loving connection with His creation, particularly the men and women He has formed in His own image. Just as a good father longs to love, protect, play with, and enjoy his children, our Father in heaven seeks to enjoy intimate personal connection with us!

He has emotion in perfect form. He feels joy, excitement, passion, laughter, as well as yearning, disappointment, and even sadness. The Bible also says that God has the capacity to "feel" jealousy, hatred, anger, and vengeance. Naturally, these negative emotions are often associated with sin, but in our wonderful Father, these personal feelings are in their perfect *and absolutely sinless* form. Emotion in our lives is often twisted and difficult—causing conflict in our relationships and within ourselves. In God, however, His emotion is in pure and perfect manifestation—never violating His love or justice. God's emotion is complete, balanced, and within the total control of His righteousness. Jesus Christ, God's Son, is the only one who has ever lived a human life with each of these divine emotions in perfect display. He is the only true example of emotion in pure form, and seeking to know Him better will help each of us bring balance to our often unstable, emotional lives.

> "As the bridegroom rejoices over the bride, so shall your God rejoice over you" (Isaiah 62:5b).

> "The Lord your God is in your midst, the Mighty One, will save; He will rejoice over you with gladness, He will quiet you with His love, He will rejoice over you with singing" (Zephaniah 3:17).

GOD IS GOOD

> "The Lord your God will make you abound in all the work of your hand, in the fruit of your body, in the increase of your livestock, and in the produce of your land for good. For the Lord *will again rejoice over you* for good as He rejoiced over your fathers" (Deuteronomy 30:9).

One of the most often repeated statements in the Bible is, "The Lord is good" (Jeremiah 33:11). God's goodness refers to His kind and generous nature towards people, especially His own children. The fact that God is good is one of the most important and vital truths we can ever know about Him. The gods of the pagan world are typically fickle, capricious, and often mean-spirited. But the God of Scripture longs to be kind and generous to people who seek Him (Hebrews 11:6). He is not cruel, and His goodness is available to everyone (Psalm 145:9).

There are ways in which God demonstrates His goodness to the world. First, the Bible speaks of the *universal goodness of God.* This is revealed in the ways God shows Himself as Caretaker and Provider for all His creation. He gives sunlight, rain, and natural beauty to everyone. Jesus said that the Father makes the rain to fall on the crops of the righteous as well as the unrighteous. He keeps the forces of nature operating in seasons and cycles that allow human life to survive and flourish. He provides natural gifts and wisdom to men and women who do not know Him, and permits them to make free choices to live, prosper, marry, raise families, and use their skills to benefit others. He allows all people to enjoy the beauty of His planet. He desires to forgive sinners, and it is by His goodness that He leads us to repentance and faith (Romans 2:4).

However, there is another way in which God demonstrates His good nature. This is known as the *covenant goodness of God.* Our heavenly Father has made special promises to demonstrate His goodness in a special way to His own children who have entered into covenant with Him through Jesus Christ. A *covenant* is an agreement made between two parties to provide, protect, and perform services for one another. Covenants also unite the debts, enemies, and burdens of the two parties. When we receive Jesus Christ as our Savior, we enter into a legal covenant with God Himself. In this new covenant, God promises to show His special goodness to us as His own sons and daughters. This new covenant is a binding spiritual contract through which God has obligated Himself to demonstrate His love towards us by showing us special favor, provision, protection, and future promises.

As a father of three sons, our home has always been a welcome environment for our children's friends. Some of these young people would spend days at a time at our home. We'd feed them, let them enjoy our pool, camp in our recreation room, and take them to church. We were good to them. However, they did not experience the same kind of goodness that we reserved for our own children. Only our own sons received the benefits of having their own room, free access to our pantry, our family name, our parental love, discipline, medical care, education, and the many other benefits of being a member of our family. In the same way, we need to recognize that while God is often good to all people—even those who deny His existence—He has a special goodness that He has reserved for His own children.

The Bible teaches that He longs to give desirable and perfect gifts to his children (James 1:17). His goodness is behind His plan to care for His people and to demonstrate His generosity to us in the ages to come (Ephesians 2:7). The goodness of God is the reason He longs to answer our prayers, heal our bodies and wounded hearts, and prosper our relationships and finances (Luke 12:31-32; Psalm 42:8; Acts 10:38).

When God Doesn't Seem Good

When life gets difficult and we suffer things we don't understand, it is common for us to doubt God's goodness. Sometimes we attribute our suffering to Him, and assume He somehow gets pleasure from our pain. But the Lord never intends to cause injury to us through our pain. Much of the pain in our lives is self-inflicted. At other times, our suffering is a result of the choices of others, the work of the Devil, or the dangers of living in a fallen world. Some pain is necessary for us to grow and learn right from wrong. We must distinguish between what God *sends* and what God *uses* in our lives. While God does not send every pain we experience, He always has a purpose to use it *for our benefit.* It is in these moments that we need to remember that our God is good, and His mercy endures forever (1 Chronicles 16:34).

We need to develop strong faith in the goodness of God.

> "Oh, taste and see that the Lord is good; blessed is the man who trusts in Him!" (Psalm 34:8).

> "For the Lord is good; His mercy is everlasting, and His truth endures to all generations" (Psalm 100:5).

> "I would have lost heart, unless I had believed that I would see the goodness of the Lord in the land of the living" (Psalm 27:13).

> "Oh, how great is Your goodness, which You have laid up for those who fear You, which You have prepared for those who trust in You in the presence of the sons of men!" (Psalm 31:19).

GOD IS HOLY

God is a *holy* God. This means that He is without any moral flaw and is perfect in every way. The Lord does not merely possess holiness, He is the essence of holiness itself. Everything that is right, that is pure, that is unstained and clean, finds its source in God. The Bible describes God's holiness as unapproachable light (1 Timothy 6:16).

> "Who is like You, O Lord, among the gods? Who is like You, glorious in holiness, fearful in praises, doing wonders?" (Exodus 15:11).

> "For thus says the High and Lofty One who inhabits eternity, whose name is Holy: 'I dwell in the high and holy place, with him who has a contrite and humble spirit" (Isaiah 57:15).

> "Exalt the Lord our God, and worship at His holy hill; for the Lord our God is holy" (Psalm 99:9).

Around His throne are angels that continuously cry out "Holy, holy, holy is the Lord God Almighty." This attribute of God is absolutely essential to understanding everything else that involves the Lord and His actions. His purity is so absolute and so potent, that no imperfect being can approach God and look directly at Him without instantly being consumed and destroyed.

Read this passage slowly and thoughtfully. Imagine that you are the Prophet Isaiah: Suddenly you are transported into the throne room of the Almighty God. Let this scene fill your heart and mind.

> "In the year that King Uzziah died, I saw the Lord sitting on a throne, high and lifted up, and the train of His robe filled the temple. Above it stood seraphim; each one had six wings: with two he covered his face, with two he covered his feet, and with two he flew. And one cried to another and said: 'Holy, holy, holy is the Lord of hosts; the whole earth is full of His glory!' And the posts of the door were shaken by the voice of him who cried out, and the house was filled with smoke. So I said: 'Woe is me, for I am undone! Because I am a man of unclean lips, and I dwell in the midst of a people of unclean lips; for my eyes have seen the King, the Lord of hosts" (Isaiah 6:1-5).

Perhaps more than any other of His attributes, God's holiness is what causes man to feel both a sense of attraction and repulsion. It is His holiness that causes us to fear Him. In the garden of Eden, the moment Adam and Eve fell into sin, they immediately sensed their nakedness and hid from God's presence. It was His holiness—His purity—they were avoiding. When Isaiah saw the Lord, he was instantly aware of his own uncleanness.

God's holiness is also beautiful. The Scripture calls us to worship God in "the beauty of holiness" (Psalm 29:2). When we sense His presence, it is His holiness that draws us towards Him. Aware of our own impurities, we are drawn to the only One who can change and restore us. Only He can do this.

Thankfully, God is not merely pure; He is also a purifier. He desires to share His holiness with the creatures He has made, and delights in removing our sin. Just as He cleansed Isaiah with fire from the altar before His throne, God longs to cleanse people from their sins. His beautiful light chases away the shadows in our souls and pulls us into His orbit again and again.

DAY 4 EXERCISES

1. Why would you say it is so vital to our faith that our God be personal?

_____

_____

_____

2. When we receive Jesus as our Savior, we enter into a covenant. What is a covenant?

_____

_____

_____

3. There are Scriptures all over the Bible attesting to the goodness of God. Why do you think it is so important that we believe God is good? What happens if we think God is capable of evil?

_____

_____

_____

4. What are some causes of pain in your life?

_____

_____

_____

5. _____ _____ is what causes man to feel both a sense of attraction and repulsion toward God. Why?

_____

_____

6. It's worth repeating—what you think about God affects you in every facet of your life. And we find in the Bible that our God loves us and wants a close personal relationship with each of us. He wants to be part of everything we do. He offers unconditional love, real freedom, and a life of the highest personal fulfillment in His perfect plan for us. He has done the work; we have only to trust Him. Write a short prayer of thanks here.

_____

_____

_____

_____

_____

CHAPTER THREE

THE GIFT OF RIGHTEOUSNESS

CHAPTER THREE
The Gift of Righteousness

DAY 1: GOD'S ORIGINAL DESIGN

You and I have a major problem. You've probably figured out by now that there is a serious gap between us and God—it is called holiness. God is holy and we are not. That's why the primary message of the Christian faith is one of redemption and restoration. The term *redemption* means to regain possession of something in exchange for payment or clearing of a debt. Any story that involves a message of redemption also implies that something terrible has occurred, making the redemption necessary in the first place. You don't search for things that are found. You don't buy back something that was never lost. You can't save someone who isn't in danger of great injury or death.

This is why Christians tell the good news of Jesus Christ by first discussing the tragic story that required His coming into this world. The Bible tells us that God made this universe and all that is in it and called it "good." But something happened to the universe—and to our little planet in particular.

From a distance this world is a most beautiful place. But the closer we get to Earth, the sooner its flaws begin to emerge. We see cities packed with malnourished children; vast savannahs with villages of impoverished mothers and starving babies; decaying urban communities filled with violence and drug abuse; smoke rising from war-torn nations; hospitals filled with suffering victims of disease. All of these stark images may be seen every day all over the earth.

It doesn't take a rocket scientist to figure out that even though this world displays the majesty of our Creator, something has gone terribly wrong. The beauty is marred, the earth's vistas are scarred. It appears something has been let loose on this otherwise magnificent planet. Something is corrupting it. There is a battle afoot—a long-standing, observable fight between the goodness we hope for and the evil we see. Physical scientists have a term for this corrupting force. They call it *entropy*, which is a scientific term for "decay." However, this principle is much more than a natural process or a scientific concept. The Bible tells us that there is a very real spiritual force that is eating away at the edges of our world and all who live here. It teaches us that the physical presence of death, sickness, famine, and human evil finds its source in a very real spiritual force called *sin*.

> *Sin is not just a religious invention or philosophical idea. It is a moral disease that constantly works to corrupt our hearts and infect our world.*

The problem of evil is so great and its corrupting influence has so thoroughly saturated our world that God went to the ultimate lengths and paid the highest possible price to remove it. The Christian faith is the story of what happened to our world, to us, and what God has done to reverse the progress of evil and restore us to Himself. It is a story of redemption.

LET US MAKE MANKIND IN OUR IMAGE

Humanity: The Crowning Achievement of God's Creation

> "What are mere mortals that you should think about them, human beings that you should care for them? Yet you made them only a little lower than God and crowned them with glory and honor. You gave them charge of everything you made, putting all things under their authority" (Psalm 8:4-6 NLT).

There is a spiritual law that is evident throughout the Bible and is an important key to understanding the purpose of anything in existence. It's called the *law of original design*. This law teaches that in order to understand the purpose of something, one must first go back and discover its original intended design. The book of Genesis is sometimes called the book of beginnings and gives us important spiritual information about what God intended for His creation, for our world.

In the first chapter of Genesis, we find that God has carefully prepared the earth for living things. The story builds to a climax as it describes the activities of God in a succession of six days. The crowning achievement of His creation was reserved for the final day. He saved the best for last! On the sixth day, He made man.

Seven Gifts That Separate Mankind from the Rest of Creation

There are seven important characteristics that separate man from every other being or thing God has created. Understanding these is essential to discovering our purpose on earth and God's plan for our future.

> *While man is a creature that is beneath God in every way, in our human form God has left us an imprint of Himself.*

1. The Gift of Image Bearing

The final act of God's physical creation was the formation of man and woman. Humans are the crowning achievement of God. The Scripture tells us that God made man's body from the dust of the earth, but breathed a spirit into the body He had formed. This means that man is both a physical and a spiritual creature. Man is also the only creature of whom God said;

> "Let us make human beings in our image, to be like us....So God created human beings in his own image" (Genesis 1:26-27a NLT).

This is an astounding statement because it tells us that humans are the image or reflection of God Himself. We can actually understand God's nature by looking at ourselves. God has a spiritual form that is similar to the human form. God is spirit (John 4:24) and man is a spiritual being living in a material body. God is intelligent, passionate, and emotional, just as we are. He has emotions, desire, love, and creativity! While man is a creature that is beneath God in every way, in our human form God has left an imprint of Himself.

2. The Gift of Speech

We alone among God's creatures have been given the power of creative speech. This is another mark of image bearing. God's angels are only permitted to speak what He has commanded. Animals communicate through various means of sight, sound, and instinct. Only the human race has been given the capacity to express desires, dreams, and prayers in the form of intelligent words.

3. The Gift of Marriage

God is a relational being. When God initially formed the first man, Adam, he was a single being. God then divided man into two equal, but distinct, genders and called them together for the purpose of a relationship.

> "In the image of God He created him; male and female He created them. Then God blessed them, and God said to them, 'Be fruitful and multiply; fill the earth and subdue it'" (Genesis 1:27-28a).

> "Then the Lord God said, 'It is not good for the man to be alone. I will make a helper who is just right for him.'…So the Lord God caused the man to fall into a deep sleep. While the man slept, the Lord God took out one of the man's ribs and closed up the opening. Then the Lord God made a woman from the rib, and he brought her to the man. 'At last!' the man exclaimed. 'This one is bone from my bone, and flesh from my flesh! She will be called "woman," because she was taken from "man." This explains why a man leaves his father and mother and is joined to his wife, and the two are united into one" (Genesis 2:18, 21-24 NLT).

The first human relationship between two beings of different genders was called marriage, and is the foundation of family and the bedrock of human society. In the marriage relationship, we discover a complete reflection of the image of our Creator. God is therefore a being who encompasses the total strengths of each gender—masculine and feminine. This is why marriage is a sacred union. It demonstrates the total image of God in a way that no other relationship can. In marriage we also discover the wonderful gift and creative energy of sexual union. Our sexual selves were designed by God for the unique pleasure of human marriage.

This is also why there is such an effort made by God's enemy, Satan, to destroy, diminish, distort, and redefine the covenant of marriage. No other relationship demonstrates God's love for us like the relationship of covenant marriage.

God delights in marriage! It is called "the Lord's holy institution which He loves" (Malachi 2:11). Scripture teaches that all believers are to hold a high and honorable view of marriage, as it uniquely demonstrates the image of God and His relationship with His people (Ephesians 5:31-32).

> "Give honor to marriage, and remain faithful to one another in marriage" (Hebrews 13:4a NLT).

4. The Gift of Dominion

God made humans both rulers and caretakers over everything He created. This dominion means that we have been given both authority over the earth and its creatures, as well as the responsibility to care for it. The earth is a precious gift that every Christian is to enjoy and preserve. By caring for the earth and its creatures, we demonstrate our love for God and appreciation for the work of His hands (Psalm 8; Psalm 115:16).

> "Then God blessed them, and God said to them, 'Be fruitful and multiply; fill the earth and subdue it; have dominion over the fish of the sea, over the birds of the air, and over every living thing that moves on the earth'" (Genesis 1:28).

> "The heavens belong to the Lord, but he has given the earth to all humanity" (Psalm 115:16 NLT).

While humans have a responsibility to care for God's creation, we must remember we are unique in creation. Nature is not our "mother," and man is much more than a glorified animal.

Today there is a great effort to blur the line between the hierarchy God set in nature. Secular and evolutionary philosophy sees humans as little more than animals with overgrown brains who just happen to stand at the top of the food chain. Some religions teach that man and animals are both persons who simply appear in different forms.[12] These pagan concepts diminish the dignity and uniqueness of human beings and often create a basis to justify behaviors that God calls evil. After all, if we are just intelligent animals, then we may take our behavioral cues from the animal kingdom. Genocide has often been justified as the "survival of the fittest." Sexual behavior is little more than satisfying an animal instinct. The Bible warns about what happens when we serve creation and forget the Creator. It says:

> "For ever since the world was created, people have seen the earth and sky. Through everything God made, they can clearly see his invisible qualities—his eternal power and divine nature. So they have no excuse for not knowing God. Yes, they knew God, but they wouldn't worship him as God or even give him thanks. And they began to think up foolish ideas of what God was like. As a result, their minds became dark and confused. Claiming to be wise, they instead became utter fools. And instead of worshiping the glorious, ever-living God, they worshiped idols made to look like mere people and birds and animals and reptiles. So God abandoned them to do whatever shameful things their hearts desired. As a result, they did vile and degrading things with each other's bodies. They traded the truth about God for a lie. So they worshiped and served the things God created instead of the Creator himself, who is worthy of eternal praise! Amen" (Romans 1:20-25 NLT).

5. The Gift of Work and Rest

From the opening verses of the Bible, we learn one very important thing about God: He is a Being devoted to work and productivity. The Bible describes the Lord's work as taking

---

12. Hinduism is an example of this idea. Hinduism teaches that all life is unity, and that the differences between humans and other life forms are distinctions in degree, not essence.

place over a period of six days. This was followed by a seventh day in which He ceased from all work—He rested and reflected. Naturally, God did not rest because He was tired. His power is inexhaustible. Rather, He was setting a pattern for human life and healthy productivity. When He made man, He gave him the special command to "subdue," "work," and "maintain" the earth (Genesis 1:26, 2:15). No other creature has the capacity or the calling to cultivate, build, and manage the earth.

Human labor is not a curse or a burdensome necessity that is to be avoided. When humans work, they are cultivating the potential God placed into the earth, and fulfilling their creative purpose to develop that hidden potential.

For this reason, Christians place a high value on every kind of honest labor. Whether our work is physical or mental, blue collar or white, agricultural or academic, manufacturing or marketing, all labor that develops and enables human potential is profitable and sacred (Colossians 3:23).

In the same way, God commands us to rest. We need to take one day each week to cease from focusing on external productivity and spend time in restful enjoyment of all that God has provided. We are to take this time to gather with other believers and worship our Creator, spend time with our families and friends, and enjoy the fruit of our labors.

6. The Gift of Righteousness
The most wonderful and significant characteristic of the human race is that we are the only beings in the universe specifically designed to have an intelligent, intimate, personal relationship with God. He designed us for relationship with Himself. Scripture says that Adam walked with God (Genesis 3:8). No other animal or plant shared the unique privilege of being called to walk with God in fellowship.

Adam and Eve enjoyed perfect righteousness. *Righteousness* may be defined as the right to stand in the presence of God without any sense of guilt or fear of judgment. Righteousness, simply put, is right standing with God. Without complete righteousness, it would have been impossible for the first humans to know God, much less have an intimate relationship with Him. This awesome gift was also the most delicate. It was upon this foundation of right standing with God that Adam and Eve were able to enjoy every other gift God had given. All it took was one act of disobedience—one selfish act of betrayal—to destroy the perfect harmony our first parents enjoyed.

7. The Dangerous Gift of Free Will
The last important characteristic that God gave humanity was a distinct and free capacity to think, reason, and choose. He gave us an individual will. The animal kingdom operates primarily on instinct. Their behaviors are motivated by biological drives and environmental conditioning as opposed to reasoned choices. Humans alone possess the capacity to weigh the moral consequences of their choices, imagine and dream of what might be, and choose to act opposite of those feelings and drives. By giving each human being a distinct will, God gave people a very dangerous gift. True freedom means that one has the capacity to choose for themselves, independent of the will of another. This means that by giving us a free will,

God gave us the power to choose to either follow Him or depart from Him, to love or to hate Him, to serve Him or serve ourselves.

Human freedom requires responsibility. In the world today, we prize our freedoms. The idea of liberty was the fundamental concept upon which our nation was born. As Americans, we celebrate and demonstrate our rights, and historically have paid a great price to fight for the freedoms of other nations. Freedom without responsibility will result in anarchy and chaos. The greater freedom you possess, the more self-control you must exhibit. The first humans were given this gift of freedom. In allowing freedom for His creatures, God also allowed the possibility of evil and the need for redemption.

DAY 1 EXERCISES

1. The long-standing battle that we see in the world today is between what?

_____

2. What is the primary message of the Christian faith?

_____
_____
_____
_____

3. What is the law of original design?

_____
_____
_____
_____

4. What does true freedom mean?

_____
_____
_____
_____

5. Explain how being able to work is a gift of God.

_____
_____
_____
_____

DAY 2: EFFECTS OF THE FALL OF MAN

The Fall of Man

Although mankind was created without flaw, he was given freedom to continue in His trust relationship with God or to walk away from it. When God placed Adam and Eve in the garden of Eden, He gave them only one commandment. It was a test of faith. He told them not to eat of a tree that would open the door to the knowledge of good and evil. The Lord was quite clear in His instructions: "In the day that you eat of it you shall surely die" (Genesis 2:17b).

You would think that God's warning would have been sufficient to keep the first humans from opening the door to evil. The sad truth, however, is that they did open that door, but not without some assistance from a talking snake.

Enter Satan

The reality and role of Satan in Scripture is clear and comprehensive. While he only appears by name five times in the Old Testament, his influence and operation is evident throughout. Once Jesus comes upon the scene in the New Testament, the existence of Satan and his role in corrupting God's creation is vividly detailed. The only figure more regularly and literally mentioned in the New Testament is God Himself. Paul, Peter, James, John, and Jude all speak of Satan as the enemy of God and His church. It is popular today to minimize and allegorize the Devil as a minor character or as a metaphor for human evil. But if Scripture is to be taken seriously at all, the place of Satan in our world is an undeniable fact that we must contend with.

The Origin of Satan
The Bible reveals that Satan was once a glorious and exalted angel named Lucifer. While very little is revealed in Scripture about the time before the creation of Adam and Eve, we know that God's holy angels once roamed the universe. They too were given some measure of free will and were tested. Lucifer became entranced by his own beauty, became jealous of God, and used his freedom to lead a rebellion against God (Isaiah 14:12-17; Ezekiel 28:11-19; Revelation 12:7-9).

The Punishment of Satan
Naturally, God dealt severely with Lucifer. Jesus said that He was an eyewitness of Lucifer's rebellion and fall (Luke 10:18). God cast Lucifer and the angels that followed him out of heaven, banishing them to the ancient earth. Lucifer became known as Satan, or "adversary," and has become the sworn enemy of God.

Locked in the murky chaos of his spiritual prison, he could only watch in wonder as God began to reform the elements of earth and create from the dust the first man and woman. Imagine what it must have been like for this once-glorious creature to watch as God formed creatures of dirt in His own image, breathed into them His own nature, and began to love them as His own children. It isn't any wonder that this powerful, spiteful, fallen being would immediately seek to destroy the relationship God enjoyed with these lowly creatures of dirt—a relationship that Satan himself had lost.

The Plan of Satan

The only way Satan and his army of fallen spirits could take their revenge on God was by attacking these newly formed children of God. He knew the only way he could gain authority on this earth would be to dispossess the rightful rulers: Adam and Eve. He also knew from his own experience that to do this, he had to entice them to betray God's trust by breaking God's commandment. The Lord, in His wisdom, permitted this test of Adam's love. He allowed the first humans real freedom by permitting them to act against His will. In the course of time, Satan entered the garden in the form of a serpent and deceived our human parents (Genesis 3:1-8). Then, they willfully broke their relationship with God by eating of the tree the Lord had forbidden. This act of treason had monumental consequences for the human race and our little planet (Romans 5:12).

The Power of Satan

Through this one act of human selfishness, Satan gained entrance into our world and dominion over the human race (2 Corinthians 4:4; Ephesians 2:2). Satan's power in this world is real, and Scripture teaches that he has the right to test, attack, afflict, and deceive fallen men and women. This, however, was only the beginning of the sad results of Adam's fall.

> *While God uses everything in our experience (including our suffering) to lead us to truth, He is not responsible for the presence of evil in this world.*

CONSEQUENCES OF THE FALL: LOSS OF RIGHTEOUSNESS

The results of Adam's fall were immediate and devastating. His right standing and fellowship with the Father was instantly broken. Through Adam's experience we learn the real lesson of sin's danger. God hates and warns against sin because of what it does to us and our capacity to love. Sin destroys our ability to relate with God and, ultimately, one another.

1. Spiritual Death

As God had foretold, their sin instantly flooded their spiritual beings with darkness. Evil and selfishness replaced righteousness and love. Spiritual death ensued. When we speak of spiritual death, we are not suggesting that their spiritual selves ceased to exist. Spiritual death is disconnection from the source of life: God. Like a dropped call, Adam and Eve's communication with, and connection to, the Father was cut off; and in its place was spiritual isolation and the growing drive of selfishness.

2. Guilt and Fear

The glory of God that once covered Adam and Eve was lost. Now they felt their naked exposure to a world that would no longer respond to their authority. Guilt and fear flooded their beings as they sought to hide from God's presence (Genesis 3:7-8).

3. Futile Human Works

Terror and shame filled their once innocent hearts as they desperately tried to cover their own nakedness. In this, we see the roots of all human religion: a futile attempt to fix what has been broken. There is something in every human that knows they are flawed, broken, and in need of redemption. The religions of the world are various examples of fallen humanity creating new methods of alleviating the problem of human evil and guilt. Buddhism seeks to address evil by denying the very existence of the self.[13] Islam prescribes a rigid adherence to a code of exacting laws and submission to a deity that can never be known as "father."[14] Even "Christian" religions can fall into the trap of thinking that humans can fix their problem with sin through a combination of God's grace and their own good deeds and efforts.

The Scriptures, however, clearly teach that our sin is so great and our blindness so complete that nothing we can do will remedy the corruption in our hearts (Isaiah 59:9-13). The problem is that a fallen man can't get up on his own—any attempt we make to try to fix ourselves will be corrupted by our own brokenness.

4. Loss of Authority

Instead of possessing spiritual dominion over the earth, humanity became servants of sin. The deception of sin is such that while it promises to please and satisfy, it only serves to enslave and dominate our natures. The earth became a difficult place to live as the opened door of sin infected the animal kingdom, and creation no longer yielded its bounty with ease (Genesis 3:17).

5. The Dominion of Darkness

Whatever you submit to becomes your master—good or bad. By yielding to Satan's deception, Adam gave his rightful rule over to God's adversary. Satan now has the right to flood our planet with his own brew of wickedness. The Scripture teaches that the whole world is now under the control and influence of Satan (1 John 5:19; 2 Corinthians 4:4). When Jesus encountered Satan, he tempted the Lord by promising Him the stolen authority of Adam (Luke 4:5-7). Paul called Satan the "prince of the powers of the air" (Ephesians 2:2; Colossians 1:13). Three times Jesus called Satan the "ruler of this world" (John 12:31; 14:30, 16:11). Scripture teaches that when a man or woman comes to Christ, they are delivered from the authority or dominion of darkness (Colossians 1:13; 1 Peter 2:9; Acts 26:18).

With the loss of love came the entrance of sin, selfishness, and human mortality. Pestilence, sickness, mental illness, and death were born. With the loss of righteousness came poverty, war, famine, violence, and natural disasters that would fill human experience. These were never part of God's original design for us. We cannot blame God for our human condition.

Many people wrongfully harbor resentment towards God, believing that He is the author of their suffering. By confusing what God has *permitted* with what He has *performed*, they resist God

---

13. The Buddhist philosophy has one goal: the annihilation of individual consciousness by absorption into the great impersonal universal force or energy.

14. One of the primary tenets of Islam is that God has no children. This includes humans. It is strange and offensive to Muslims every time they hear of Christians speaking of God as "Father."

and His love. While God uses everything in our experience (including our suffering) to lead us to truth, He is not responsible for the presence of evil in this world.

We opened the door to the Devil by opening the door to sin. When looking for the reason for evil, we have to look no further than ourselves.

THE CORRUPTION OF THE HUMAN RACE

There are several facts regarding our fallen condition that we must understand in order to fully appreciate what God has done to redeem us to Himself. Until each of us understands our real problem, we will not look for the right answer.

Born Bad

> "When Adam sinned, sin entered the world. Adam's sin brought death, so death
> spread to everyone, for everyone sinned" (Romans 5:12 NLT).

One of the most unpopular teachings of the Christian faith is the teaching of original sin. The term *original sin* simply means that all sin and suffering has its roots in Adam and Eve, and that as a result, we have inherited their corruption. It is common today to hear self-help gurus and pop-religious coaches say things like, "You are a good person. We are all children of God. The reason evil exists is because we are ignorant of our inner divine light." But if God's Word is correct, nothing could be further from the truth.

Both Old and New Testaments speak clearly and frequently on the subject of humanity's fallen and wicked nature. No one is exempt from sin. We are born broken, and with age we become increasingly selfish and wicked. The Prophet Jeremiah said that the human heart has become desperately wicked beyond anything else (Jeremiah 9; 11; 18; 16:12; 17:1; 18:12). Isaiah wrote explicitly about the total corruption of every man. He calls us "dead men in desolate places" (Isaiah 59:10). David said,

> "There is none who does good. The Lord looks down from heaven upon the
> children of men, to see if there are any who understand, who seek God. They
> have all turned aside, they have together become corrupt; there is none who
> does good, no, not one" (Psalm 14:1b-3).

This does not mean that we are incapable of performing some positive and good deeds. Rather, it implies that even on our best days, our good intentions are insufficient to fully remove the shadow of our selfish and evil desires. No one does good perfectly. All around us we see the sad evidence of this truth. Scandals, corruption, and human brokenness mar the records of philanthropists, humanitarians, politicians, celebrities, athletes, and evangelists alike. Hardly a day passes in which another human we thought beyond reproach is revealed to be broken in some way. It should not surprise any of us, however. Why? Because each of us has been inflicted with the same disease—as the Apostle Paul taught,

> "For everyone has sinned; we all fall short of God's glorious standard"
> (Romans 3:23 NLT).

Incapable of Seeking and Finding God on Our Own

Another sad reality of our fallen human condition is that while each of us knows there is something wrong with us, if we are left to ourselves, we will never successfully seek or find the answer. It is common in Christian circles today to refer to non-Christians as "seekers." But Scripture teaches that fallen humans are actually running from God.

Like Adam, our sin causes us to hide from God. If it were not for His gracious intervention, we would all avoid God like a plague. Our search is for a way out of the dark. But our blindness keeps us groping for fig leaves. Our search to cover our nakedness leads us to drugs, immoral sex, alcohol, materialism, unhealthy relationships, power-seeking, self-improvement, good deeds, and human religious works. Yet none of these will lead us back to right standing with God.

> "They don't know where to find peace or what it means to be just and good. They have mapped out crooked roads, and no one who follows them knows a moment's peace. So there is no justice among us, and we know nothing about right living. We look for light but find only darkness. We look for bright skies but walk in gloom. We grope like the blind along a wall, feeling our way like people without eyes. Even at brightest noontime, we stumble as though it were dark. Among the living, we are like the dead....We look for justice, but it never comes. We look for rescue, but it is far away from us. For our sins are piled up before God and testify against us. Yes, we know what sinners we are. We know we have rebelled and have denied the Lord. We have turned our backs on our God. We know how unfair and oppressive we have been, carefully planning our deceitful lies. Our courts oppose the righteous, and justice is nowhere to be found. Truth stumbles in the streets, and honesty has been outlawed. Yes, truth is gone, and anyone who renounces evil is attacked. The Lord looked and was displeased to find there was no justice" (Isaiah 59:8-10, 11b-15 NLT).

Heading toward Eternal Separation from God

No one likes to think about hell. While many of us want our enemies to go there, most rational people would do anything to avoid it themselves. The biblical doctrine of hell is very unpopular. It isn't a mystery as to why we don't like this idea. It simply isn't in our best interest for hell to exist. But refusing to believe in something doesn't make it go away. I can deny the existence of South America, and even teach others to believe the same, but that doesn't change the fact that it is there. In 1879, a pseudo-Christian religious philosophy surfaced called Christian Science. It taught that evil, Satan, and sickness were illusions and that by simply denying their existence they would disappear. Many believed that by the sheer force of denial, evil could be banished from the world. But when we look at the twentieth century, we see the bloodiest one hundred years in human history.

Atheists deny the existence of God. But that won't make Him go away. God is real. Furthermore, we all know it in our hearts. God is holy and sinless. We are broken and sinful. Someday, we will all be held accountable for our sin. The place of ultimate accountability and justice for human sin is a spiritual prison called hell. The Bible teaches that for the high crime of human treason against our Creator, all of us are destined to this prison and eternal separation from

God. Some people flippantly minimize the idea of hell by embracing it as the ultimate party house. But God's Word says that hell will be anything but a party.

No one can know exactly what hell's "fires" are like. But we know it will not be enjoyable. The greatest torment of hell will most certainly be the conscious knowledge that one is separated from God's eternal love. Hell is a place of incredible loneliness because it is there, in eternal blackness, that each sinner will feel the full weight of his sin without the presence of friends, family, or God to comfort them.

God did not create hell for humans originally. He prepared it for Satan and his demonic army. While God is perfectly just in sending each of us to this prison and punishing us according to our individual sins, He chose to make a way for us to return to His love. God had a plan to restore fallen humanity to right standing with Himself. In order to accomplish this, God would have to do something about our sin by finding a man who could win back for the human race what Adam had lost.

> "For I looked, and there was no man; I looked among them, but there was no counselor, who, when I asked of them, could answer a word" (Isaiah 41:28).

DAY 2 EXERCISES

1. True or false: Satan is an allegorical figure used in the Bible to illustrate spiritual concepts.

   _____

2. Satan is what type of creation? _____

3. If you were witnessing to someone about Jesus, and they said a loving God would never allow such suffering in the world, how would you address this?

   _____

   _____

4. What is original sin? _____

   _____

5. Are we capable of finding God on our own? Why or why not? _____

   _____

   _____

6. Another unpopular idea today is the confession of sin. I am not referring to going to a priest, but simply confessing our sins to God. As we admit our sins and ask for God's help, we release the Holy Spirit's power into those areas. (Sin committed against another person should be confessed to them as well—so healing and forgiveness can flow through that relationship.) Write 1 John 1:9 here. Jesus is faithful and just; He is our righteousness!

   _____

   _____

   _____

   _____

   _____

   _____

DAY 3: RESTORING RELATIONSHIP

GOD'S PLAN TO RESTORE RIGHTEOUSNESS

As soon as man fell, God promised to send a Redeemer. In Genesis 3:15, God declared war on Satan and his demonic army. He said,

> "And there will be war between you and the woman and between your seed and her seed: by him will your head be crushed and by you his foot will be wounded" (Genesis 3:15 BBE).

The battle was on. In this single prophecy, we learn that God would work through the descendants of Adam and Eve to bring forth a new warrior. We also learn that the Redeemer would come through a female descendent of Eve. This Redeemer would be deeply wounded by the battle with Satan (His foot would be wounded); but ultimately He would crush the serpent's head.

The Prophet Isaiah, observing the awful condition of the human race, was given a picture of God's plan. The Lord intended to redeem, or buy back, Adam's descendants, as well as restore the earth from all that was lost. This is what Christians mean when we speak of salvation. God made a way to deliver humanity from sin and its eternal consequences.

> "'Behold, the Lord's hand is not shortened, that it cannot save; nor His ear heavy, that it cannot hear. But your iniquities have separated you from your God; and your sins have hidden His face from you, so that He will not hear.... The Redeemer will come to Zion, and to those who turn from transgression in Jacob,' says the Lord" (Isaiah 59:1-2, 20).

The Need for a Second Adam

> "He saw that there was no man, and wondered that there was no intercessor; therefore His own arm brought salvation for Him; and His own righteousness, it sustained Him" (Isaiah 59:16).

God's plan to restore man's righteousness required a perfect human representative. Since there was no human untainted by the problem of sin, a second Adam was needed. If you and I are to be saved from the penalty of sin, we need a perfect substitute to pay our penalty for us. This truth is difficult for many to accept. Yet Scripture is clear that just as Adam represented the entire human race in sin, only one representative was needed to represent the entire human race in redemption.

> *The Old Testament reveals how imperfect we all are and how incapable we are of restoring our right standing with God through our own best efforts.*

The western world is made up of nations with representative democracies. We elect individuals to represent us collectively in local, state, and federal government. Once a representative is selected, the law gives this single individual the right to speak for the entire constituency for a designated period of time. These representatives carry the *vox humana*, which is a Latin term for the "human voice " or "the voice of the people." In the ancient world, nations would often send a single warrior to fight on behalf of the people. Facing his opponent on the field of battle, the hopes and fears of an entire country rested on the victory or defeat of their representative. This is illustrated in Scripture when Israel and the Philistines battled each other through their champions—David and Goliath. When David killed Goliath, all of the Philistine nations accepted their defeat. Today, we see this idea shadowed in athletic contests between national teams representing cities. When New York plays Boston in the American game of baseball, entire cities of millions consider their team's victory or loss as their own.

Adam was our representative. He was representing our team. When he lost, we all lost. We needed a new warrior—a human representative who wouldn't fall to the work of Satan or stumble under the weight of the battle. Therefore God's answer was to raise up a second Adam to face Satan and pay the price for all of us. God's promise to Adam and Eve in the garden was that someday He would send His *Messiah* to deal with both sin and Satan. The word *Messiah* means "anointed one" and is translated to the English word "Christ." The Old Testament is the story of how God raised up a human family, the nation of Israel, through which He would send His Christ into the world (1 Corinthians 15:45).

God's Covenant Family—Israel

In Genesis 12, God made a special agreement with a man named Abraham. He promised him that He would bless and multiply his descendants so that through them, all the families of the earth would be blessed (Genesis 12:1-6). Abraham and his descendants grew into a mighty nation, just as God had promised. After migrating to ancient Egypt, the family of Abraham grew to over one million people and fell into slavery under the whips of their Egyptian masters. God raised up a redeemer from among their ranks—a man named Moses. Moses confronted the wicked power of Egypt and, by a series of miraculous events, led the entire nation of Israel out of bondage, across the Red Sea, and into the Arabian Desert to meet God at Mount Sinai. It was there that God gave His people the Law and taught them how to make blood atonement for their sins as they awaited His promised Messiah.

GOD'S PROVISION FOR SIN UNDER THE OLD COVENANT

The Spiritual Law of Blood Atonement

In order to restore man's righteousness and bring us back into fellowship with God, the problem of our sin had to be dealt with. God is holy and just. His law demands that for sin to be removed, it must be punished, or atoned for. The word *atonement* means to restore a relationship by removing a barrier. Atonement can be understood by looking at each part of the word: at–one–ment. It is the process by which God brings humans back into perfect unity with Himself. Scripture says that the price for sin is death. The shedding of blood is the only thing that can remove human sin.

"And according to the law almost all things are purified with blood, and without shedding of blood there is no remission" (Hebrews 9:22).

"For the wages of sin is death" (Romans 6:23a).

The Purpose of the Law

This is why God instituted an elaborate process of worship through ritual sacrifices and offerings for Israel. By shedding the blood of animals, the Lord was demonstrating to His people that sin must be paid for by blood. God was also teaching them that by putting their faith in a substitute, or sacrificial animal, their sins could be covered until the promised Messiah would come to permanently take them away.

Some people think the old covenant was a failed first attempt by God to redeem us. The Law, however, was not given to restore man's lost righteousness, but to reveal man's sinfulness. It was the first stage to God's brilliant plan for salvation. God gave the old covenant law for several reasons:

1. To cover Israel's sins temporarily until a suitable and permanent sacrifice could be offered (Hebrews 10:4; 9:15-18)

2. To reveal to us our own sinfulness
"Why, then, was the law given? It was given alongside the promise to show people their sins. But the law was designed to last only until the coming of the child who was promised" (Galatians 3:19 NLT).

3. To control the growth of sin and curb evil in society
"But before faith came, we were kept under guard by the law, kept for the faith which would afterward be revealed" (Galatians 3:23).

4. To teach us we need a Savior
"Therefore the law was our tutor to bring us to Christ" (Galatians 3:24).

5. To illustrate God's redemptive plan
God loves to speak in pictures and images. Jesus used imaginative parables and images throughout His teaching. The old covenant law is filled with ceremonies, rituals, and patterns of worship that beautifully teach God's redemptive plan and point towards the work of Jesus Christ.

The Insufficiency of Self-Righteousness

Far from failing in its purpose, the law worked just as God intended it. Primarily by giving a strict code of holy conduct and requiring exact compliance, the Lord was showing the human race just how broken we really are. A child is usually very proud of his or her own artwork until it is compared to that of an older, more developed child. We all judge ourselves to be fairly decent until we are compared to absolute perfection. In this way, God's Law was a perfect measuring stick that revealed to the human race just how crooked our lives had become. In spite of Israel's best attempts to keep God's Law, the Old Testament is the story of their repeated failures. In this way, the Old Testament reveals how imperfect we all are and how incapable we are of restoring our right standing with God through our own best efforts.

HOW THE OLD TESTAMENT PREPARED US FOR HIS SON

By prescribing a work of sacrifice for every infraction and broken commandment, Israel's worship was filled with unceasing offerings of blood. Each sacrifice and death of an innocent animal was continuously illustrating the pain and suffering that was required to pay for human sin. There was one particular sacrifice that perfectly foreshadowed God's plan for a future final substitute.

The Day of Atonement (Yom Kippur)

The highest and holiest day of the Jewish calendar has always been *Yom Kippur*, or the Day of Atonement. On this day, one man, known as the high priest, was commanded to make an annual sacrifice to atone for the sins of the people. In a very real sense, the high priest was a representative substitute of the entire Jewish nation. Leviticus 16 describes this ritual in great detail. It involved the offering of two male goats.

The People's Goat

The first goat was killed as a substitute in place of the people. Its blood was taken by the high priest into the holy sanctuary, where the ark of God's covenant was kept. This ark was a special and beautiful golden chest over which God's presence resided. The high priest alone was allowed into this sacred place, and only on the Day of Atonement. Once inside, the high priest would sprinkle the blood of the people's goat upon the lid of the ark, known as the mercy seat, to satisfy God's justice for their sin and secure His forgiveness and mercy for another year.

The Lord's Scapegoat

The second goat was called the scapegoat. It was the sin-bearing part of the offering and was known as the Lord's goat. It was presented alive to the high priest. Laying his hands upon its head, he would confess the sins of Israel, and symbolically transfer their transgressions to the animal. Then the goat was sent into the wilderness, where God's wrath would fall upon the goat. In this way, the scapegoat would carry the sins of Israel away, thus opening the door for another year of God's blessing.

This sacred ritual perfectly illustrated God's future plan of redemption. It spoke of the need for a perfect sacrifice, representing both parties in the broken relationship of God and man. This sacrifice would be provided by God Himself in the person of His one and only Son, Jesus Christ.

JESUS: OUR RIGHTEOUSNESS

"But when the fullness of the time had come, God sent forth His Son, born of a woman, born under the law, to redeem those who were under the law, that we might receive the adoption as sons" (Galatians 4:4-5).

One of the wonderful distinctions of the Christian faith, which distinguishes it from every other religion and faith on earth, is the *doctrine of the incarnation*. Christianity is the only faith in which God becomes one of us in order to redeem us. This remarkable truth displays the amazing depth of God's love for us and the length to which He has gone to bring us back into right standing in our relationship with Him.

WHEN GOD BECAME A MAN

Hundreds of years before Jesus was born, the Prophet Isaiah proclaimed, "'Behold, the virgin shall be with child, and bear a Son, and they shall call His name Immanuel,' which is translated, 'God with us'" (Matthew 1:23). Jesus was nothing less than God in human form. The miracle by which God became a man is called the *incarnation*, which literally means God "in flesh." Jesus was more than a prophet, a moral teacher, or a divine angel. He was the complete union of God and man in one perfect form. It is important to understand that this miracle did not diminish either Jesus' humanity or His divinity. He was not 50% God and 50% human. He was, and is, 100% God and 100% man in one Person.

Jesus is God

The divine nature of Jesus is something that we must not fail to grasp. Jesus declared His deity or Godhood many times in His teachings. The Apostle Paul stated that "For in Him dwells all the fullness of the Godhead bodily" (Colossians 2:9), and "For God in all his fullness was pleased to live in Christ" (Colossians 1:19 NLT). Perhaps one of the most powerful examples of Jesus revealing His divine nature occurred in a conversation He had with His disciple Philip:

> "Philip said to Him, 'Lord, show us the Father, and it is sufficient for us.' Jesus said to him, 'Have I been with you so long, and yet you have not known Me, Philip? He who has seen Me has seen the Father; so how can you say, "Show us the Father"? Do you not believe that I am in the Father, and the Father in Me?'"
> (John 14:8-10a).

In order to redeem us and restore the human race to right standing with God, Jesus could not be anything less than God the Son. Only His infinite righteousness would be sufficient to overcome the wickedness of the human race.

Jesus is a Man

> "The law of Moses was unable to save us because of the weakness of our sinful nature. So God did what the law could not do. He sent his own Son in a body like the bodies we sinners have. And in that body God declared an end to sin's control over us by giving his Son as a sacrifice for our sins" (Romans 8:3 NLT).

As the second Adam, Jesus needed to be complete in His human nature. Through divine conception in the womb of a young Jewish virgin named Mary, the Lord was born into the total human experience. The Bible teaches that Jesus' physical form was genuine in every way. He possessed a human body, mind, and spirit. Notice this list of human experiences that the New Testament reveals about Jesus' human nature.

- He had a human birth, and grew physically and intellectually as a human (Galatians 4:4; Luke 2:52).
- He became hungry and ate real food (Luke 4:2; 5:30). He became thirsty and drank (John 19:28; 4:7).
- He grew weary and slept (John 4:6; Mark 4:38).
- He had human emotions such as joy, compassion, sorrow, anger, grief, and astonishment (Luke 10:21; 7:9; Matthew 26:37-38; Mark 3:5).

- He felt deep anguish, anxiety, fear, and rejection (Matthew 27:46; Luke 22:44; Mark 8:12; John 13:21; 11:33).

- He felt pain, experienced agony of physical torture, bled and died a human death (Matthew 27:26-50; Luke 22:44; 24:26).

- He was tempted with every kind of sin and category of temptation. This is one of the most important truths of the humanity of Jesus. If Jesus only appeared to be human, then He would not have had the full human experience of temptation. He could not fully relate to our daily struggles in life. But the astounding teaching of the Bible is that Jesus had a full human experience—including the experience of deep, persistent, burning, demonically-inspired temptation (Luke 4:2; Mark 1:13).

> "Therefore, it was necessary for him to be made in every respect like us, his brothers and sisters, so that he could be our merciful and faithful High Priest before God. Then he could offer a sacrifice that would take away the sins of the people. Since he himself has gone through suffering and testing, he is able to help us when we are being tested" (Hebrews 2:17-18 NLT).

JESUS IS THE PERFECT REPRESENTATIVE

By choosing to bring Jesus into the world through a young virgin, God fulfilled the prophecy in Genesis 3:15 that the seed of a woman would crush the serpent's (Satan's) head. Because the Father supernaturally placed His Son as a seed in Mary's womb, Jesus carried the full nature and righteousness of His divinity. In this way, Jesus is the Son of God.

It is important to remember that the Son of God did not begin in Mary's womb. He was always one with the Father in eternity. Hundreds of years before His birth in Bethlehem, the Prophet David asked "Who has ascended into heaven, or descended?...Who has established all the ends of the earth? What is His name, and what is His Son's name, if you know?" (Proverbs 30:4; See also Psalm 2:7-12). John said, "In the beginning the Word already existed. The Word was with God, and the Word was God....So the Word became human and made his home among us.... And we have seen his glory, the glory of the Father's one and only Son" (John 1:1, 14 NLT). Jesus added a human nature to His divine nature. How God accomplished this is a mystery, but the Bible tells us a few things about this miracle:

> "Though he was God, he did not think of equality with God as something to cling to. Instead, he gave up his divine privileges; he took the humble position of a slave and was born as a human being....he appeared in human form" (Philippians 2:6-8a NLT).

When Jesus took a human body, He laid aside some of the privileges of being God. He willingly laid aside and did not access some of His divine powers as a man upon the earth. This is why He had to grow in knowledge and wisdom. His human nature needed to grow up, and His body experienced the same limitations and urges that our bodies feel. Without ceasing to be God, Jesus added to Himself a fully human nature. In this way, the Bible refers to Jesus as the Son of Man.

Jesus is Our Substitute

As we have learned, humanity needed a substitute—a second Adam to represent us before God (1 Corinthians 15:45). Jesus was God's choice as the perfect and final substitute. A substitute takes the place of another. In Jesus we see every Old Testament sacrifice, shadow, and promise fulfilled. Jesus lived a perfect and flawless human life. As a Jewish male, He did for us what no human could ever do.

Jesus is Our High Priest

The book of Hebrews says that Jesus is also our perfect High Priest (Hebrews 2:17). Israel had a high priest who would make sacrifices for the people and go to God on their behalf. Jesus is our new and permanent High Priest. He goes to God on our behalf and makes atonement for our sins. He represents us in front of God, and came to earth as His representative for us.

Jesus is Our Passover Lamb

Every year on Passover, all Israel would kill an unblemished lamb and spread its blood over their doorposts in the shape of a cross. The blood of the Passover lamb protected Israel from the death, disease, and poverty that was coming upon the Egyptians. They had to put their faith in the blood in order to be saved.

The Bible teaches that Jesus is "the Lamb slain from the foundation of the world" (Revelation 13:8). When John the Baptist first saw Jesus approaching, he cried out, "Behold! The Lamb of God who takes away the sin of the world!" (John 1:29). Paul calls Jesus our Passover (1 Corinthians 5:7). When Jesus died on the cross, He did so on the day of the Jewish feast of Passover. He was the final Passover sacrifice. His blood covers all who put their faith in it. It protects us from the wrath of God and the work of Satan.

Jesus is Our Scapegoat

Just as the scapegoat was sent into the wilderness on the Day of Atonement to bear away the sins of Israel, Jesus took our sins and carried them away. The Bible says that on the cross, the Father laid upon Jesus the sins of the whole world, and then punished Jesus in our place as our scapegoat.

It is important to know that Jesus did not merely bear the penalty for our sins, but actually became the sin itself. Jesus absorbed the sins of the world and "became sin" with our sinfulness (2 Corinthians 5:21). Scripture says that God "laid on Him the iniquity of us all" (Isaiah 53:6).

After He died, His spirit descended into hades, or the abyss (Acts 2:27; Romans 10:7; 1 Peter 3:18-19). He carried our sins to hell—the ultimate place of judgment. After suffering, Jesus preached to those who had been waiting for the Messiah—all the saints from the Old Testament, who were held in a special place of comfort, waiting for the day they could be made righteous and taken to heaven (1 Peter 4:6; Ephesians 4:8-9).

When Jesus was raised from the dead, He was taken from that place of prison and judgment and left our sins behind! (Isaiah 53:8). This means that for believers in Jesus Christ, our sins have already been carried into hell, judged, and left there forever. We can rejoice knowing that as Christians we will never go to hell because Jesus already went there—with our sins—and suffered in our place!

> "Great is the mystery of godliness: God was manifest in the flesh, justified in the Spirit, seen of angels, preached unto the Gentiles, believed on in the world, received up into glory" (1 Timothy 3:16 KJV).

DAY 3 EXERCISES

1. What is the meaning of the word *atonement*?

_____

_____

2. The Law separated and protected the people of Israel. Name two more purposes of the Law mentioned in today's reading.

1._____

2._____

3. Jesus is the perfect representative of the human race. List two roles He fulfilled on our behalf.

1._____

2._____

4. What is the incarnation?

_____

_____

_____

5. Jesus was: (circle one)
   a. 50% God and 50% man.
   b. 100% God and 50% man.
   c. 100% God and 100% man.

DAY 4: WALKING IN RIGHTEOUSNESS

Receiving the Gift of Righteousness

God went to great lengths to redeem fallen humanity from their sins. He put His own "skin in the game," by sending His one and only Son to live the life we could not live and die the death we should have died. God could have demanded anything He wished for the incredible gift of eternal life and complete forgiveness of sins. But the Father chose to provide the sacrifice for our sins to be removed from us. He chose to pay the price Himself (Romans 6:23)! He wants to freely give this gift of forgiveness and restored righteousness, at no cost to us. In fact, the only condition He has placed upon receiving His gift of righteousness is that we do not try to earn, purchase, or be worthy of it ourselves. He simply wants us to believe that His Son did it all for us, and to accept Jesus as our Savior and Lord (Ephesians 2:8).

> *Faith is the hand that reaches out and receives the gift God has offered. It does not earn the gift, but simply accepts it.*

But this is the problem for many people. As humans, we resist trusting God to provide for us. There is something inside us that wants to earn our own righteousness. We want at least some credit for spiritual exaltation. We don't want to be dependent on God's provision alone. But this is not acceptable to God. To try and add anything to the perfect work of His Son Jesus is the ultimate insult. It implies that Jesus' work as our substitute was not quite enough. This human tendency to try and establish our own righteousness before God is the single greatest hinderance to receiving God's free gift of righteousness.

"For the wages of sin is death, but the free gift of God is eternal life through Christ Jesus our Lord" (Romans 6:23 NLT).

"But now the righteousness of God apart from the law is revealed, being witnessed by the Law and the Prophets, even the righteousness of God, through faith in Jesus Christ, to all and on all who believe" (Romans 3:21-22a).

"But now God has shown us a way to be made right with him without keeping the requirements of the law, as was promised in the writings of Moses and the prophets long ago. We are made right with God by placing our faith in Jesus Christ. And this is true for everyone who believes, no matter who we are" (Romans 3:21-22 NLT).

Repentance from Dead Works

The Bible teaches that all of our human efforts to fix ourselves and our sins are insults to God. There is nothing men or women can do to change themselves by their own strength. The Bible says that when humans try to achieve right standing with God, they fail every time.

> "Because they did not seek it by faith, but as it were, by the works of the law. For they stumbled at that stumbling stone" (Romans 9:32).

> "We are constant sinners; how can people like us be saved? We are all infected and impure with sin. When we display our righteous deeds, they are nothing but filthy rags" (Isaiah 64:5b-6a NLT).

> "Therefore by the deeds of the law no flesh will be justified in His sight" (Romans 3:20a).

> "Being conscious that a man does not get righteousness by the works of the law, but through faith in Jesus Christ, we had faith in Christ Jesus, so that we might get righteousness by faith in Christ, and not by the works of the law: because by the works of the law will no flesh get righteousness" (Galatians 2:16 BBE).

The Bible teaches that until we actually repent from our own empty, futile, religious efforts to save ourselves, we cannot come to God through faith (Hebrews 6:1).

Working for a Gift Insults the Giver

There are some branches of the Christian faith that teach that we are saved by what Jesus has done on the cross *and* our own good deeds. In other words, they say we have to earn the gift of righteousness. But this is a terrible mistake, and is displeasing to God.

Imagine a small boy on Christmas morning racing to the family room to join his family around the tree. Under the tree are beautiful packages with different name tags attached to each one. The father begins distributing the gifts and finally calls the name of the anxious little boy, "Tommy, this is for you!" Tommy reaches up and begins to touch the beautiful package, only to pull his hand back with a concerned look crossing his face. Immediately Tommy leaps up, races into the kitchen, and begins washing the dishes, working intensely. The father rises curiously and follows his son into the kitchen. "Tommy, what are you doing? Don't you want to join us and receive the rest of your gifts?" The boy pauses, looks up, and says, "Daddy, I really want those gifts. That's why I am working for them. Pretty soon I'll have this kitchen cleaned and I'll start on the laundry." "But son," the father declares in disbelief, "I am not giving these gifts to you because of your goodness or your work; I am giving them to you because I love you! I worked for the money to buy these presents. I don't want you to earn them! I already did!"

Our Work: Belief

Once some men came to Jesus to ask how they could please God. Jesus said: "This is the work of God, that you believe in Him whom He sent" (John 6:29b).

Having faith in Jesus' finished work on the cross is the way in which we receive the free gift of God's righteousness.

Righteousness Received by Faith Alone

The Apostle Paul was given the assignment to proclaim one central message to the newly formed church: Anyone can be made right with God by putting their total trust in Jesus Christ.

Writing to the Ephesian church Paul said, "By grace you have been saved through faith, and that not of yourselves; it is the gift of God, not of works, lest anyone should boast" (Ephesians 2:8-9).

This revelation of salvation by faith alone is repeated continuously in the New Testament. When we come to God on the basis of our own self-righteousness and good works, we are standing on faulty ground. But when we approach God the Father through faith in His own Son, God accepts us completely. Faith is the hand that reaches out and receives the gift God has offered. It does not earn the gift, but simply accepts it.

The Great Exchange

When a person puts their faith in the gospel—the good news of Jesus' death and resurrection for our sins—a real and permanent miracle takes place in their human heart. The moment a person believes in the completed work of Jesus Christ and confesses His Lordship over their lives, their spiritual condition instantly changes. All of their sin—past, present, and future—is transferred to the cross of Jesus Christ, our scapegoat. God considers the death of His Son full payment for your sins; and your guilt before God is removed.

At the same moment, God transfers Jesus' perfect righteousness to you. The fullness of all that Christ earned in His life of perfect obedience to God becomes yours. This transfer of Christ's righteousness occurs in two distinct ways:

1. Legally Righteous
When we are saved, God declares us righteous. God is a judge. The moment a man, woman, or child believes upon Jesus, God declares them righteous, and transfers Christ's perfect standing before God to their account. It is similar to a new immigrant taking the oath of citizenship. The moment they pledge their allegiance to their new country, the judge declares them full citizens, with all the rights and privileges that come with it. That country's constitution outlines rights and privileges, military and police protections, social services' benefits—the fullness of their new country's opportunities is instantly transferred to their account. In the same way, when a person receives Christ, all the benefits that Christ's blood has purchased—all the protections against the claims of Satan and his forces, and full legal standing with God as Father—becomes the possession of the believer.

2. Internally Righteous
Secondly, God makes us righteous by putting His name in our hearts. Christ's actual righteousness is infused and bonded into the very spirit of the believer. This means that a Christian does not merely carry Christ's righteousness like a driver's license or passport. His righteousness is transferred into the believer's essential nature. Paul said this:

> "For He [God] made Him [Jesus] who knew no sin to be sin for us, that we
> might become the righteousness of God in Him" (2 Corinthians 5:21).

The Gift of Righteousness is Permanent

One of the most wonderful and important truths about God's free gift of righteousness is that it changes the believer's standing before God *forever.* Our right standing before God is not only instant and complete, it is also permanent. If our salvation rests in any way upon our good behavior, before or after we receive Christ, then our salvation stands in part upon our good works. Once we are born again, in God's eyes we've been perfected forever.

> "For by that one offering he forever made perfect those who are being made holy" (Hebrews 10:14 NLT).

We have already seen that our good works cannot be the basis of our relationship with God. It must be Christ's righteousness alone in which we put our faith. Any Christian doctrine that teaches our salvation is maintained by works is, in essence, a doctrine of salvation by works. This will lead the believer back into a new kind of religious bondage.

Continuing by Grace

Grace is God's unearned and unlimited favor. When we become children of God, we receive not only the gift of Christ's righteousness, but something called *the abundance of grace*. This overflowing measure of God's special favor enables us to continue in our right standing with God. When we stumble and sin as Christians, God's abundant grace is standing ready to cleanse, restore, and keep us in that wonderful state of righteousness before God.

> "And the result of God's gracious gift is very different from the result of that one man's sin. For Adam's sin led to condemnation, but God's free gift leads to our being made right with God, even though we are guilty of many sins. For the sin of this one man, Adam, caused death to rule over many. But even greater is God's wonderful [abundant] grace and his gift of righteousness, for all who receive it will live in triumph over sin and death through this one man, Jesus Christ" (Romans 5:16-17 NLT).

Kept by Grace

Our ongoing relationship with God is rooted in Christ's righteousness. Although we all continue to fall as we learn to walk with God, our relationship with Him as our Father is permanent. When you were saved, you became completely righteous in your spiritual nature. You will never lose it and can never add to it. You cannot become more righteous than Jesus Christ. His righteousness is freely and fully given to every believer for eternity. Our faith must be in Christ, and His finished work, alone.

Ongoing Cleansing

The Bible says there are consequences to our sin. Accepting God's righteousness does not mean that God does not care about our behavior as Christians. Paul asked the Romans after teaching them about righteousness, "What shall we say then? Shall we continue in sin that grace may abound? Certainly not! How shall we who died to sin live any longer in it?" (Romans 6:1-2). But the quality of our life on earth and in heaven will be decided by how we apply the work of Christ to our daily lives. When a believer sins, it affects his or her fellowship with God. Although the believer's relationship with God is secure, our fellowship with God is deeply impacted by unconfessed sin. The wonderful news is that when we sin as Christians, there is a way to be instantly cleansed. The Bible says, "If we confess our sins, He is faithful and righteous to forgive us our sins and to cleanse us from all unrighteousness" (1 John 1:9 NASB).

In later chapters, we will examine how a believer can overcome sin in their personal life while always carrying the assurance that their standing before God in righteousness is secure.

THE WORK OF RIGHTEOUSNESS

Finally, let's examine the wonderful effects of God's gift of righteousness in the life of the believer.

Peace with God

Romans 5:1 says that "having been justified by faith, we have peace with God through our Lord Jesus Christ." The first evidence that a person has received God's salvation is a deep, abiding, and genuine sense of peace. A warmth, a glow, a sensation of inner connection with God fills the heart that trusts in Christ. When a person is saved, God is no longer the Judge whom they will face in eternity, but a loving Father who receives and favors them for all time. This creates a wondrous peace that passes all understanding. The feeling of guilt and fear that has plagued the unbeliever their whole life melts away.

Confidence

Isaiah said, "The work of righteousness will be peace, and the effect of righteousness, quietness and assurance forever" (Isaiah 32:17). Right standing with God makes the believer confident in the presence of God and Satan. Righteousness restores to us the dominion that Satan stole from Adam. This is why the Scripture says, "those who receive…the gift of righteousness will reign in life" (Romans 5:17). The believer no longer needs to fear Satan or any earthly enemy. God's righteousness makes us qualified to enjoy our full inheritance upon the earth.

Direct Access to the Father

Righteousness means we can access the very presence of God in worship, prayer, and in petition. Paul said that because of Christ and our faith in him, we can come boldly and confidently into God's presence (Ephesians 3:12). Heaven is never closed for the believer. God is ready to hear and answer our prayers.

Many Christians fail to understand that the God of the universe is their own Father, and that they are worthy to approach Him and receive what they need and desire. Many Christians pray as if God were distant, irritable, and about to strike them with a lightning bolt. This behavior is a result of religious training, and not New Testament teaching.

We do not approach God as beggars hoping for a morsel, or as slaves asking their master for a favor. We approach God as nothing less than sons and daughters of a King. We come boldly before His throne, reciting His own promises and expecting to receive His favor and blessing. Our confidence is not in our own works or efforts, but in the gift of His righteousness which we have received in Christ.

> "Let us therefore come boldly to the throne of grace, that we may obtain mercy and find grace to help in time of need" (Hebrews 4:16).

Authority to Receive Our Inheritance

A final, but wonderful, effect of righteousness in our lives is that as believers we have a right to the full inheritance of our Father. Paul taught that, "In Him also we have obtained an inheritance" (Ephesians 1:11). Jesus is our Lord and our older brother. The Scriptures teach that He has qualified us to receive the inheritance of the saints (Colossians 1:12). This inheritance includes authority over Satan and demons (Mark 16:17), healing from sickness and disease (Mark 16:18; Matthew 8:17; James 5:14-15), deliverance from poverty and material lack (2 Corinthians 8:9; 9:11) and the right to be led in life by the Holy Spirit (Romans 8:14).

> "Open their eyes, in order to turn them from darkness to light, and from the power of Satan to God, that they may receive forgiveness of sins and an inheritance among those who are sanctified by faith in Me" (Acts 26:18).

Establishing A Righteousness Consciousness

This wonderful teaching of righteousness has been neglected by the church. For centuries, these amazing truths have been ignored by religious traditions that have emphasized our human sinfulness instead of our right standing with God. Many churches teach believers to be sin conscious rather than righteousness conscious. It is important to learn the difference between right and wrong, and to point out the dangers of sin, but if that is what we focus on, it will produce bondage.

Many Christians live and die without really enjoying the benefits of their right standing with God. They are ignorant of it, so the enemy keeps them riddled with guilt over their past sins, thus paralyzing their prayer life. Their worship and praise in church and at home is hindered by their deepening sense of unworthiness. There is little more that Satan has to do in order to keep this believer from being effective. By reminding them of their sins and struggles daily, the enemy captures the mind of the believer and their faith withers.

But it is a lie—and one we must fight against! Believers must firmly establish that in spite of their past sins and temporary struggles with the flesh, God has declared them righteous on the basis of Jesus' perfect sacrifice. We stand sinless and holy before God, washed in the blood of His own Son (Revelation 1:5b). The Bible teaches that we must become skilled in the teaching about righteousness or we will remain in spiritual infancy (Hebrews 5:13). Here are some steps to establish righteousness in your thinking:

1. Don't Trust Your Feelings
Our feelings are not a good indicator of our spiritual condition. They cannot always be trusted to communicate the truth. Emotions are based on circumstances and external events which change daily, sometimes even hourly. In contrast, our right standing with God is based on spiritual, concrete Bible facts. No matter what your feelings tell you, see yourself as a blameless, forgiven child of the King.

2. Constantly Affirm and Confess Your Righteousness
When we speak what the Word of God says about us, we release its power into our lives. Write down the Bible verses that declare your right standing with God and speak them out loud to yourself daily.

- I am the righteousness of God in Jesus Christ (2 Corinthians 5:21).

- I am holy and without blame before Him (Ephesians 1:4).

- If God is for me, who can be against me? (Romans 8:31).

- I have received God's abundant grace and the gift of righteousness. Therefore I will reign as a king in my life, through my Lord Jesus Christ (Romans 5:17).

- I have been made righteous by faith, therefore I have peace with God through my Lord Jesus Christ (Romans 5:1).

- God has forgiven all of my sins (Colossians 2:13).

- I therefore come boldly before the throne of His grace, and I will obtain mercy and find grace to help me with whatever I need (Hebrews 4:16).

Righteousness versus Religion

Human religion always looks to our own flesh and cries out, "Do! Do! Do!" But the gift of God's righteousness looks to Christ's cross and cries out, "Done! Done! Done!" In Ephesians chapter 2, Paul writes the story of every person who comes to Jesus Christ and has their lost righteousness restored. It is a story that captures our fall into sin, our bondage under Satan's cruel dominion, and the wonderful work that God performed to restore us to favor with Himself. Please read it carefully, prayerfully, and then spend a few moments worshipping God openly.

> "Once you were dead because of your disobedience and your many sins. You used to live in sin, just like the rest of the world, obeying the devil—the commander of the powers in the unseen world. He is the spirit at work in the hearts of those who refuse to obey God. All of us used to live that way, following the passionate desires and inclinations of our sinful nature. By our very nature we were subject to God's anger, just like everyone else. But God is so rich in mercy, and he loved us so much, that even though we were dead because of our sins, he gave us life when he raised Christ from the dead. (It is only by God's grace that you have been saved!) For he raised us from the dead along with Christ and seated us with him in the heavenly realms because we are united with Christ Jesus. So God can point to us in all future ages as examples of the incredible wealth of his grace and kindness toward us, as shown in all he has done for us who are united with Christ Jesus. God saved you by his grace when you believed. And you can't take credit for this; it is a gift from God. Salvation is not a reward for the good things we have done, so none of us can boast about it. For we are God's masterpiece. He has created us anew in Christ Jesus, so we can do the good things he planned for us long ago"
> (Ephesians 2:1-10 NLT).

DAY 4 EXERCISES

1. What is the single greatest hindrance to receiving God's free gift of righteousness?

_____

_____

2. The Bible teaches that our human efforts to fix ourselves and our sin are _____
   to God. Why?

_____

_____

_____

3. How do we receive the free gift of righteousness?

_____

_____

4. In what two ways are we made righteous before God?
   1._____
   2._____

5. What else do we receive along with Christ's righteousness when we become children of
   God?

_____

_____

6. Name the two results of the work of righteousness in the believer's life.
   1._____
   2._____

7. As we grow as Christians, it is vital that we apply the Word of God to our lives. Its truth is
   necessary for us to live in our inheritance. Choose two verses used in this section and write
   them in your journal and below. Read them over to yourself this week, say them out loud,
   and declare their truth over your life. Faith comes by hearing, so speak them out loud!

_____

_____

_____

_____

_____

CHAPTER FOUR

THE NEW CREATION

CHAPTER FOUR
The New Creation

DAY 1: HEART TRANSPLANT

In the last chapter, we learned that when a person believes in Christ, they receive the wonderful gift of righteousness—an eternal and complete right standing with God. But exactly *how* does God place His gift of perfect righteousness inside the heart of a person who still struggles with sin? How can something so holy reside in a sinful person without becoming corrupted by the sinner? How can Christ "live" in my heart if my heart is desperately wicked? (Jeremiah 17:9).

The Miracle of the Christian Faith

Most people today think that being a Christian involves joining a church or religious group and trying to live life by following the teachings of Jesus. We often speak of "making a decision for Christ," and sing songs that declare that we have decided to follow Jesus.

However, being a Christian is far more than membership in a religious organization, following a moral code, or even making a decision to believe in Christ and the Bible. When a person is saved, God does much more than make an entry in a heavenly ledger. All of these things may occur, but none of them explain what actually happens to a person when they receive Jesus as their Lord. All the major religions of the world teach that to embrace their particular path involves little more than choosing to adopt a set of beliefs and a code of behaviors. True Christianity, however, makes a far more radical claim.

The Bible teaches that when a person is saved, they actually undergo a complete and total transformation of their human spirit. The core nature of the believer is powerfully, pervasively, and permanently changed. The Christian faith, then, is built not upon a behavioral code, but upon an actual miracle that occurs in the human heart. The Apostle Paul said, "Therefore, if anyone is in Christ, *he is a new creation*; old things have passed away; behold, all things have become new" (2 Corinthians 5:17).

In this chapter, we are going to learn about the greatest miracle we will ever receive from God—the miracle of becoming born again.

God did not just promise to send the Messiah to save us, He promised to change us—to take out of our being the old sinful heart and to create a new one that could contain His very presence.

The Promise of a New Heart

The prophet Ezekiel was given a vision of a day when God would do a supernatural work in the very heart of His own people. He prophesied, "Then I will sprinkle clean water on you, and you will be clean. Your filth will be washed away, and you will no longer worship idols. And *I will give you a new heart, and I will put a new spirit in you.* I will take out your stony, stubborn heart and *give you a tender, responsive heart.* And *I will put my Spirit in you* so that you will follow my decrees and be careful to obey my regulations" (Ezekiel 36:25-27 NLT). Hundreds of years before Jesus was born, God shared a secret plan to not only save us from sin, but to change us into *saints*!

The Prophet Jeremiah was given similar insight. He said, "Behold, the days are coming, says the Lord, when I will make a new covenant with the house of Israel…I will put My law *in their minds*, and write it *on their hearts*; and I will be their God, and they shall be My people.…They all shall know Me, from the least of them to the greatest of them, says the Lord" (Jeremiah 31:31, 33-34).

God did not just promise to send the Messiah to save us, He promised *to change us*—to take out of our being the old sinful heart and to create a new one that could contain His very presence.

Changing Wineskins

When Jesus walked the earth, He taught the parable of the wineskin. He said you cannot put new wine into old wineskins. The wineskins will burst and both will be ruined (Matthew 9:17). His meaning was clear. The new wine of God's Spirit cannot be contained in the old wineskins of the human heart. Man needed a new wineskin. God could not put His gift of perfect righteousness and the power of the Holy Spirit into a sin-stained human vessel.

In order for us to carry His presence, He would need to change us—to place a new container inside of us that could hold, protect, and preserve His gift of salvation. *This is exactly what God does to every person who receives Jesus Christ as their Lord and Savior*—He makes us new creations. The Gospel of John declares,

> "But to all who believed him and accepted him, he gave *the right to become children of God. They are reborn*—not with a physical birth resulting from human passion or plan, but *a birth that comes from God*" (John 1:12-13 NLT).

Jesus and Nicodemus: You Must Be Born Again!

In John chapter 3, Jesus encountered a very religious Jewish leader. This man was a Pharisee—a devoted and careful follower of the Law of the Old Testament. He came to Jesus under the cover of darkness to secretly express his appreciation for Jesus as a divinely-sent teacher. Jesus immediately identified what Nicodemus really needed. He said, "I tell you the truth, unless you are born again, you cannot see the Kingdom of God" (John 3:3 NLT). This statement greatly confused this proud and religious man. "How can an old man go back into his mother's womb and be born again?" asked Nicodemus. It seemed a preposterous notion that Nicodemus would need anything to see the kingdom of God. After all, he was a leader of the one true world religion, Judaism. He followed the law of Moses faithfully. Here again, we see that our own religious works are insufficient to save us from our sins. We need new hearts.

Jesus went on to explain, "I assure you, no one can enter the Kingdom of God without being born of water[15] [human childbirth] and the Spirit [spiritual rebirth]. Humans can reproduce only human life, but the Holy Spirit gives birth to spiritual life. So don't be surprised when I say, 'You must be born again'" (John 3:5-7 NLT). In order for us to be saved and qualified to enter God's kingdom, we need much more than religious good works. We need to have our spiritual natures reborn. This gives us one very important truth: *To be a Christian, one must be born again; and if one is not born again, it cannot be said one is a Christian.*

There are those today who think born-again Christians are a new type of Christian. They speak as if "born-again churches" were strange cults or offshoots of genuine historic Christianity. Nothing could be further from the truth. In fact, according to Jesus, all genuine Christians *must* be born again. It is not one's church group or denomination that identifies one as a Christian. It is the indwelling of Christ in our hearts that identifies us as His own. Throughout the Christian era this has always been the case. Being born again is not a phenomenon born of some recent understanding of the Bible. The apostles, the early church, and the people of God from then to now have all been born again. *This means that all true Christians are born again, and unless one is born again, he or she is not a true Christian!* We repeat this because it is vitally important; in fact, it is so important that Jesus repeated it three times in His conversation with Nicodemus that evening. We'll examine the miracle of spiritual rebirth more closely in the next section.

---

15. The term "born of water" refers to the breaking of the amniotic sac when a baby is born. Human babies are delivered into this world in a "rush of waters."

DAY 1 EXERCISES

1. According to the Bible, what happens when a person is saved?

_____

_____

2. The Christian faith is built upon what?

_____

_____

3. According to Ezekiel 36:25-27, what does God give us in place of our "stony, stubborn heart?"

_____

_____

4. In order for us to carry His presence, what did God need to do?

_____

_____

_____

5. According to John 3:5-7, what must happen in order for us to enter the kingdom of heaven?

_____

_____

DAY 2: THE THREE-FOLD NATURE OF MAN

THE NATURE OF THE HUMAN BEING

Understanding the Three-fold Nature of Man

Just as God is a community of three distinct persons in a single being, so man, formed in His image, is a single being comprised of three distinct dimensions. In the New Testament, Paul clearly identifies these three aspects of human nature when writing to the Thessalonians. He prayed, "Now may the God of peace make you holy in every way, and may your whole *spirit and soul and body* be kept blameless until our Lord Jesus Christ comes again" (1 Thessalonians 5:23 NLT). In the original language, each word is separated. This indicates that the human spirit, soul, and body are separate components with each part carrying unique characteristics.

Studying these three parts of our being will help us understand the way God's salvation comes into our lives and transforms us over time. Let's examine each component, starting from the outside and moving in.

> *One of the greatest struggles of the Christian life arises from confusion about the differences between the spirit, soul, and body.*

The Body

The word "body" is from the Greek word *soma* and refers to the physical part of our being. The New Testament also uses the term "flesh," or *sarx* in Greek, when speaking of the body and its ongoing appetite for sin. There are four important truths the Bible teaches about our physical bodies.

1. Your Body is Your Earth Suit

Our bodies are our "earth suits," or the material houses we live in while on earth. It is our link to the physical realm. God formed the body from the earth and He gave it five senses with which we navigate, process, and interact with the physical world. Our bodies were never designed to rule us, but to be our servants during our lives on earth.

You are *not* your body. Your body is not the "real you" any more than the house you live in is the real you. For example, someone might throw an egg at the front door of my house, but that does not mean they have thrown an egg at me. Our spiritual selves require a physical vessel through which to navigate this life. God designed the body to be our earth suit—the servant of the believer's spirit.

2. Your Body is Mortal

Through Adam's fall, corruption invaded our physical beings and humans became mortal, or subject to death. From the moment we are born into the world, we begin our long march towards physical death. Though God graciously equipped our bodies with survival instincts and immune defenses, the effects of sin continue to age and erode our physical beings. Sickness and disease assault our bodies and, sooner or later, our physical homes can no longer support our inner spiritual beings. Each of us departs our bodies at physical death. Because of this corruption, our physical bodies need care, rest, exercise, and nourishment in order to maximize our lives on earth.

3. Our Bodies Are Naturally Inclined towards Sin

Our bodies have a wild side. In fact, the body is the primary source of temptation. James said, "What is the cause of wars and fighting among you? Is it not in your desires which are at war in your bodies?" (James 4:1 BBE). Paul said, "For when we were in the flesh, the evil passions…were working in our bodies to give the fruit of death" (Romans 7:5 BBE).

The new birth does not immediately change this. Our bodies carry the appetite for sin even *after* we are saved. "Put on the Lord Jesus Christ, and make no provision for the flesh, to fulfill its lusts" (Romans 13:14). Therefore every Christian must learn to bring his body into subjection (1 Corinthians 9:27). Although our body has been infected by sin and contains a nature that responds to temptation, it can be restrained and controlled by the Holy Spirit. There is a divine purpose for the body, and with God's help, it can be retrained to be used for God's service (Romans 6:13; Romans 12:1).

4. Our Bodies Are Not Yet Saved

While the Christian can retrain and restrain the physical body, it will remain mortal. The body, then, cannot be what Paul was referring to when he said "if any person is in Christ, he is a *new creature*" (2 Corinthians 5:17 NASB). Therefore the body is not born again.

The Soul

The word "soul" is translated from the Greek word *psuche*, from which we get the English words psyche and psychology. It refers to the mind, emotions, intellect, and human will. The human soul is the mental and emotional aspect of our nature. It processes the information it receives from the body. There are several important characteristics of the human soul:

1. Your Soul is Your CPU, or Central Processing Unit

Your soul is the seat of your mind, emotions, and will. It is where we process thoughts, experience feelings, and make decisions. As such, your human soul is like a computer. It receives input from the body and processes it into beliefs and actions. With your soul, you contact the social and intellectual realms of life. The human soul is continuously forming patterns of thought and feeling—from which we make decisions. And, like a computer, it is only as good as the information we program into it. The soul, then, can be trained or untrained. It is a highly changeable part of our being.

2. The Soul is the Battlefield of the Christian Life

There is a war for your thought life. Because the soul sits between the spirit and the body, it is constantly choosing which side to obey. Both God and Satan seek to gain influence in your life by capturing the attention of your soul. The New Testament has much to say about our minds and the vital role our thinking plays in living a positive Christian life. This is why we will devote an entire chapter to studying the human soul and God's plan to renew it through His Word.

3. Our Souls Are Being Saved

The soul is in a *process* of transformation. James said, "Humbly accept the word God has planted in your hearts, for it has the power to save your souls" (James 1:21 NLT). This passage was written to people who were already saved. They were new creatures in Christ. Yet their souls (*psyche*: minds) still needed to be "saved" (*sozo*: to heal or transform). Although they were Christians, there was an aspect of their being that needed further transformation. Therefore, it cannot be the soul or mind of the person that is born again and made a new creation. There is a final and deeper aspect to the human being. This is the part of us that receives salvation.

The Spirit

The spirit of a person is the real person. We are a spirit-being, possessing a soul, and living in a physical body. While the Old Testament sometimes uses the terms *heart, soul,* and *spirit* interchangeably, the New Testament writings to the church make a clear distinction between the mental and spiritual aspects of our being. There are several important things we need to know about the human spirit in order to appreciate God's gift of salvation.

> *The spirit of a person is the real person. We are a spirit-being, possessing a soul, and living in a physical body.*

1. Your Spirit is Not Your Soul

Failing to distinguish between the spirit and the soul will leave the student of the Bible highly confused— especially when studying the New Testament. Paul taught that there was an important distinction between the soul and spirit that could only be understood by the Word of God.

> "For the word of God *is* living and powerful, and sharper than any two-edged sword, piercing even to the division of soul and spirit" (Hebrews 4:12a).

> "For the word of God is alive and powerful. It is sharper than the sharpest two-edged sword, cutting between soul and spirit" (Hebrews 4:12a NLT).

If the soul and spirit can be divided, they cannot be the same thing. Only by appreciating this important truth can one fully understand the miracle of the new birth. It is not the soul that is made new in salvation; it is the human spirit that is reborn.

2. Your Spirit is the Eternal You

The human spirit is the eternal person on the inside. Animals have a body and soul (mind). But only humans have been given a spirit. When God breathed into Adam's body the breath of life, He placed an eternal essence into the core of man's being. This is the part of man that is made directly in the image of God. Jesus said "God is [a] Spirit" (John 4:24). Therefore, if man is made in His image, man must also be a spirit-being. Your spirit has a form and shape that is similar to your physical being, but it is incapable of decay and will *always* exist, whether you receive Christ *or not.*

> "For we know that if our earthly house, this tent, is destroyed, we have a building from God, a house not made with hands, eternal in the heavens. For in this we groan, earnestly desiring to be clothed with our habitation which is from heaven, if indeed, having been clothed, we shall not be found naked. For we who are in this tent groan, being burdened, not because we want to be unclothed, but further clothed, that mortality may be swallowed up by life. Now He who has prepared us for this very thing is God, who also has given us the Spirit as a guarantee. So we are always confident, knowing that while we are at home in the body we are absent from the Lord" (2 Corinthians 5:1-6).

3. Your Spirit is a Direct Creation of God

Every human being has a spirit that was formed as a creation of God. "Thus says the Lord, who...*forms the spirit of man within him*" (Zechariah 12:1). When a child is conceived, his human parents provide the genetic material for his human body and mind, but God alone can create the human spirit. This is why Scripture teaches that at death the body returns to the dust from which it came, but "the spirit will return to God who gave it" (Ecclesiastes 12:7).

> "The Spirit of God has made me, and *the breath of the Almighty gives me life*" (Job 33:4).

> "If God were *to take back his spirit* and withdraw his breath, all life would cease, and humanity would turn again to dust" (Job 34:14-15 NLT).

> "Thus says God the Lord, who created the heavens and stretched them out, who spread forth the earth and that which comes from it, *who gives breath to the people on it, and spirit to those who walk on it*" (Isaiah 42:5).

4. It is Our Spirit Which is Saved or Born Again

Jesus said to Nicodemus, "that which is born of the Holy Spirit is [*your*] *spirit*" (John 3:6-7). When a person is born again, their bodies do not substantially change. If one has a bald head and a big nose before they are saved, they will likely have that same nose and hairline after they are saved. Similarly, the intellect, thought patterns, and knowledge of a person does not suddenly change when one receives Christ. If a person didn't know how to cut hair or play football before salvation, chances are they will not suddenly possess that knowledge after salvation. The body and mind do not substantially change. Yet Scripture says that in at least one aspect of our beings, "old things have passed away; behold, *all things have become new*" (2 Corinthians 5:17). Salvation then is work that occurs in the *human spirit.*

5. Seeing Yourself as a Spiritual Being

Scripture teaches that God is a spirit-being. We have learned that mankind has been made in the image and likeness of God. Therefore, as bearers of His image, *we are essentially spirits as well.*

One of the greatest struggles of the Christian life arises from confusion about the differences between the spirit, soul, and body. When lust, temptation, or sinful urges arise, many believers mistakenly think that those impulses are coming from their inner, true selves. The Bible, however, is very clear that it is the corruption of sin dwelling in our flesh or bodies that is the source of every unrighteous desire. You are not your body!

Physical Death Does Not Fragment the Real You

We do not become a fragmented person when we leave our bodies upon physical death. This is one of the strongest evidences for the fact that you and I are first and foremost spiritual beings.

If you were not a distinct person apart from your body, then when you died you would only be a partial person, some strange remnant of what you once were. However, Scripture teaches that when your body dies, it is your *complete self* that goes to either heaven or hell. Paul, speaking of his own death, said, "For to me, to live is Christ, and to *die is gain.* But if I *live on in the flesh,* this will mean fruit from my labor…For I am hard-pressed between the two, having a desire *to depart and be with Christ,* which is far better. Nevertheless to remain in the flesh is more needful for you" (Philippians 1:21-24).

If we were not complete and distinct beings apart from our physical bodies, Paul could not have said that to die is "gain" (Philippians 1:21). It would not be "far better," because death would be a *fracturing* of our self—a loss of some kind. This truth should give great encouragement to every believer because regardless of what temptations we suffer in our flesh, they are not originating inside of us if we are new creations in Jesus Christ.

Characteristics of the Human Spirit

Because our spirit is not visible to the physical eye, it is often assumed that our spiritual bodies are ethereal, vapor-like, and formless. Scripture, however, tells us that the spirit is the seat of the soul. It possesses thought, memory, personality, desire, and the capacity to feel pain, fear, love, and guilt. Jesus told the story of a poor beggar named Lazarus who died and went to paradise while an unrighteous, rich man died and went to hell. This teaching gives us insight into the capacities of the human spirit after physical death, even when separated from God.

> "And his soul went to the place of the dead. There, in torment, he saw Abraham in the far distance with Lazarus at his side. The rich man shouted, 'Father Abraham, have some pity! Send Lazarus over here to dip the tip of his finger in water and cool my tongue. I am in anguish in these flames.' But Abraham said to him, 'Son, remember that during your lifetime you had everything you wanted, and Lazarus had nothing. So now he is here being comforted, and you are in anguish. And besides, there is a great chasm separating us. No one can cross over to you from here, and no one can cross over to us from there.' Then the rich man said, 'Please, Father Abraham, at least send him to my father's home. For I have five brothers, and I want him to warn them so they don't end up in this place of torment'" (Luke 16:23-28 NLT).

From this story we learn,

- The human spirit exists as a real and complete person after it has left the human body.

- The human spirit is conscious and self-aware.

- The human spirit looks similar in form to the human body (a voice, eyesight, tongue, finger, etc. See verses 23 and 24).

- In our spiritual form, we will consciously recognize one another, including past friends, family, and acquaintances (verse 23).

- The human spirit feels both pain and comfort (verses 24 and 25).

- The human spirit has memory of life and loved ones on earth (verses 27 and 28).

- The human spirit has the emotional capacity to desire, grieve, fear, and feel guilt (verses 24 and 27).

- The human spirit does not wander the earth like some lost ghost, getting stuck in graveyards, closets, or former dwellings. It leaves the earth for either comfort or punishment.

Therefore we see that man is an eternal spirit, possessing a mind and living in a physical body. Since the spirit is the heart and core of our being, it is also the place where the nature of sin finds its roots. It is the spirit that must change if we are to become children of God.

DAY 2 EXERCISES

1. We are made in three parts just like God! What are those three parts?

    1. _____

    2._____

    3. _____

2. Which part of us receives new birth and becomes a new creation?_____

3. Which part of us is a battlefield?_____

4. Which part of us has yet to be saved? _____

5. According to Philippians 1:21-24, what happens to the believer at death?

_____

_____

6. From the story in Luke 16, name four characteristics of the human spirit outside of the body?

    1. _____

    2._____

    3. _____

    4. _____

DAY 3: THE REBIRTH OF THE HUMAN SPIRIT

The new birth is the process by which God accomplishes what He promised through the Prophets Ezekiel and Jeremiah: "Then I will give them one heart, and I will put a new spirit within them, and take the stony heart out of their flesh, and give them a heart of flesh" (Ezekiel 11:19). In the book of Hebrews, God is called "the Father of *our* Spirits" (Hebrews 12:9 NLT). There are two "births" that the Bible speaks of—natural birth and spiritual birth.

> *Through the new birth, God literally removes the corruption of sin from the human heart and replaces it with His own nature.*

Born of the Flesh

Each living person has been "born of the flesh" and is therefore a member of the family of Adam. The nature of sin is present in each human from infancy—a nature that pulls us away from God and separates us from His family.

1. Children of Adam

Our natural birth places each of us "in Adam," and as a result under the curse of spiritual death.

> "For as *in Adam all die*, even so in Christ all shall be made alive....The first man was of the earth, made of dust; the second Man is the Lord from heaven. As was the man of dust, *so also are those who are made of dust*...And as we *have borne the image of the man of dust*" (1 Corinthians 15:22, 47-49b).

Because each of us carries the nature of Adam through our natural birth, all humans must have a new birth to enter God's kingdom (John 3:3).

2. Children of Satan

The sad fact is that Satan is the father of sin and the spiritual leader of everyone who is not born again. Jesus said to those who did not believe in Him, "You are of *your father the devil*, and you want to do the desires of your father. He was a murderer from the beginning, and does not stand in the truth" (John 8:44a NASB). Later the Bible says, "The *children of the devil* are manifest: Whoever does not practice righteousness is not of God" (1 John 3:10).

The Apostle Paul taught the Ephesians, "Once you were dead because of your disobedience and your many sins...just like the rest of the world, *obeying the devil*—the commander of the powers in the unseen world. *He is the spirit at work in the hearts of those who refuse to obey God*" (Ephesians 2:1-2 NLT).

The implications of these statements are clear: Every unsaved person has the nature and spirit of God's enemy actively working in their lives. This does not mean that lost people have become as wicked as possible, or that every unsaved person is knowingly serving the Devil. It simply means that Satan has access *to*, and lordship *over*, their spiritual natures.

Through the sinful nature, Satan is constantly luring and corrupting the human heart so that it can never be free from sin, or acceptable to God.

3. Children of Wrath

This is perhaps the most frightening aspect of our inheritance from Adam. Paul went on to tell the Ephesians that before they received Christ, "we all once conducted ourselves in the lusts of our flesh…and were *by nature children of wrath*, just as the others" (Ephesians 2:3). In Adam, each of us is heading towards the ultimate consequences for our sin: the wrath of Almighty God.

It is popular in today's culture to imagine that God is only capable of love and reward—that He has somehow lost the characteristics of holiness and judgment that are described in the Old Testament. We love to hear sermons about God's mercy and grace and often stay away from messages that speak of God's judgment and our need for holiness. Our culture, however, does not have the right to strip God of the aspects of His personality that make us uncomfortable.

Scripture speaks directly and consistently in both the Old and New Testaments about God's anger with the sin of the human race. The New Testament is clear about God's coming day of wrath. John the Baptist begins with this: "Then he said to the multitudes that came out to be baptized by him, 'Brood of vipers! Who warned you to flee from the wrath to come?'" (Luke 3:7). Jesus warned openly of the consequences of rejecting Him: "He who believes in the Son has everlasting life; and he who does not believe the Son shall not see life, but *the wrath of God abides on him*" (John 3:36).[16] Many people imagine today that hell is the place where Satan's wrath is experienced by sinners, but the Bible teaches that Satan is not yet in hell. In fact, Scripture clearly teaches that at this time, Satan lives on the earth (John 14:30; 12:31; 16:11; Ephesians 2:2). Hell was prepared by God. It is His prison for sinful human spirits. When a person dies without Christ, they are taken to hell, where they experience not the wrath of Satan, but the fierce wrath of a holy God (Revelation 20:1-3; Matthew 25:41).[17]

What about the Children?

When we begin to really understand what the Bible teaches about our fallen human nature, the question naturally arises: What about infants and young children who cannot understand or believe the gospel? Most Christians agree that God has made special provision for the salvation of children, infants, and those who lack the mental capacity to understand and believe the gospel.

In Romans 7, the Apostle Paul teaches that the sin nature dwells in our bodies. He says that, "I was alive once without the law, but when the commandment came, sin revived and I died" (Romans 7:9). The life and death Paul is speaking of is not physical life and death, it is spiritual life and death. He taught that before he knew the law, he had spiritual life. Being raised in a devoted Jewish family, Paul could only be describing his life from infancy through childhood.

---

16. See also: Romans 1:18; 2:5; 2:8; 3:5; 5:9; 9:22; Ephesians 5:6; Colossians 3:6; 1 Thessalonians 1:10; 2:16; Revelation 6:16-17; 11:18; 14:10, 19; 15:1, 7; 16:1, 19; 19:15.

17. The notion that Satan lives in hell is more of a medieval idea than a biblical teaching. Scripture clearly says that Satan is the prince of this world—he rules the powers of the air—and that demons fear the day they will be cast into hell. Scripture never places Satan as a current occupant in hell, and actually teaches that he will be upon the earth until a future day when God Himself will cast him into the abyss, or pit. Eventually Satan will be cast into the lake of fire.

In other words, when he was a child, he was spiritually alive towards God, even though sin was dwelling in his flesh, or body.

This passage gives hope to every parent who has lost a child. It reveals that when a child comes into the world, their spiritual natures are alive to God. The Lord is merciful to children and to those who lack the capacity to know and respond to the law of God. However, as children grow, they reach an age where they understand the difference between right and wrong. At this point, the sin of Adam awakens in their flesh and, like all of us, they sin and experience spiritual death. It is at this point that they must be born again and receive a new nature through faith in Jesus Christ.

Born of the Spirit

For all of these reasons, each man, woman, and child needs a *second* birth. This is why Jesus told Nicodemus, "you must be born again." Even our best religious efforts cannot change the condition of our hearts. Through the new birth, God literally removes the corruption of sin from the human heart and replaces it with His own nature. Instead of remaining a "child of Adam," the believer is now reborn "in Christ." There are several important steps that occur in the new birth.

1. The Heart is Awakened

Scripture says that our sinful nature blinds us to our need for Christ. Paul declares that we are dead in our trespasses and sins. It is only through the preaching of the gospel that the Holy Spirit awakens us from spiritual death and creates within us a realization of our sinful condition and gives us a yearning for the love of Jesus. "And you He made alive, who were dead in your trespasses and sins" (Ephesians 2:1), "I am not ashamed of the gospel of Christ, for it is the power of God to salvation for everyone who believes" (Romans 1:16). The first step in being born again is hearing the gospel.

2. The Heart Believes

Scripture says, "Faith comes by hearing, and hearing by the word of God" (Romans 10:17). Whenever the message of Christ is preached, the Holy Spirit is present to enable our hard and stony hearts to believe it. There is a supernatural work of God that draws fallen people to Christ through the gospel message. Jesus said, "No one can come to Me unless the Father who sent Me draws him" (John 6:44). God not only tells us what we must believe (the gospel), but He also gives us the capacity to do so! In this way our salvation is completely the work of God. "By grace you have been saved through faith, and that not of yourselves; it is the gift of God, not of works, lest anyone should boast" (Ephesians 2:8-9).

3. The Heart is Changed

This is the great miracle of salvation. We call this *regeneration*. Once a person trusts in Christ, the miracle of the new birth occurs. In our final section, we will learn about the astounding things that occur when we become born again.

DAY 3 EXERCISES

1. What does it mean to be "born of the flesh"?

_____

_____

2. What are the implications of Ephesians 2:1-2?

_____

_____

_____

3. What did Jesus warn were the consequences of rejecting Him?

_____

_____

4. What does the Holy Spirit do in us when we hear the preaching of the gospel?

_____

_____

5. What is the first step in being born again?

_____

_____

6. Why do we NEED a second birth?

_____

_____

_____

7. What happens to our hearts when we are born again?

_____

_____

_____

DAY 4: THE TRANSFORMED HEART

CHARACTERISTICS OF THE TRANSFORMED HEART

Many Christians live and die having never fully understood or appreciated the exact nature of what happened to them the day they became born again. Recently I spoke to a couple who had been struggling to pay their bills. They both worked very hard and were praying for some extra income. One day, during the local state fair, the man was walking past various displays in one of the public buildings and noticed a booth that had been set up by the state. Upon inquiry, he discovered the station was designed to help people discover unclaimed funds that had been kept on the state books. When this man entered his information, he was thrilled to discover that he had over one thousand dollars in unclaimed refunds due him. He simply filled out a claim form and received his check.

> "But to all who believed him and accepted him, he gave *the right* to become children of God. They are reborn—not with a physical birth resulting from human passion or plan, *but a birth that comes from God*" (John 1:12-13 NLT).

Very often we struggle to live the Christian life, completely unaware that God has already given us "all things that *pertain* to life and godliness" (2 Peter 1:3). When a person is born again, a miracle has taken place in their human spirit, and they instantly receive a bounty of gifts, grace, and special rights that belong to them as citizens of the kingdom of God, but you cannot take advantage of anything you don't know you have. The Bible is a book that was written to inform us of what belongs to us in Christ, and to teach us how to claim the blessings that God has deposited in the accounts of every one of His children.

Instant and Complete Transformation

Becoming born again is not a gradual process that takes place over time. It occurs the moment we believe the gospel and confess Jesus as our Lord. God instantly transfers the believer out of the kingdom of darkness and into the kingdom of His dear Son. You do not develop gradually into a Christian.

> "He has delivered us from the power of darkness and conveyed us into the kingdom of the Son of His love" (Colossians 1:13).

There may be a long process prior to the new birth, in which God works with your life and draws your heart and mind towards Christ. There is a lifelong process after the new birth in which the believer learns to walk in their new nature. But between them, there is a single moment in which the actual transaction occurs. One moment you are living under the dominion of darkness, and the next you are a child of God (Colossians 2:9-10).

BORN A REAL CHILD OF GOD

"Behold what manner of love the Father has bestowed on us, that we should be called children of God! Therefore the world does not know us, because it did not know Him" (1 John 3:1).

"And because you are sons, God has sent forth the Spirit of His Son into your hearts, crying out, 'Abba, Father!'" (Galatians 4:6).

Many people believe that everyone is a child of God just by virtue of being born into this world. But as we have seen, the opposite is true. Natural birth makes one a child of sin. The second birth makes one a child of God. Being a child of God is not a metaphor or turn of phrase either. One is not merely "counted" or "adopted" as a child of God. The Bible teaches that when a person is born again, their entire spiritual nature is regenerated with the life and nature of God Himself. God's very own life force, His holy seed, is planted into the human heart.

"In this the love of God was manifested toward us, that God has sent His only begotten Son into the world, that we might live through him" (1 John 4:9).

Becoming born again is not a gradual process that takes place over time. It occurs the moment we believe the gospel and confess Jesus as our Lord.

BORN INTO HIS FAMILY

God desired a family. When He first formed Adam and Eve, His plan was to raise up a family of sons and daughters who would be in His likeness, and who would love Him with free hearts. When a person is born again, they not only receive God as their Father, but they are instantly connected to every other child of God that has ever lived. The Apostle Paul called God the Father "from whom the whole family in heaven and earth is named" (Ephesians 3:15). This means that we have an instant spiritual family made up of children of God from every race, nation, tribe, and tongue.

God's family on earth is called His church. Wherever God's children live on earth, we are instructed to join together in local churches in order to worship, learn, give, grow, and serve together. In later chapters, we will learn about God's church and how we may fully benefit from a dynamic relationship with our spiritual family.

BORN IN HIS LIKENESS

Children bear the physical image and characteristics of their natural parents. The same can be said of the children of God. We carry in our spirits the imprint of God's own nature. We have been created to be *like* God Himself in character.

Completely Righteous and Holy

Paul taught the Ephesian Christians that our new spirit has been "created according to God, in true righteousness and holiness" (Ephesians 4:24). This astounding statement tells us that our born-again spirit is recreated in the very righteousness and holiness of God. While our minds may grow in our knowledge of God and our bodies must learn to walk in greater righteousness in our daily lives, the born-again spirit is instantly righteous and holy. It never becomes more righteous. Our spirit does not increase in holiness. We carry perfect righteousness and holiness the moment we are born again! This righteousness is not our own. As we have already learned, our hearts are made righteous with Christ's own perfect righteousness. Our confidence is not in our religious performance, but in Christ's perfect work on our behalf.

Filled with Divine Love

The Bible says that "the love of God has been poured out in our hearts by the Holy Spirit who was given to us" (Romans 5:5). God's highest attribute is love. In the new birth, God's own loving nature is deposited in us. In fact, the primary assurance that we have of our salvation is the attribute of love. The highest attribute of Islam is obedience to the Koran and submission to Allah. The highest value of Buddhism is self-denial. But the highest value of Christianity is love (1 John 3:14; 4:7-8).

Receivers of the Divine Nature

When we are born again, the imprint of Adam is erased from our hearts and a new nature takes its place. Peter said we have become "partakers of the divine nature, having escaped the corruption that is in the world through lust" (2 Peter 1:4). The Apostle John taught that "we may have boldness in the day of judgment; because as He [Jesus] is, so are we in this world" (1 John 4:17). This new nature desires to obey God and keep His Word.

Included in this divine nature is the fruit of the Spirit. Just as a healthy tree grows fruit according to its nature, our new heart produces fruit in our lives according to God's nature. This fruit is found in Galatians 5:22: Love, joy, peace, patience, goodness, meekness, kindness, faithfulness, and self-control. These divine character traits are present in every believer's heart right now, and are waiting to be developed in our natural lives.

BORN IMPERISHABLE

Natural birth is a permanent and irreversible entrance into a human family. Once a child is conceived and born, they will always carry the DNA of their parents. There is nothing we can do to change our birth parents. We carry their image in our genes. In the same way, when a person is born again, they are recreated to be the actual spiritual offspring of God. This occurs by the power of the Holy Spirit and is part of God's eternal plan, which He determined before the foundation of the world. This means the new birth is a radical, powerful, and permanent change in the human spirit. It cannot be reversed because God Himself has determined to keep His own children and finish the work He has begun in them (Philippians 1:6).

Peter teaches that we have been born again "not of corruptible seed but of incorruptible, through the word of God which lives and abides forever" (1 Peter 1:23). The Apostle John, speaking of the born-again heart, makes the remarkable statement: "Whoever has been born of God does not sin, for His Seed remains in him; and he cannot sin, because he has been born of God" (1 John 3:9). John is not implying that Christians do not ever sin. In the first chapter of this same letter, John says that if we (believers) say that we have no sin we "deceive ourselves," and "if we confess our sins, He is faithful and just to forgive us our sins" (1 John 1:8-9). Naturally, as long as we live in our mortal bodies, we are susceptible to fall into sin. John is saying that the part of us that is born of God, however, does not sin. In other words, our born-again spirits are not the source of temptation and sin in our lives. It is our born-again spirit that pulls us towards righteousness every time. The word "seed" in 1 John 3:9 is the Greek word *sperma*. It is the word that is directly translated in English as the seed of the male. God's seed, His very nature and life, has given birth to the Christian heart. Therefore it remains a child of God for eternity.

Sealed by the Holy Spirit

This concept of being permanently a child of God is possible because once the Holy Spirit changes our heart, He seals it. In Ephesians, the Apostle Paul reveals this wonderful truth.

> "In whom also, having believed, you were sealed with the Holy Spirit of promise,
> who is the guarantee of our inheritance until the redemption of the purchased
> possession, to the praise of His glory" (Ephesians 1:13-14).

> "And do not grieve the Holy Spirit of God, by whom you were sealed for the
> day of redemption" (Ephesians 4:30).

The Greek word translated "sealed" in these verses is the word *sphragizo*. It is a word developed from the idea of a king sealing a royal document with his personal insignia ring. Once sealed, the document could not be opened or the seal broken by anyone but the king himself. These seals also contained date stamps that indicated when the document should be opened and the king's desires fulfilled. By using this special word, God is telling us that once we believe on Christ and are born again, God seals our salvation into our spirits. This sealing protects our eternal relationship with Him until the day of our final redemption. This is why a believer may fall into sin with their bodies and minds, but our hearts are kept by His own power until He comes to finish what He started in our lives.

Receives Eternal Life

Jesus said that "My sheep hear My voice, and I know them, and they follow Me. And I give them eternal life, and they shall never perish; neither shall anyone snatch them out of My hand" (John 10:27-28). Later Jesus said, "I am the resurrection and the life. He who believes in Me... shall live" (John 11:25). Eternal life is the very essence of God's own life coming into our spirits. It is called eternal for three reasons: its quality, effects, and duration.

1. Quality of Eternal Life
Because we receive God's own life the moment we believe in Christ, we receive something of eternal value and quality. God is eternal, so anything that comes from Him bears the quality of His own eternal nature.

2. Effects of Eternal Life
Once God's life comes into our hearts, it begins to transform our lives. Nothing will ever be quite the same again. His life instantly changes our spirits and then goes to work on our souls, bodies, relationships, vocations, and lifestyle. The life of God blesses everything it touches. It impacts our feelings, our finances, and our families. Most

believers never fully allow the divine life that is in them to govern their lives. It is powerful and effective.

3. Duration of Eternal Life

As Jesus taught, once one receives eternal life, they shall never perish. He made it clear that His life, once imparted to our hearts, guarantees we will belong to Him and the Father for all eternity.

Many Christians bristle at this idea of our salvation being permanent. They imagine that if one believes they are eternally children of God, there will be no reason to continue to pursue a righteous life. No doubt there are many who take advantage of God's gracious gift and behave poorly, looking for quick and easy forgiveness. Paul warns against those who would turn the grace of God into a license to sin (Jude 1:4).

There are many good Christians who teach that salvation can be undone by a believer's personal sin, and then redone again through the believer's faith. In some of these circles, the miracle of the new birth might occur many times in a person's life—going from lost to saved and back and forth—based on particular behaviors and beliefs in a person's life. God, however, has not based His salvation upon something as flimsy as our behavior. As we have learned, salvation is based upon the work of Christ alone. Any salvation that must be maintained by works of personal virtue is ultimately a salvation based upon it.

The Scripture does contain many warnings against sin and its consequences. A number of these verses indicate that salvation could be forfeited if we were to continue in sin without interruption (Hebrews 6:4-6). But God also has a plan that includes discipline for His children who fall into sin, and it simultaneously works in their lives in such a way that ultimately they will be kept as children of God.

> "Dear friends, even though we are talking this way, we really don't believe it applies to you. We are confident that you are meant for better things, things that come with salvation" (Hebrews 6:9 NLT).

The *true* doctrine of eternal salvation *does not teach* that one can become saved and then live any way they want to without consequence. It actually teaches that if one is *genuinely* saved and truly born of God, they are no longer satisfied with sin. *They have been changed.* They *will want* to live for God. When a believer stumbles into sin, it will grieve their born-again hearts.

If you have been born again, *the real you doesn't want to sin anymore.* Your flesh and unrenewed mind may still feel the tug of temptation, but the regenerated spirit will always want to do what is right. If a person says they have been born again, but continues to practice sin without any sense of conviction or desire to change, *their conversion is a fable.* They are not true children of God, because he that has been born of God does not continue to practice sin. The new birth *really* changes our hearts—powerfully, perfectly, and permanently.

The Dual-Nature Error

It is important to understand that once a person is born again, they do not have two natures in their spirits. Scripture says that once we are saved, the old is gone and the new has come. No person can have two natures in their spirits at the same time. One is either a child of the Devil or a child of God. You cannot be both (Matthew 12:30; 1 John 3:10).

The fight in the Christian life is not within the spirit of the believer. Our fight is between our inner man and our outer man. It is a war between the believer's born again spirit, made in the likeness of God, and the believer's flesh, or body, which still bears the nature of Adam. Understanding and engaging this battle successfully will be the subject of the next section in this book. God has placed our new nature in the same old body we had before we were saved. The key to winning this battle is to realize who we are in Christ, and to boldly confess what the Bible says about us.

GOD'S INDWELLING PRESENCE

The final wonderful truth we will examine about the new birth is that when a person receives the new birth, the fullness of the Triune God comes to live inside them. John said "You are of God, little children, and have overcome…because He who is in you is greater than he that is in the world" (1 John 4:4). Paul taught that "He who raised Christ from the dead will also give life to your mortal bodies through His Spirit who dwells in you" (Romans 8:11b).

In our next chapter, we are going to talk about the Holy Spirit's work in our lives through a special gift known as the baptism of the Holy Spirit. But it is important to note that every Christian has the Spirit of God living inside of them. One of the most amazing and wonderful truths in the New Testament is the revelation that God Himself has come to make His home inside of us. The indwelling of God's presence is not a mere philosophical concept or religious notion. It is a real fact, and perhaps the most wonderful part of being born again.

This brings us back to an ancient prophecy from Ezekiel. Remember he said that a day was coming in which God would take the stony heart out of our flesh, and give us a new spirit? "And I will put My Spirit within you" (Ezekiel 36:27a). When we trust in Jesus Christ, the Father supernaturally takes the old heart out of us and creates a new heart into which He can pour Himself. There is nothing more wonderful than being born again!

The new birth is the greatest work of God on earth. It is a miracle of transformation in which God changes the human heart and removes the curse of sin and imprint of Adam's nature from our very being. This supernatural work sets the Christian faith apart from every other religion in the world. Human religion seeks to alter man's heart through codes of behavior. Believing in Jesus Christ changes our hearts instantly so that He can work through us to change our behavior.

Boldly confess:

- "I am a new creation in Christ Jesus."

- "Old things have passed away; all things have become new in me."

- "I have received eternal life, and I shall never perish."

- "Greater is He that is in me, then he that is in the world."

- "He that has begun a good work in me will perform it until the day of Jesus Christ."

- "I have been translated out of the kingdom of darkness, and transferred into the kingdom of His dear Son."

DAY 4 EXERCISES

1. What happens to the believer in Colossians 1:13?

_____

_____

2. When a person is born again, what happens to their entire spiritual nature?

_____

_____

3. What is God's family on earth called? _____

4. According to 1 Peter 1:23, of what kind of seed have we been born again?

_____

_____

5. According to Ephesians 1:13-14, how long are we to be sealed with the Holy Spirit?

_____

_____

6. When we are saved, we are changed inside. We may not always feel different, but the change is real. We ended our reading with a list of affirmations to boldly confess. Choose one of them today to write here. Keep it in front of you all day and say it to yourself over and over again.

_____

_____

CHAPTER FIVE

THE GIFT OF THE HOLY SPIRIT

CHAPTER FIVE
The Gift of the Holy Spirit

DAY 1: THE PERSON OF THE HOLY SPIRIT

Transformation requires power. Whether we are speaking of physical transformation, social transformation, or personal transformation, genuine change requires great power. This is especially true when it comes to experiencing the kind of transformation God desires for our lives.

While there are many things we can do ourselves, the kind of spiritual transformation that we need can only be accomplished through a power that is greater than ourselves. The good news is that God *has made this power available to us* through the gift of His Holy Spirit. In fact, *everything God does in your life and in this world* is accomplished through the direct action of the Holy Spirit. The Spirit of God acts on the Word of God to produce the change that God desires. We see this in the very first few verses of the Bible, as God prepares a dark and chaotic planet earth to be transformed into a beautiful home for life and creation.

> "In the beginning God created the heavens and the earth. The earth was without form, and void; and darkness was on the face of the deep. *And the Spirit of God was hovering over the face of the waters*. Then God said, 'Let there be light'; *and there was light*" (Genesis 1:1-3).

In this passage, the Holy Spirit acted upon the spoken Word of God to bring transformation to the dark condition of the earth. Today, God works the same way to bring transformation to the broken places in our lives. As we act in faith upon the Word of God, the Holy Spirit goes into operation enabling the change we need in our lives.

> *Everything God does in your life and in this world is accomplished through the direct action of the Holy Spirit.*

In this chapter we are going to learn how God's Spirit works to bring about our transformation through two distinct works—the new birth and the baptism of the Holy Spirit.

UNDERSTANDING THE HOLY SPIRIT

The Holy Spirit is Our Earthly Companion

None of us want to be alone. We all need connections with real people in order to be emotionally healthy and fulfill our mission in this world. In the gospel of John, Jesus prepared His disciples for the massive transition that they were about to experience. Jesus was going to die, and while He would be raised again from the dead, His next mission was going to be carried out at His

Father's side in heaven. Jesus had spent three years loving and leading these men and women. He had been a constant presence in their lives, and they were not mentally or emotionally ready to lose the best friend they had ever known. So Jesus prepared them by promising to leave them in the best hands possible. Jesus said,

> "Nevertheless I tell you the truth. It is to your advantage that I go away; for if I do not go away, the Helper will not come to you; but if I depart, I will send Him to you" (John 16:7).

> "These things I have spoken to you while being present with you. But the Helper, the Holy Spirit, whom the Father will send in My name, He will teach you all things, and bring to your remembrance all things that I said to you" (John 14:25-26).

> "I still have many things to say to you, but you cannot bear them now. However, when He, the Spirit of truth, has come, He will guide you into all truth; for He will not speak on His own authority, but whatever He hears He will speak; and He will tell you things to come. He will glorify Me, for He will take of what is Mine and declare it to you" (John 16:12-14).

The Holy Spirit is a Person

> "And I will pray the Father, and He will give you another Helper, that He may abide with you forever—the Spirit of truth, whom the world cannot receive, because it neither sees Him nor knows Him; but you know Him, for He dwells with you and will be in you" (John 14:16-17).

The first thing we learn about the Holy Spirit is that He is a *person*. Many people today refer to the Spirit like He is some kind of spiritual energy that exists similar to the physical forces of electricity or magnetism. They sometimes describe Him by using the word "it" in statements like, "I really sensed the Spirit in church today. *It* was really strong." The problem is that language like this fails to acknowledge the Holy Spirit as a divine person. The Holy Spirit is a *spiritual person*—like the Father, Jesus, you, and I. Jesus referred to the Spirit as "He." He is the third person of the Godhead who shares the qualities of Jesus and the Father, yet has a specific mission on the earth and in the life of the believer. The Bible teaches:

- The Holy Spirit forbids (Acts 16:6).

- He may be grieved (Ephesians 4:30).

- He can be resisted, ignored, and sinned against (Acts 6:10; 7:51).

- Jesus said that He speaks and hears (John 16:13; Acts 21:11).

- He has a mind (1 Corinthians 2:11) and a will (1 Corinthians 12:11).

- He teaches us and reminds us of things spoken by Jesus (John 14:26).

- He serves as our personal guide (John 16:13).

All of these are characteristics that belong to a person, not an energy or force. This is an important truth because it enables us to have a relationship with the Holy Spirit. You can only have a relationship with a conscious, thinking, feeling person. A number of cults teach the Spirit of God is a force[18] and this false doctrine robs the believer of the richness of a personal relationship with the Holy Spirit!

The Holy Spirit is God

As a member of the Trinity, the Holy Spirit Himself is God. He shares all the qualities of God along with the Father and the Son. This doctrine is called *the deity[19] of the Holy Spirit*. His divine nature is revealed in the following facts:

1. The Holy Spirit is Referred to as God

"But Peter said, 'Ananias, why has Satan filled your heart *to lie to the Holy Spirit*…You have not lied to men *but to God"* (Acts 5:3-4).

"Do you not know that you are *the temple of God* and *that the Spirit of God dwells in you*?" (1 Corinthians 3:16).

"Now *the Lord is the Spirit*; and where the Spirit of the Lord is, there is liberty" (2 Corinthians 3:17).

2. The Holy Spirit Possesses the Qualities of God

He is life (Romans 8:2), truth (John 16:13), love (Romans 15:30), and holiness (Ephesians 4:30). He is eternal (Hebrews 9:14), and omnipresent, or everywhere present in time and space (Psalm 139:7). He is omniscient, or has all knowledge of all things (1 Corinthians 2:11). He is also omnipotent, or all powerful; nothing is impossible for Him to do.

3. He Performs the Works of God

He is our Creator (Genesis 1:2; Job 33:4; Psalm 104:30), Redeemer (Isaiah 63:10-11; Ephesians 4:30; 1 Corinthians 12:13), and He performs miracles (Acts 1:8; Galatians 3:2-5; Hebrews 2:4).

4. The Holy Spirit is Mentioned Equally in the Trinity

"The grace of *the Lord Jesus Christ,* and the love *of God,* and the communion of *the Holy Spirit* be with you all. Amen" (2 Corinthians 13:14).

"Go therefore and make disciples of all the nations, baptizing them in the name of the *Father* and of the *Son* and of the *Holy Spirit*" (Matthew 28:19).

"And the *Holy Spirit descended* in bodily form like a dove upon Him, and *a voice came from heaven* which said, 'You are *My beloved Son*; in You *I am well pleased'"* (Luke 3:22).

---

18. Jehovah's Witnesses.
19. The qualities making one God.

5. The Holy Spirit is Sent from the Father and Son

While our God is one in essence, He is three in person. There is total equality between the Father, Son, and Holy Spirit, but there is a *functional* submission among them. Jesus was sent to be with the Father. The Holy Spirit is sent by the Father and the Son. The Spirit draws us to Jesus, and Jesus brings us into direct relationship with the Father (John 14:16, 26). The Bible teaches that the submission of the Holy Spirit and Jesus to the Father is an act of love amongst equals, not a pecking order of superiority (Philippians 2:1-15).

6. The Holy Spirit is the Active Agent of God on the Earth Today

Since Jesus returned to heaven and sat down at God's right hand, He works continuously to advocate for His children before the Father. The Scripture teaches that Jesus "*must remain in heaven* until the time for the final restoration of all things, as God promised long ago" (Acts 3:21 NLT).

Therefore the Holy Spirit is the member of the Trinity who is present on the earth today. The Father and the Son work in the earth through the ministry of the Holy Spirit. This means that as believers, we must have a deep knowledge of what the Bible says about the Holy Spirit, and grow daily in our relationship with Him.

THE THREE RIVERS OF GOD'S WORK ON EARTH

I grew up on a beautiful family property in a place known as Three Rivers in central New York state. It was here where the Seneca and the Oneida rivers meet, mingle, and flow together into a third river—the Oswego. From there, its waters travel twenty miles to Lake Ontario, then into the Saint Lawrence River, and finally to the Atlantic Ocean.

Centuries ago, the intersection of these three rivers was one of the traditional meeting grounds of the Iroquois League. The Six Nations of the Iroquois League would convene annually at this natural intersection of waters. According to legend, it was here that these ancient warring factions built a lasting peace between their tribes by agreeing to a law written on wampum. Some of the facets of this law would later be used by the founding fathers in crafting the U.S. Constitution.

My dad used to stand on our dock and tell me, "John, from Three Rivers, you can go anywhere in the world!" I felt like our magical little dock was the gateway to the entire world. In much the same way, there are three "rivers" that God uses to accomplish His transforming work in our lives. Each one is essential to our personal growth and development.

This natural phenomenon illustrates the three rivers, or forces, that God uses to accomplish His ministry on earth.

1. The River of the Holy Spirit

The first river is the work of the Holy Spirit. Jesus said, "He who believes in me…out of his heart will flow rivers of living water" (John 7:38). The Holy Spirit carries the will, power, and authority of God into the world.

2. The River of the Word

The Spirit of God must work with and through the Word of God. It is the Word of God that the Holy Spirit is sent to enforce and establish. *This is why we must be students of the Bible.* The Holy Spirit confirms the Word. If there is no Bible teaching or preaching, the Spirit has nothing with which to work (Isaiah 55:9-11; Mark 16:20).

3. The River of the Local Church

Finally, both the Word of God and the Spirit of God require a channel through which to operate—a body that will carry God's voice and Spirit to the people who need it. That third river is *the local church.* God's church is the *assembly of God's people* in a local city, village, or region. God uses this spiritual community to carry Christ's work to the world. We need to understand the need for these three vital rivers of ministry working together with the Spirit and the Word operating through the local church. When we commit our lives to each of these "rivers," we will enjoy the Lord's work carried out to the "waters" of this world—the teeming sea of unsaved humanity that Jesus died to save, heal, and deliver.

"And they went out and preached everywhere, the Lord working with *them* and confirming the word through the accompanying signs. Amen" (Mark 16:20).

DAY 1 EXERCISES

1. Fill in the blanks: The _____ of God acts on the _____ of God to produce the _____ that God desires.

2. As related in this section, the Holy Spirit is God and not an "it." He is a real person, and extremely powerful. Read John 14:16-17. In these verses, Jesus calls the Holy Spirit "the Spirit of _____."

3. In your reading, there are seven characteristics listed that demonstrate that the Holy Spirit is a person. List four of them here.
   1. _____
   2. _____
   3. _____
   4. _____

4. There are six facts that reveal the Holy Spirit as God. What are they?
   1. _____
   2. _____
   3. _____
   4. _____
   5. _____
   6. _____

5. What are the three rivers of God's work on the earth?
   1. _____
   2. _____
   3. _____

DAY 2: THE WORK OF THE HOLY SPIRIT

T he Holy Spirit actually has a written job description. When Jesus promised to pour out the Holy Spirit, He described exactly what His work on earth would involve. We need to study the duties and responsibilities assigned to Him by Jesus so that we have a basis to believe for His ministry in our lives.

THE WORK OF THE HOLY SPIRIT IN THE NEW BIRTH

God begins His work of transformation in our lives through a special work of the Holy Spirit called *the new birth*. We refer to those who experience this work as having been born of the Spirit, saved, or born again.

Drawing the Unbeliever to Jesus

The first work of the Holy Spirit is to draw each of us to Jesus. He does this by working through the church to preach and teach the gospel of Jesus.

> "In Him you also trusted, after you heard the word of truth, the gospel of your
> salvation; in whom also, having believed, you were sealed with the Holy Spirit
> of promise" (Ephesians 1:13).

Whenever a person is truly saved, we can be assured that the Holy Spirit was working in their lives long before the day they received Jesus as their Savior. He works in the world to draw future believers to a place where they can hear the message of Jesus. He works through local churches and existing believers to get the message of Jesus to those who have not yet believed.

In this way, the Holy Spirit's work in bringing sinners to salvation is dependent upon the obedience of Christians operating through the local church. If Christians do not witness for Christ, if pastors do not preach the work of Christ, if local churches do not send finances and missionaries to proclaim Christ, then the Holy Spirit has nothing with which to work.

Convicting the World of Sin

Jesus said that the Holy Spirit would begin His work by convicting the world of sin, righteousness, and judgment. Whenever the gospel, or good news, of Jesus Christ is shared, the Holy Spirit immediately goes to work in the hearts of lost or non-Christian men and women. He enables their ears to hear the message and opens their spiritual eyes to "see" the truth of Jesus Christ. He works through the message of Jesus to convict each person of their sinful condition and their disconnection with the God who created them.

This does not mean that He works to condemn the innocent, but rather to convince the guilty of their existing sinful condition. He does this so that the unbeliever may reach out to God for salvation. Before you can help a person in a burning building, you must convince them that there is indeed a deadly fire. It is this discomfort that urges the victim to escape by reaching out to the rescuers. In the same way, the Holy Spirit first makes the sinner uncomfortable and disturbs their sense of safety by pointing out their separation from the God who made them.

Revealing the Need for Righteousness

Once convicted of their sin, the Holy Spirit immediately points the heart of the unbeliever to their only hope—faith in Jesus Christ. He gives each one who receives the gospel the capacity to believe that Christ died for them. Finally, He opens for them an opportunity to be made righteous by faith in Christ and escape God's judgment upon their lives. This is what was meant when Jesus said in John 16:8-11:

> "And when he [the Holy Spirit] comes, *he will convince the world of its sin, and of God's righteousness, and of the coming judgment.* The world's sin is that it refuses to believe in me. Righteousness is available because I go to the Father… Judgment will come because the ruler of this world [Satan and his kingdom] has already been judged" (NLT).

Changing the Heart of the Unbeliever

When a person believes the gospel of Jesus from their heart, the Holy Spirit immediately goes to work in their spirits to remove the sinful nature they have inherited from Adam, and replace it with His own nature and righteousness. As we learned in chapters three and four, we become spiritually reborn, receive the indwelling presence of the Holy Spirit, and are sealed into Christ for all time and eternity.

Transferring Us from the Dominion of Darkness to Light

God is in complete control of the world. It is divided into two different spiritual kingdoms—the kingdom of light and the kingdom of darkness. Every person on earth occupies one of these two spiritual kingdoms. There are only two kinds of people in the world: the lost and the found, the saved and the condemned, the forgiven and the guilty, the children of light and the children of darkness. This darkness has nothing to do with color, race, or social status. Darkness is the absence of light. It is moral and spiritual darkness that commits us to an eternity outside of God's love.

When a person is born again, they are transferred totally and permanently out of Satan's dominion of darkness and become eternal children of God.

Read these passages carefully:

> "And you were dead in your trespasses and sins, in which you formerly walked according to the course of this world, according to the prince of the power of the air, of the spirit that is now working in the sons of disobedience. Among them we too all formerly lived in the lusts of our flesh, indulging the desires of the flesh and of the mind, and were by nature children of wrath, even as the rest" (Ephesians 2:1-3 NASB).

> "Giving thanks to the Father, who has qualified us to share in the inheritance of the saints in Light" (Colossians 1:12 NASB).

"To open their eyes so that they may turn from darkness to light and from the dominion of Satan to God, that they may receive forgiveness of sins and an inheritance among those who have been sanctified by faith in Me" (Acts 26:18 NASB).

"Do not be bound together with unbelievers; for what partnership have righteousness and lawlessness, or what fellowship has light with darkness?" (2 Corinthians 6:14 NASB).

"For you were formerly darkness, but now you are Light in the Lord; walk as children of Light" (Ephesians 5:8 NASB).

God's *kingdom of light* is comprised of people who have received Jesus Christ as their Savior and have accepted Jesus' death and resurrection as the full payment for their sins. *Satan's kingdom of darkness* is comprised of everyone else—for all humans have sinned and fallen short of the glory of God (Romans 3:23). The Bible says that when we are saved, we get a kingdom transfer!

"For he has rescued us from the kingdom of darkness and transferred us into the Kingdom of his dear Son" (Colossians 1:13 NLT).

Thankfully, the Holy Spirit has a ministry in both kingdoms to draw men from the dark to the light. His role is to bring all men and women to the light of Jesus Christ. As we have seen this is all accomplished by the work of the Holy Spirit operating through the preaching of the gospel by the local church.

> *Whenever a person comes to faith in Jesus, the Lord breathes the Holy Spirit into them, creating a brand new spiritual person!*

The Indwelling Presence of God

Once a person is born again, they receive the full indwelling presence of the triune God through the person of the Holy Spirit. Every true Christian has the Spirit of God dwelling in them—that is, in their spirit. The evening of Jesus' resurrection, He appeared to His disciples. This is what occurred:

"When He had said this, He showed them His hands and His side. Then the disciples were glad when they saw the Lord. So Jesus said to them again, 'Peace to you! As the Father has sent Me, I also send you.' And when He had said this, He breathed on them, and said to them, 'Receive the Holy Spirit.'" (John 20:20-22).

Jesus Gave His Disciples the Indwelling Presence of the Holy Spirit on the Day of His Resurrection

He did not make them wait. In the original Greek, this image is powerful. It indicates that Jesus went to each of His followers and actually breathed His own resurrected breath into them. The word translated "breathed on" is actually the Greek word that means "to inflate by breathing into."

This was actually Jesus reenacting the creative act by which God had created the first man in Genesis 1 and 2. He breathed into Adam the breath of life and Adam became a living soul. Through this moment, we see that whenever a person comes to faith in Jesus, the Lord breathes the Holy Spirit into them, creating a brand new spiritual person! This represents the first placement of the Holy Spirit into the believer's life, the new birth.

He Anoints and Seals Us

After creating a new spirit within us and dwelling permanently inside our new hearts, He also seals His presence and salvation inside of us, thus personally guaranteeing our final redemption. This seal is the precious work of God that marks us as God's children for all time and eternity.

Seven Benefits of Being Born of the Spirit:

1. Gives us authority over Satan and evil spirits (Mark 16:18).

2. Gives us power over sin and the flesh (Romans 8:2, 13).

3. Confirms us and assures us that we are God's children (Romans 8:16).

4. Guides us into the will of God (Romans 8:14).

5. Enables us to obey God's commands.

> "Those who obey God's commandments remain in fellowship with him, and he with them. And we know he lives in us because the Spirit he gave us lives in us" (1 John 3:24 NLT).

6. Seals us in Christ and guarantees our inheritance.

> "In Him you also trusted, after you heard the word of truth, the gospel of your salvation; in whom also, having believed, you were sealed with the Holy Spirit of promise, who is the guarantee of our inheritance until the redemption of the purchased possession, to the praise of His glory" (Ephesians 1:13-14).

> "And do not grieve the Holy Spirit of God, by whom you were sealed for the day of redemption" (Ephesians 4:30).

7. Gives us direct access to the Father in prayer.

> "For through Him we both have access by one Spirit to the Father" (Ephesians 2:18).

DAY 2 EXERCISES

1. What is the first work of the Holy Spirit? _____
_____

2. Jesus said that the Holy Spirit would begin His work by convicting the world of _____,
   _____, and _____.

3. According to Colossians 1:13 (NASB), when a person is saved, they are transferred from
   _____ to _____.

4. What does "breathe on" mean in the Greek? _____
_____

5. What are the seven benefits of being born of the Spirit?
   1. _____
   2. _____
   3. _____
   4. _____
   5. _____
   6. _____
   7. _____

6. Romans says that the Holy Spirit helps us when we pray. Prayer is an integral part of the
   Christian life. Write Romans 8:26 below.

_____
_____
_____
_____

DAY 3: THE BAPTISM OF THE HOLY SPIRIT

The Baptism of the Holy Spirit

There is a second work of the Holy Spirit in the life of the believer. This is referred to by different names in the Scriptures. It is called:

- The gift of the Holy Spirit;
- The baptism of, or in, the Holy Spirit;
- Being "filled with the Holy Spirit";
- The promise of the Father;
- Receiving the Holy Spirit.

All of these terms are used in the Scriptures to refer to this special work of the Holy Spirit in the believer's life. It is important to note that while all believers have the indwelling presence of the Spirit in the new birth, not all believers have received this special gift of being filled or baptized with the Holy Spirit.

In the new birth, the Holy Spirit creates a new spirit inside the believer and comes to dwell permanently inside of them. The baptism of the Holy Spirit is a *second* gift that God offers to all His children—one that gives the believer power to be a witness to others. This special gift is not the same thing as being born again. It is a distinct experience in which the Lord Jesus immerses the born-again believer in the power and life of the Holy Spirit.

What is the Baptism in the Holy Spirit?

Jesus said, "But you shall receive power when the Holy Spirit has come upon you; and you shall be witnesses to Me…and to the end of the earth" (Acts 1:8). Baptism in the Holy Spirit is a gift that infuses spiritual power into the life of the believer, enabling them to become effective witnesses. This power is a special anointing that produces a heightened sensitivity to the Spirit's presence, a greater operation of spiritual gifts through the believer, and a deeper hunger for spiritual things and insight into the Word of God. It also introduces the believer to a new dimension of worship and prayer.

> *The baptism of the Holy Spirit is a second gift that God offers to all His children—one that gives the believer power to be a witness to others.*

Don't I Get Baptized in the Holy Spirit When I Become Born Again?

There are different ways that Christians look at the baptism of the Holy Spirit. Some believe that when a person is born again, they also receive the baptism in the Holy Spirit—that they are one and the same experience. But there are several reasons why *this cannot be true.*

While every Christian receives *the indwelling presence of the Holy Spirit* the moment they believe on Jesus Christ, *the baptism of the Holy Spirit* is a second and distinct gift that is typically received *after* one has been born again. We have three important examples of this in the Bible.

1. The First Disciples

The apostles had two separate experiences with the Holy Spirit. Jesus appeared to His disciples the day He was raised from the dead and, "He breathed on (into) them, and said to them 'Receive the Holy Spirit'" (John 20:22).

The Holy Spirit came *into* them that day and they were born again. After many days, Jesus commanded His disciples "not to depart from Jerusalem, but to wait for the Promise of the Father, 'which,' He said, 'you have heard from Me; for John truly baptized with water, but you shall be baptized with the Holy Spirit not many days from now'" (Acts 1:4-5).

Ten days later, on the day of Pentecost, "they were all with one accord in one place. And suddenly there came a sound from heaven, as of a rushing mighty wind…and they were all filled with the Holy Spirit and began to speak with other tongues, as the Spirit gave them utterance" (Acts 2:1-2, 4).

These passages prove that the first disciples received two distinct experiences with the Holy Spirit. The first was the Spirit coming *into* them making them born-again children of God. The second was the Holy Spirit coming *upon* them in power enabling them to be witnesses.

2. The Samaritans

In Acts 8, Phillip, the evangelist, went to the city of Samaria and preached the gospel to them. The Samaritans received the gospel, and were baptized in water. Jesus taught that when a person believes the gospel and is baptized in water, they are saved (Mark 16:16). But Phillip knew that they also needed the special gift of the Holy Spirit. So he called for Peter and John to come to Samaria and lay hands upon the believers so that they could "receive the Holy Spirit. For as yet He had fallen upon none of them. They had only been baptized in the name of the Lord Jesus" (Acts 8:15-16). When the apostles laid hands upon them, they received the gift of the Holy Spirit.

If being saved automatically included the baptism in the Holy Spirit, then Phillip would not have needed to call for Peter and John to minister the gift of the Holy Spirit to the Samaritan Christians.

3. The Ephesians

In Acts 19, Paul found some young believers in Jesus who had come to Christ through the ministry of a powerful preacher named Apollos. Paul asked them a question that confirms to us that being born again is not the same thing as being baptized in the Holy Spirit. These Ephesian believers knew and spoke convincingly about their faith in Jesus, but Paul asked, "Did you receive the Holy Spirit when you believed?" (Acts 19:2a). If believing and being born again automatically gave one the gift of the Holy Spirit, then Paul would not have asked this question. The Ephesians responded, "We have not so much as heard whether there is a Holy Spirit." Apparently, Apollos spoke convincingly about Jesus, but never went any further in teaching his converts about Christian baptism or the gift of the Holy Spirit.

Paul went on to explain the difference between John the Baptist's baptism of repentance, which looked forward to the cross, and Christian baptism, which is a baptism of faith in the completed work of Christ. He evidently also taught them about the baptism of the Holy Spirit. Paul baptized the Ephesians in the name of Jesus, laid hands upon them, and the "Holy Spirit came upon them, and they spoke with tongues and [also] prophesied" (Acts 19:6).

The Promise of the Father to All Believers

In Luke 24:49, Jesus appeared to the disciples after his resurrection and promised them this: "And now I will send the Holy Spirit, just as my Father promised. But stay here in the city until the Holy Spirit comes and fills you with power from heaven" (NLT).

In Acts 1:4-5, the Bible says that Jesus commanded them not to leave Jerusalem until they received this "Promise of the Father, 'which,' He said, 'you have heard from Me; for John truly baptized with water, *but you shall be baptized with the Holy Spirit* not many days from now.'" Notice the baptism of the Holy Spirit is called the "Promise of the Father." It was not an option for some, but a commandment of Jesus for all His disciples. Jesus ascended into heaven and, just ten days later, fulfilled His promise.

On the day of Pentecost, 120 believers received this promise: "And they were all filled with the Holy Spirit and began to speak with other tongues, as the Spirit gave them utterance" (Acts 2:4). Peter told the people that Jesus Himself had ascended to heaven, and "being exalted to the right hand of God, and having received from the Father the promise of the Holy Spirit, He poured out this which you now see and hear" (Acts 2:33).

Finally, Peter went on to explain to the three thousand people who witnessed the outpouring of this promise, and heard them speak in other tongues, that the experience was not only for those select disciples, but was something God intended for every believer present and throughout the entire church age—right up until today!

> "Peter replied, 'Each of you must repent of your sins and turn to God, and be baptized in the name of Jesus Christ for the forgiveness of your sins. Then you will receive the gift of the Holy Spirit. *This promise* is to you, and to your children, and even to the Gentiles—*all* who have been *called by the Lord our God*'" (Acts 2:38-39 NLT).

This means that the experience of being baptized in the Holy Spirit and speaking with other tongues was not just an unusual occurrence for those first few disciples, but a promise for all Christians in every age.

The Baptism in the Holy Spirit is Accompanied by the Experience of Speaking in Other Tongues

Speaking in other tongues is a special experience that occurs whenever someone receives the baptism in the Holy Spirit. Very often, those seeking this experience have very real and powerful encounters with the Holy Spirit that include a sudden sense of God's presence, overwhelming feelings of God's love, and strong urges to express thanksgiving and praise to the Lord. While all of these experiences are evidence that the Spirit of God has come upon the believer, it isn't until the believer actually speaks in a language they have never learned that the believer may say that they have been baptized in the Holy Spirit.

Speaking in Tongues is for Every Believer

In Mark 16:15-17, Jesus told the disciples to "Go into all the world and preach the gospel to every creature. *He who believes* and is baptized will be saved…And these signs will follow *those who believe*: In My name they will cast out demons; *they will speak with new tongues.*"

Jesus taught that one of the outward manifestations that shows that a person has become a believer in the gospel is that they will have *signs* accompany their life. We might say that the five signs listed in this passage were intended by Christ to be the normal experience of the Christian. It is important to recognize that Jesus did not say that these signs were to follow the twelve apostles' lives only, but rather *those that believe* the message preached by the apostles. In other words, Jesus intended every believer to enjoy spiritual authority over demonic forces (verse 17). He desired for every believer to lay hands on the sick and to believe for their recovery. He promised divine protection from environmental threats (poison and serpents) for every believer. And He said that the second sign that should accompany the new life of the Christian is that they "will speak with new tongues."

By teaching that speaking in tongues was a sign that accompanies believing the gospel, Jesus made it clear to the earliest disciples that it was His plan to introduce this new kind of prayer as a normal part of the life of every Christian. Since all of the earliest Christians spoke in tongues, and since it was a priority for the apostles to insure that every new church had the experience of being baptized in the Holy Spirit and speaking in tongues, it should not be shocking or unusual for Christians today to enjoy speaking in tongues as a part of their normal daily life.

The Baptism in the Holy Spirit is the Normal Christian Life

Many Christians today think that speaking in tongues is a strange and bizarre experience that God only intended as a sign for the earliest Christians to experience. But they did not get this idea from the Bible. God never intended for any Christian to live without this powerful gift.

For many centuries, the church neglected the teaching of the Scripture and this promise. Over time, some Christians grew to believe that speaking in tongues was something that only the first apostles experienced—something that God had long ago withdrawn from Christian life. Although small groups of believers throughout the ages have had various encounters with this gift, it wasn't until the last century that people all over the world began to take Jesus at His Word and desire to experience this wonderful gift.

Today, millions of Christians all over the world have joyfully experienced for themselves the baptism of the Holy Spirit, and speak in other tongues as a normal part of their Christian life. Recent global surveys of all Christian denominations conservatively estimate between 25–33% of all Christians worldwide speak in other tongues.

DAY 3 EXERCISES

1. What is the second gift that God offers to all of His children?

_____

2. What three groups of people from the Bible demonstrated that the baptism of the Holy Spirit is typically received after a person is born again?

1. _____

2. _____

3. _____

3. What is the evidence of the baptism of the Holy Spirit?

_____

_____

4. What percentage of Christians today speak in other tongues by the leading of the Holy Spirit?

_____

5. Historically, there has always been a percentage of the church that practiced and believed in the baptism of the Holy Spirit. It is a sign of our times that mankind wants to lean on their own ideas about God and not accept Jesus' own words about Himself. Look up Proverbs 3:5-6. What does this Scripture say to you about this concept?

_____

_____

_____

_____

_____

6. The baptism of the Holy Spirit is a special anointing that produces a heightened sensitivity to the Spirit's presence, a greater operation of spiritual gifts through the believer, and a deeper hunger for spiritual things and insight into the Word of God. It also introduces the believer to a new dimension of worship and prayer. Read this description again. How important do you think it is for you to have this experience?

_____

_____

_____

_____

DAY 4: RECEIVING THE GIFT

We have seen that there is a two-fold work of the Holy Spirit in the life of the believer: the new birth and the baptism in the Holy Spirit. The new birth gives us the indwelling presence of the Holy Spirit. The baptism in the Spirit gives us the power to be witnesses for Christ. The new birth makes one a child of God (John 1:12) and the baptism of the Spirit gives one power to reach others for God (Acts 1:8). The evidence that one has been born again is an internal peace with God (Romans 5:1) and a growing external manifestation of God's love for others (1 John 3:10-14; 4:7-8). The evidence that one has been baptized in the Holy Spirit is an internal power to be a witness for Christ, accompanied by a new spiritual language of prayer and worship that flows out of your heart, called speaking in other tongues.

SEVEN BIBLICAL PURPOSES OF PRAYING IN OTHER TONGUES

1. Supernatural Power

Jesus said that "you shall receive power when the Holy Spirit has come upon you"(Acts 1:8). This power is the life and special energy of the Spirit that enables the believer to minister to others.

2. Personal Edification (Enrichment)

Paul taught, "One who speaks in a tongue edifies himself" (1 Corinthians 14:4 NASB). The word translated "edify" means to build up, strengthen, or encourage. We all need the spiritual strength that comes from spending time speaking in other tongues.

3. Direct Spiritual Communication

Paul said, "If I pray in a tongue, my spirit prays, but my understanding [mind] is unfruitful [or uninvolved]" (1 Corinthians 14:14). When we pray in tongues, our born again spirit has direct communication with God, bypassing our mind and its many natural impulses and limitations. In this way, our human spirit is able to speak to God in perfect language. While our minds may not know what we are communicating, with our spirit we can be assured we are praying according to the perfect will of God. This is an invaluable tool in Christian prayer because it enables us to pray for people, things, and circumstances that are way past the capacities of our limited knowledge.

4. Expansion of our Worship and Thanksgiving

The Bible says that when we worship God with our spirit (in other tongues) we "give thanks well," or praise and thank God with excellence (1 Corinthians 14:17).

5. Praying "Out" Divine Mysteries

Paul taught that when one prays in tongues, "in [or with] the spirit he speaks mysteries" (1 Corinthians 14:2). The word translated "mysteries" is a word that means knowledge or information that is unknown to the speaker. There are things that God knows that we do not. When we pray in tongues, we release that hidden knowledge out of our spirit. Often the Holy Spirit will reveal what we are saying in tongues to our minds through inspired thoughts, images, and internal pictures that can direct us further in our prayers according to the plan of God.

6. Praying in Tongues Refreshes the Believer

In Isaiah, the prophet foresaw this gift and said "with stammering lips and another tongue He will speak to this people…'this is the rest with which you may cause the weary to rest,' and 'this is the refreshing'" (Isaiah 28:11-12). Praying in a heavenly language actually causes our minds to become still and worry to melt away, while an instant connection is made to our own spirit. This creates a sense of rest, peace, and spiritual rejuvenation!

7. Help in Praying for Ourselves and Others

Paul said that we do not always know how to pray as we should. But the Holy Spirit will intercede for (with and through) us with deep, passionate groans and utterances (Romans 8:26). Praying in tongues is the doorway to the gifts of the Holy Spirit. It opens our hearts to other supernatural experiences and is a door to the life of spiritual power and supernatural living. God NEVER intended us to be without it. This is why Paul said "I thank my God I speak with tongues more than you all!" And, "Do not forbid anyone from speaking in tongues."

> "For he who speaks in a tongue does not speak to men but to God, for no one understands *him;* however, in the spirit he speaks mysteries" (1 Corinthians 14:2).

> "For if you have the ability to speak in tongues, you will be talking only to God, since people won't be able to understand you. *You will be speaking by the power of the Spirit,* but it will all be mysterious" (1 Corinthians 14:2 NLT).

> "For with stammering lips and another tongue He will speak to this people, to whom He said, 'This is the rest with which You may cause the weary to rest,' and, 'This is the refreshing'; yet they would not hear" (Isaiah 28:11-12).

Faith is an act of the heart responding to God by taking what He has provided.

THE GIFT OF THE HOLY SPIRIT RECEIVED BY FAITH

Everything we receive from God must be received by faith. Faith is the hand that reaches up and receives all the blessings that God offers.

Faith Does Not Beg, but Asks

The gift of the Holy Spirit is received by asking in simple faith, not by desperate pleadings, or begging. We are to approach God like a generous Father who wants to give to us, not like a stingy judge who requires us to be morally perfect or worthy before He will bestow the baptism of the Holy Spirit upon our lives.

"If you then, being evil, know how to give good gifts to your children, *how much more will your heavenly Father give the Holy Spirit to those who ask Him!*" (Luke 11:13).

Faith Requires Receiving Action on Our Part

Many people expect the Holy Spirit to seize their mouths or make them speak in tongues. Nothing could be more uncharacteristic of the nature of the Holy Spirit. He is a gentle, yet powerful being of great love. He never forces us to speak. Some people take the approach, "If God wants me to have this experience, then He will just give it to me." But this approach is passive. It requires nothing on the part of the believer. This attitude would be the equivalent of an unbeliever saying to God, "If the Lord wants me to be saved, then He will just have to save me." Such an approach may appear spiritual, but in fact it is a lazy, passive, and poor substitute for faith. Real faith always considers the promise that God has made, and takes responsibility to believe and receive. *Faith* is an act of the heart *responding to God by taking* what He has provided.

Faith Involves the Will

At Pentecost, the believers *did the speaking*, while the Holy Spirit *supplied the words*. Much like reading a book out loud, or repeating something whispered in your ear, neither the book nor the whisperer force the speaker to talk. The speaker chooses to repeat what is being read or heard. In this way, speaking in tongues involves a conscious choice to begin speaking out loud the unfamiliar words or sounds that are supplied by the Holy Spirit.

"And they were all filled (diffused throughout their souls) with the Holy Spirit and began to speak in other (different, foreign) languages (tongues), *as the Spirit kept giving them clear and loud expression* [*in each tongue in appropriate words*]*"* (Acts 2:4 AMP).

THE GIFT OF THE HOLY SPIRIT REQUIRES VOCALIZED PRAISE

Many times when praying for people to receive the gift of the Holy Spirit, there is a hesitancy to actually praise the Lord out loud. Some people are not used to openly expressing their worship to the Lord due to years of religious training to internalize their prayers and worship. But, in the Bible, we see that God's people are always encouraged to offer their prayer, praise, and worship out loud. We should never be ashamed to praise the Lord. Psalm 149 and 150 are celebrations of vocalized and expressive praise and worship. We must be willing to outwardly express our love for God, because the gift of the Holy Spirit is a gift of power to express outwardly our witness to Jesus Christ!

"But you will receive power when the Holy Spirit comes upon you. And you will be my witnesses, telling people about me everywhere—in Jerusalem, throughout Judea, in Samaria, and to the ends of the earth" (Act 1:8 NLT).

While the gift of tongues often begins as words the Holy Spirit brings into the mind, those words must be immediately spoken in bold faith out loud. The bolder one is to speak out loud, the more powerful the experience of being baptized in the Holy Spirit becomes.

THE GIFT OF THE HOLY SPIRIT INVOLVES THE SURRENDER OF OUR FLESH

Sometimes people have difficulty letting go of the mental control of their bodies and allowing their born-again spirit to take over in directing their tongue. People are often self-conscious. They fear what others may think of them, are afraid of making a mistake, or of sounding strange to others. All of these concerns are understandable, but usually involve two things that in our flesh will hinder our walk with God: fear and pride. The Scripture exhorts us to yield our bodies as instruments of righteousness to God (Romans 6:13).

1. Fear of Man

In today's world, many people are more concerned about their image, reputation, or standing in other people's eyes than they are about doing what their heart may be urging them to do. It is common today to celebrate people who conform to a group idea of acceptable behavior. Many are so afraid of being rejected by others that they are crippled when it comes to walking according to their faith in God. The Bible teaches that the fear of man brings a snare (Proverbs 29:25). Paul said, "Obviously, I'm not trying to win the approval of people, but of God. If pleasing people were my goal, I would not be Christ's servant" (Galatians 1:10 NLT). To receive the gift of the Holy Spirit, one must be willing to put aside the fear of man, and choose to be a pleaser of God.

2. Pride

Pride is the human desire to preserve one's own dignity. It is the opposite of surrender. In order to receive from God, we must surrender our pride and need to control, and be willing to yield our bodies and mouth in trust to God. There is something in our flesh that likes to be in control. Speaking in tongues is a wonderful way to crucify this selfish tendency and humbly allow our bodies to be used to glorify and magnify God. There is nothing more freeing than setting aside our fear of others, humbling ourselves in the sight of God, and joyfully expressing our prayer and praise in our Spirit-inspired language to the Lord.

YOU CAN RECEIVE THE GIFT OF THE HOLY SPIRIT RIGHT NOW!

There are several ways that the gift of the Holy Spirit may be received:

1. In Group Prayer or Gatherings with Other Believers

The first Christians were in a prayer meeting together when they "were all filled with the Holy Spirit and began to speak with other tongues" (Acts 2:4). In Acts 10, Peter was sent to preach to a house full of people when the Holy Spirit was suddenly given.

> "And the following day they entered Caesarea. Now Cornelius was waiting for them, and had called together his relatives and close friends....And as he talked with him, he went in and *found many who had come together*....Then Peter opened his mouth and said: 'In truth I perceive that God shows no partiality.'... While Peter was still speaking these words, the *Holy Spirit fell upon all those who heard the word.* And [the Jewish believers who came with Peter]...were astonished...because the *gift of the Holy Spirit* had been *poured out* on the

Gentiles also. For they *heard them speak with tongues and magnify God*. Then Peter answered, 'Can anyone forbid water, that these should not be baptized *who have received the Holy Spirit just as we have*?'" (Acts 10:24, 27, 34, 44-47).

2. By the Laying on of Hands

In Samaria and Ephesus, the believers received the Holy Spirit when God's leaders laid hands on them in prayer. It is scriptural to ask spiritual leaders or other believers who have been filled with the Holy Spirit to pray with you and lay their hands on you in faith.

> "Now when the apostles who were at Jerusalem heard that Samaria had received the word of God, they sent Peter and John to them, who, when they had come down, *prayed for them* that they might *receive the Holy Spirit*. For as yet He had fallen upon none of them. They had only been baptized in the name of the Lord Jesus. Then *they laid hands on them, and they received the Holy Spirit"*
> (Acts 8:14-17).

3. In Private Prayer Alone with God

Many believers have studied the Scriptures on the subject of the gift of the Holy Spirit, and asked God in their own private devotions to fill them with His Spirit. God is good, gracious, and always ready to give the gift of His Holy Spirit baptism to anyone who is ready to ask, believe, and act in faith. The Apostle Paul received the gift of the Holy Spirit in private prayer with only one other believer praying with him.

> "And Ananias…entered the house; and laying his hands on him he said, 'Brother Saul, the Lord Jesus, who appeared to you on the road as you came, has sent me that you may receive your sight and be filled with the Holy Spirit'" (Acts 9:17).

Have You Received the Gift of the Holy Spirit Since You Believed?

God desires all His children to enjoy the special gift of the baptism in the Holy Spirit. If you have already received Jesus Christ as your Lord and Savior, you have the indwelling presence of the Holy Spirit. He is in you and will never leave you or forsake you. He has sealed you in Christ, and enables you to be a child of God and grow as a follower of Jesus.

Now the Father has another gift for you to receive. It is a deeper and richer experience with the same Holy Spirit who saved you and lives in you today. This gift is a spiritual baptism of supernatural power that will enable you to be a greater witness for God. This gift will release a new heavenly language that will flow directly from your spirit. As you open your mouth and speak in this language by faith, God will fill you with His presence in a fresh and new way.

He is ready. As you have been reading this chapter, the Lord has been preparing your heart. The Spirit of God is with you this very moment as you read these words. You may receive this special gift right now!

Pray This Prayer Out Loud from Your Heart:

Dear Father in heaven, I thank You today for the gift of Your Son, Jesus Christ; I thank You for saving me from my sins by washing me in His precious blood. I thank You for making me

Your child, and giving me Your Holy Spirit to live and dwell inside me. Today I see that You have promised another gift that You desire for me to have—the baptism in the Holy Spirit.

Father, I desire this gift. (You said in Your Word, that if I asked You for bread, You would not give me a stone, so how much more will You give the Holy Spirit to those who ask You!) So right now I ask You, Lord Jesus, to baptize me in Your Holy Spirit, filling me to overflowing, just as You did on the day of Pentecost—with the evidence of speaking in other tongues! Fill me now with Your Holy Spirit, in Jesus' mighty name!

I believe that I receive the gift of the Holy Spirit and right now by faith I will begin praying and speaking in other tongues, as Your Spirit gives me the words. I thank You, Father, for this right now, in the name of Your Son, Jesus Christ!

Now lift your hands and begin to thank and praise God out loud for this wonderful gift! Do not ask Him again, but instead begin to joyfully thank Him by faith. After a few moments of joyful praise, switch from using your natural language to thanking Him with the new language that is bubbling up inside you right now. Open your mouth and begin speaking the words and sounds that are forming inside you! At first, this may be only a few words, unusual sounds, or syllables, but speak them out loud in faith!

As you begin yielding your tongue to these new sounds, more will come. Continue to worship in this wonderful new language for as long as you desire.

Some things to remember:

- Now that you have begun to speak in tongues, you may do so at any time. Paul said. "I will pray with the spirit [in other tongues], and I will also pray with the understanding [my native language]" (1 Corinthians 14:15). You now have the opportunity to pray and worship with your mind and with your spirit in other tongues!

- Make a decision to pray in tongues at least once a day for ten minutes. The more you pray in tongues, the less self-conscious you will be in prayer and the greater the flow of heavenly language will become.

- When you speak in tongues for the first time, if you are alone, make sure to call someone who has been filled with the Spirit and tell them what God has done for you! Your witness will strengthen the power of the Spirit in your life!

- If you are reading *The Transformed Life* as part of a group Bible study, report your experience to your group leader or teacher. Share what happened when you prayed. If you have any questions, or would like to have prayer to receive this gift, ask those present to pray with you.

- When you come to church, be sure to come on time for worship. Use your heavenly language to worship God in church. Make sure your worship flows along with what God is doing in the congregation. The volume of your worship in tongues should flow along with the general volume and spirit of worship coming from the congregation. In this way, your experience of worship is neither repressed nor distracting from the overall experience of what is happening in the congregation. Naturally, it is much easier to use your prayer language in congregational worship if the church you attend believes in the gifts of the Holy Spirit and encourages open and demonstrative worship expression in the congregation.

- Whenever using your prayer language in corporate worship or in church services, make sure your volume and expression of praise does not rise above the praise of others. If this occurs, some may expect that you are delivering a message in tongues to the entire church body. There is a special gift of speaking in various kinds of tongues that God gives to some members of the body of Christ. This is different from the private devotional prayer language that every believer receives when they are baptized in the Holy Spirit.

DAY 4 EXERCISES

1. What does the word *edify* mean?

_____

_____

_____

2. What is the two-fold work of the Holy Spirit in the life of the believer?

   1. _____

   2. _____

3. According to Luke 11:13, what is the key to receiving good gifts from our Father?

_____

_____

4. What two things in our flesh will hinder our walk with God?

   1. _____

   2. _____

5. What are three ways that you can receive the gift of the Holy Spirit?

   1. _____

   2. _____

   3. _____

6. Earlier in the book, we read Romans 8:26. Today write the next verse as well: Romans 8:27.

_____

_____

_____

_____

CHAPTER SIX

THE TRANSFORMED MIND

CHAPTER SIX
The Transformed Mind

DAY 1: CHANGING THE WAY WE THINK

It may come as a shock to hear this, but nearly all of your problems are in your head. In fact, the majority of the struggles we face in our daily lives are *head* problems. This doesn't mean you need to check in to the psych ward at the nearest hospital. Nor does this mean that your problems are imaginary or hallucinations. The reason most of our problems are head problems is because most of the ongoing challenges we face in life result from *the way we think*. We have thinking problems. Therefore, until we change the way we think *within* our lives, we are incapable of finding the answers we need to actually *change* our lives.

The transformed life requires radical change. You can change your address, change your job, change your wardrobe, change your friends, you can even change your name. However, your life will not change until you change the way you think. Becoming a Christian begins the process of transformation. Your spirit becomes new, your eternal destination changes, your relationship with God changes. Yet even with all these wonderful adjustments, we are left in the world, remain in a body, and are stuck with a mind that is pretty much the same.

"For as he thinks within himself, so he is" (Proverbs 23:7a NASB).

"And do not be conformed to this world, but *be transformed by the renewing of your mind*, that you may prove what is that good and acceptable and perfect will of God" (Romans 12:2).

"Don't copy the behavior and customs of this world, but let *God transform you into a new person by changing the way you think*. Then you will learn to know God's will for you, which is good and pleasing and perfect" (Romans 12:2 NLT).

The Mystery of the Mind

We are living in unprecedented times. In the last twenty years, our generation has witnessed the greatest advances in our collective understanding of one of God's greatest gifts—the human mind. For centuries, doctors, psychologists, philosophers, sociologists and biologists have sought to understand the workings of the human mind and the physical container which holds it—our brain.

Much work had been done to understand how our life experience, environment, and heredity impacts how we think, feel, and behave. Yet the greatest mysteries of the mind remained unsolved. For example, how exactly does an image seen by the eye become stored in the soft gray tissue of the brain so that it can be vividly recalled, described, and even artistically recreated? Where does an idea actually come from? How and why does thought affect our bodies? Why do persistent kinds of thinking show up in our physical bodies—either in health or sickness?

Because of wonderful breakthroughs in science and technology, the rapidly growing science of neurology has begun to deliver remarkable answers to these and many other questions. We have begun to see that our brains are organs that can be developed, trained, and enhanced. Much like a muscle, the brain may also grow in both strength and precision. Parts of the brain that are neglected or left unused actually begin to shrink and become more difficult to access. Amazingly, we have just begun to learn that even the weakest, least stimulated parts of the brain may be energized, rewired, and provoked to grow when intentionally stimulated over time.

This means that the brain you were born with has the capacity to change—for the better or for the worse! It also implies that even if your brain has been "wired" for depression, negativity, addiction, or anxiety, given the right stimulus and placed under the right healthy "stresses," it can be rewired, changed, and renewed.

This comes as no surprise to Christians. The Bible said long ago that our minds could be changed. God's Word was given to help us to rewire our thinking and change our minds so that we may transform our lives.

God Transforms Us Progressively

One of the most important truths of the Christian faith is the teaching of *how* God transforms us from sinners to saints. When we become born again, we instantly become the children of God. Something in our hearts has changed. Yet we know that as powerful as that spiritual transformation is, there is still much about us from the human standpoint that is far from complete. We rejoice in our new relationship with God, yet struggle each day with persistent desires in our flesh, feelings, and minds that seem contrary to the change that our hearts have received. The question often persists, "If I am born again, why do I still struggle with my mind and flesh?"

The answer to this question is found in the biblical doctrine of sanctification. *Sanctification* simply means, "to be set apart for special purpose." It refers to the process by which something is cleansed, purified, and prepared for special use. It means, "to make holy." The teaching of sanctification, then, is the Christian understanding of how God takes us from a worldly life and begins to cleanse us and prepare us for His purposes.

The Bible teaches that this process occurs in three stages: *present, progressive,* and *promised.* These three stages are important to understand because they correspond to three different aspects of our human nature—*spirit, soul,* and *body.*

God's plan for our salvation extends to the whole of our being. In 1 Thessalonians 5:23, Paul prayed, "Now may the God of Peace Himself *sanctify* you completely; and may your whole *spirit, soul,* and *body* be preserved blameless [holy] at the coming of our Lord Jesus Christ." Just as God created us as spirit, soul, and body, God's purpose is to redeem us in all three dimensions of our being through a series of stages. These stages correspond with the three parts of our human architecture mentioned in the above passage.

> *The reason most of our problems are head problems is because most of the ongoing challenges we face in life result from the way we think.*

STAGES OF SALVATION

In one sense, the believer has been saved. In another sense the believer is being saved. And in yet another sense, it is perfectly correct to say that the believer has yet to be saved. These are not contradictory ideas; rather they beautifully explain the stages of salvation God has designed in His plan of redemption.

1. The Born Again Spirit is Saved

When a person is born again, they instantly receive the gift of eternal life. The spirit of the believer is instantly and completely transformed the moment one hears and believes the gospel. We become new creations in Christ *in our spirits*. At that moment, it may be said that we are *presently saved*.

As we learned in chapter four, this new birth is radical, complete, and permanent. While our spirit may grow in knowledge, grace, faith, and power, it does not become more perfect or righteous over time. At the moment we believe in Jesus, we become the *saved* children of God.

> "[God] made us alive together with Christ (by grace *you have been* saved)" (Ephesians 2:5).

> "For by grace *you have been saved* through faith, and that not of yourselves; it is the gift of God" (Ephesians 2:8).

> "These things I have written to you who believe in the name of the Son of God, *that you may know that you have eternal life*, and that you may continue to believe in the name of the Son of God" (1 John 5:13).

2. The Believer's Soul is Being Saved

The new birth, however, does not cause the same transformation in the believer's mind or *soul*. Often we use the terms *soul* and *spirit* interchangeably, but in the New Testament Epistles (or letters), God makes a clear distinction between the two. The word *soul* comes from the Greek word *psuche*, or *psyche* and is typically used to refer to the mind, emotions, and will of human nature. The Greek word *psyche* is the root for our English words *psychology* and *psychiatry*, which are sciences devoted to understanding and healing the human mind.

The soul comprises the human mind, intellect, reason, emotions, and will. While your spirit is the eternal and essential "you," the human soul, or mind, is the intellectual and emotional "you." You use your soul in order to think, feel, relate to others, and process the data you receive through the senses of your physical body. With your spirit you touch God; with your body you touch the earth; but with your soul or mind you process and decide how to live in this world. In this chapter, we are going to use the word soul and mind interchangeably.

When we are born again, our minds still contain the memories, the patterns of thinking, the feelings, and the general outlook or our pre-Christian life. The soul requires transformation. It must be changed to reflect the true condition the believer has achieved through faith in Christ. This process of transformation occurs over the believer's lifetime. By renewing our minds, we transfer the genuine experience of our spirit into our visible natural lives.

> "So get rid of all the filth and evil in your lives, and humbly accept *the word God has planted* in your hearts, for it has *the power to save your souls*" (James 1:21 NLT).

> "Do not be conformed to this world, but be transformed by the renewing of your mind" (Romans 12:2a).

> "And be renewed in the spirit of your mind" (Ephesians 4:23).

3. The Body Has Yet to Be Saved

The Bible teaches in 2 Corinthians 4:7 that our salvation is a "treasure [contained] in earthen vessels" or "clay jars" (NLT). The "clay jars" Paul is referring to are our physical bodies. We have this wonderful, brand-new, born-again spirit in the same, old, unchanged physical body. In the next chapter we will learn about God's plan for the salvation of our bodies, but for now it is enough that we understand that it is clear that the change we experience when we are saved does not substantially happen in our bodies. After salvation, our bodies continue to age, to weaken, and ultimately, to die.

However, the Bible does promise that there is coming a day where the Lord will raise up our lowly earthly bodies and transform them to be like Jesus' glorious body! In this sense, we have yet to be saved—but it's only a matter of time.

> "For our citizenship is in heaven, from which we also eagerly wait for the Savior, the Lord Jesus Christ, *who will transform our lowly body* that it may be conformed to His glorious body, according to the working by which He is able even to subdue all things to Himself" (Philippians 3:20-21).

> "And we believers also groan, even though we have the Holy Spirit within us as a foretaste of future glory, for *we long for our bodies to be released* from sin and suffering. We, too, wait with eager hope for the day when God will give us our full rights as his adopted children, *including the new bodies he has promised us"* (Romans 8:23 NLT).

Dividing the Soul and Spirit

> "For the word of God is quick, and powerful, and sharper than any twoedged sword…dividing asunder soul and spirit, and of the joints and marrow, and is a discerner of the thoughts and intentions of the heart" (Hebrews 4:12 KJV).

Only the Word of God can correctly help us to divide or see the difference between the human soul and the human spirit. Understanding whether a thought or urge is coming from your human soul or born-again spirit is critical to growing up in God. This is why Paul said that it is only once we renew our minds, that we can prove what God's will is for our lives.

> "Be transformed by the renewing of your mind, *so that you may prove what the will of God is"* (Romans 12:2 NASB).

The primary reason believers in Jesus do not experience lasting and ongoing change is because they have not changed the way they think. They have brand-new spirits, but the same old heads.

Receiving Christ changes your heart, your eternal destination, and your relationship with God; but until you change the way you think, your life will remain largely unchanged. This is why Peter teaches us,

> "As newborn babes [in Christ], desire the pure milk of the word, that you may grow thereby" (1 Peter 2:2).

DAY 1 EXERCISES

Fill in the blanks.

1. The born again_____ *is* saved.

2. The _____ has *yet to be* saved.

3. The believer's _____ is b*eing* saved.

4. What helps us to correctly divide, or see, the difference between the human soul and human spirit?

_____

_____

5. What is the primary reason believers in Jesus do not experience lasting change?

_____

_____

_____

6. The Word of God has the power to expose our thought life. It brings clarity and help to us and strengthens us as we read it. Commit Romans 12:1-2 to memory. To help in that process, write it here.

_____

_____

_____

_____

_____

_____

DAY 2: HOW THE MIND WORKS

THE ARCHITECTURE OF THE MIND

The human mind is a wonderful and fascinating gift from God. While the brain is the physical organ that houses and enables the mind to operate in the body, it is through a network called the central nervous system that the mind is able to make sense of the world. The central nervous system is an intricate network of communication that transmits, receives, and interprets billions of chemical and electrical signals, which are continuously flowing between the mind and the physical world around us. Thinking is a function of interpreting these signals, giving them meaning, and ultimately choosing to act upon them.

For this reason, it is absolutely essential that the "data" we are receiving is accurate, appropriate, and interpreted correctly. When we have bad data, we will make inaccurate interpretations, and ultimately, wrong decisions. Therefore, we must make sure we are receiving the right data, avoiding the wrong data, and developing the skills of processing and interpreting that will lead to decisions that are good, God-pleasing, and conducive to living a transformed life.

> *While we cannot stop every thought that arises, we alone are responsible for what we allow to engage our minds.*

God and Your Thought Life

God cares about your mind. He is very clear that our thoughts are both visible and important to Him. Psalm 19:14 says, "May the words of my mouth and the meditation of my heart (mind) be pleasing to you, O Lord, my rock and my redeemer" (NLT). That means that God sees what we think in our hearts and minds. Our thought life can either be acceptable or unacceptable to God. In Hebrews 4:13, the Bible teaches us that "all things are naked and open to the eyes of Him to whom we must give account." Not only does God see our thoughts, He will hold us accountable for them.

You cannot be held accountable for something over which you have no control. Many people have bought the modern lie that "I can't help what I think," or that the Devil somehow has the power to control our thought life. Often people blame others for how they think, saying, "You made me think that." But in reality, if either Satan or other people truly had the power to make you or I think something, then it would be highly unfair for God to hold us responsible for our thoughts. Yet over and over in the Bible we are told not only what to think, but that our thought life is our responsibility. This means we can possess our own minds, manage our thought life, and choose what we will allow to play on the screen of our minds.

That doesn't mean that we can control every thought that arrives in our mind from the world around us. Every day, thoughts inspired by other people, our environment, and even evil spirits will come knocking on the door of your mind. These thoughts provoke many feelings that seek to take root in our minds. While we cannot prevent thoughts from coming to the door of our minds, we can choose which thoughts we are going to allow inside. Whether or not we invite a thought inside, entertain it in our mental living room, or let it live in a spare bedroom in our heads is *entirely up to us.* A wise man once said, "Thoughts will come and thoughts will go, but thoughts that are not put into word or action will die—unborn."

Our minds are like the wide-screen TV in your home. You cannot choose what the broadcasters will play on a given channel at a given time, but you can choose what channels you are going to allow to play in your home. This is why we must take ownership of our minds, and win the battle over the "remote." Because whatever you allow to fill your mind will eventually show up in your life. Proverbs 4:23 says "Keep your heart [mind] with all diligence, for out of it spring the issues [experiences and events] of life." Show me your mind, and I'll show you your future. You cannot fill your mind with worldly thinking, ungodly entertainment, unclean language and images, negative news reports, and fear-filled imaginations, then expect your life to be filled with the blessings and promises of God.

Components of Your Mind

1. The Intellect (The mind's "library")
The intellect has the capacity to gain knowledge and use it in thought. It has the ability to learn and associate.

2. Imagination (The mind's "eye")
The imagination has the capacity to create possibilities and form new ideas with the mind, and to envision them internally. It has the ability to create pictures in the mind.

3. Memory (The mind's "flash drive")
The memory has the capacity to recall information, experiences, events, feelings, and thoughts experienced by the mind. It has the ability to remember.

4. Emotion (The mind's "voice")
The emotions have the capacity to experience inner passions in association with particular events, memories, experiences, or thoughts. It has the ability to feel. Emotions are the voice of our thoughts. Emotion "tells" us what and how we are thinking. Emotion may also arise in response to physical events occurring in the body—hormonal changes, illness, or various stressors.

5. Reason/Will (The mind's "judge")
The will has the capacity to consider information, make judgments between conflicting options, viewpoints, or courses of direction, and initiate action by the mind or body. It has the ability to choose.

You Are What You Think

> "As he thinks in his heart, so is he" (Proverbs 23:7a).

Whatever we allow to captivate our thought life will eventually control our lives. The life you are experiencing today is largely a result of your thought life yesterday. Look at Proverbs 4:23 again. The New Living Translation puts it this way, "Guard your heart above all else, for *it determines the course of your life.*" Whatever we continually meditate upon will begin to program our reason, feelings, and will. Over time, we will subconsciously make choices to speak and act in ways that are consistent with the prevailing thoughts in our minds.

> *If you change your mind, you change your life.*

Simultaneously, our thoughts carry the force of attraction. As we develop patterns of thinking, we begin to draw into our lives experiences, events, people, and resources that resonate with our thought life. This phenomenon is so consistently observed that nearly all world religions, philosophies, and sociological observers confirm it.

The great news about this law of the mind is that if you don't like the condition of your life, you can change it. If you change your mind, you change your life.

YOUR MIND IS YOUR RESPONSIBILITY

As we have previously discussed, it is common today for people to speak as if they were not responsible for their thoughts, feelings, and actions. We are disempowering ourselves from making real change by denying our responsibility over our own minds. Our thoughts are our responsibility, and while we cannot stop every thought that arises, we alone will be held accountable for what we allow to engage our minds.

Take Responsibility for Your Thoughts and Feelings

The first step to renewing your mind is to take ownership of your own thought life. The truth is that we are powerless to change anything for which we refuse to accept responsibility. Becoming aware of what and how you think is an important first step to developing a new mind that reflects the plans and purposes of God. What are the limiting and defeating thoughts that you find yourself returning to repeatedly during the day? When you are left alone to your thoughts, what patterns of thinking do you find your mind drifting towards? Do you keep your life full of activity with little time to be alone because you are afraid of your own thoughts, feelings, and fears? These are all signs that in some way you have to regain control of your thought life. Begin by saying out loud the following confession by faith:

> *In the name of Jesus Christ, I take responsibility for my own mind. I take authority over my thoughts, feelings, meditations, and imagination. I own the thoughts and images I allow to play on the screen of my mind. Satan cannot force me to think, feel, or meditate on anything I refuse to permit. My mind is a gift from God and I choose to fill it with thoughts that will draw me into the life God has planned.*

Evaluate Your Thought Life by Examining Your Feelings

Feelings come from *thinking*. One of the best ways to evaluate the condition of your mind is to keep a journal of the negative and fearful things that enter your mind during the day. Just write words or phrases that reflect any thoughts or feelings that naturally come to your mind. Writing these things down gets them *out* of your mind and onto paper where you can evaluate them. One or two days should be enough. You will probably be amazed at how many times your mind drifts in the direction of fear, anger, lust, pride, jealousy, and self-condemnation. This is the natural state of the human mind that has not been renewed in Christ. Don't allow this exercise to discourage you.

Once you have a couple of days of thoughts recorded, look at each thought or fear and ask yourself how you could think differently about the situation. Ask yourself, *Is this thought valid? Is it worth yielding control of my mind to think like that? What are other ways I could view this? Is thinking about this changing anything for the better? What would happen if I replaced this thought or image with something hopeful and positive?* Then make a quick list of three to five positive things that you want in your life, and how you could think about them. Ask yourself, *What if I spent this time thinking about these things instead?* This exercise works because it gives you self-awareness and empowers you to take control over what you allow into the theater of your mind.

DAY 2 EXERCISES

1. What Scripture proves that our thoughts are both visible and important to God?

_____

_____

2. What are the five components of the mind, and how can each one be described?

   1. _____

   2. _____

   3. _____

   4. _____

   5. _____

3. What we allow to captivate our thoughts will eventually _____

_____   _____.

4. What does it mean that our thoughts carry the force of attraction?

_____

_____

5. What is the first step to renewing your mind?

_____

_____

6. Look up Philippians 4:8 and write it here.

_____

_____

_____

7. Consider what this verse means and how to apply it to your life. Ask Jesus to show you anything that occupies your mind that needs to be cut out of your life. If anything comes to mind immediately, write it here.

_____

_____

DAY 3: RENEWING OUR MINDS

THE PROCESS OF RENEWING YOUR MIND

Installing a New Operating System

The modern computer is a marvel of human progress. Yet in almost every way, the computer was conceived, designed, and produced *as a replica of the human mind*. Consider this: a computer has three basic elements—a screen, a CPU (central processing unit) and an operator (programmer). For the purpose of this illustration, consider these three components as metaphors for your own spirit, soul, and body. The screen is your natural or physical life. The operator is the spirit. The CPU represents the human soul or mind.

Before we knew Christ, we were using an old operating system. Because we were lost, we programmed all kinds of wrong things into the CPU—bad language, bad behavior, bad "short-cuts," and had some really bad "web-surfing" habits as well. This filled our CPU with ungodly material. Then, one day, we became born again. On that day the operator or programmer changed. A brand-new righteous and spiritually alive operator was placed behind the same old computer and told to produce new images and results on the screen. However, because the CPU had already been programmed and operated by the person that *used* to sit there, it still produces those bad images. When you try to "surf the web" of your mind, the old habits, bookmarks, and historical data of the former user keep popping up. The old programs are still running behind the scenes even though new applications or thoughts are installed. Viruses and spyware from the world continuously try to enter and corrupt our new applications. Sometimes, the whole system crashes, and we fall back into our old patterns of thinking, speaking, and behaving. Thankfully, God has given us a special "recovery system" that will always restart and restore our minds—prayer, confession of sin, and faith in God's Word.

The only way to consistently change what is displayed on the screen of our lives is to reprogram our minds! Old files have to be meticulously found, deleted, and replaced with new data. For a while, as you look at the results on the screen, you may be tempted to think that nothing has changed. But if you will stick with the process, delete the old, and replace it with the new and good information, eventually the screen will display what the programmer desires. You will begin to see the reflection of Jesus in you.

This is really a large part of living the transformed life. We must devote ourselves to the task of deleting the old programmer's files, applications, and history, while simultaneously replacing them with new files and applications that reflect our new life in Christ. Just because your screen keeps displaying old programs, doesn't mean you have not changed. It just means you have to renew your CPU—your mind.

If your thoughts are fixed on God, His Word, and you trust Him with your problems, you will have real inner peace.

The Law of Exchange

God's Word does not just tell us what we shouldn't think about. Renewing your mind is not emptying your mind and using your willpower to keep wrong thoughts out. That is a nearly impossible task. The biblical concept of renewing your mind involves a spiritual principle that we will call *the law of exchange*. The law of exchange teaches that life operates on a constant stream of "trades" or exchanges. You must trade something you have in order to get something else. A student trades their time, attention, finances, and efforts to a college in exchange for knowledge that will help the student achieve their goals in life and a diploma that corroborates that they have completed the outlined degree. A single man trades his bachelorhood in exchange for a committed relationship with his wife in order to experience the joys of marriage and family. We all make decisions every day to trade our thinking, our time, our energies, and our attention to places, people, and things. Those decisions are producing the life that you are currently living.

The life that you are living today is largely the result of the trading choices you have made in the past about your time, talents, diet, money, words, friends, and thoughts. If you don't like the results—in other words, if you want to change some part of your current life—you are going to have to make some different trades. This may seem too simple, but the key to changing your life really isn't any more complicated than making the right exchanges. When you became born again, you exchanged the old, negative, sinful condition of your heart for a new heart that is softened by the grace, love, and life of Jesus Christ. Renewing the mind is God's way of extending the life of Jesus into every area of your life and relationships.

DEVELOPING NEW MINDSETS

"If then you were raised with Christ, seek those things which are above, where Christ is, sitting at the right hand of God. *Set your mind on things above*, not on things on the earth" (Colossians 3:1-2).

"For those who live according to the flesh *set their minds* on the things of the flesh, but those who live according to the Spirit, [*set their minds on*] the things of the Spirit" (Romans 8:5).

In these verses, the Apostle Paul tells us to exchange our earthly way of thinking for Christ-centered thinking. He says we must "set our minds." Mindsets are more than just fleeting thoughts or ideas. A *mindset* is a deeply entrenched pattern of thinking that develops over time. They result from repeatedly thinking about something in a particular way until that perspective becomes second nature to us. Mindsets are hard to change. This is a good thing if our mindsets are positive, helpful, and based on the Word of God. A godly mindset affords great peace and strength. In order to change wrong mindsets, we need to exchange our old thoughts for new ones. We must feed our hearts and minds on the truth of God's Word and keep those right images in our minds until they replace our old mindsets. Paul goes on to instruct the believer what kinds of "negative" or worldly thoughts and behaviors we need to "put off," and what new thoughts and actions we need to "put on":

"But now you yourselves are *to put off all these*: anger, wrath, malice, blasphemy, filthy language out of your mouth. Do not lie to one another, since *you have put off the old man* with his deeds, *and have put on the new man who is renewed in knowledge* according to the image of Him who created him…Therefore, as the elect of God, holy and beloved, *put on* tender mercies, kindness, humility, meekness, longsuffering…But above all these things *put on love*, which is the bond of perfection. And let the peace of God rule *in your hearts*, to which also you were called in one body; and *be thankful. Let the word of Christ dwell in you richly* in all wisdom, teaching and admonishing one another in psalms and hymns and spiritual songs, singing with grace in your hearts to the Lord" (Colossians 3:8-10, 12, 14-16).

The Power of Meditation

"Let the words of my mouth and *the meditation of my heart* be acceptable in Your sight, O Lord, my strength and my Redeemer" (Psalm 19:14).

"This Book of the Law shall not depart from your mouth, but you shall meditate in it day and night, that you may observe to do according to all that is written in it. For then you will make your way prosperous, and then you will have good success" (Joshua 1:8).

"My eyes are awake through the night watches, that I may meditate on Your word" (Psalm 119:148).

Believe it or not, the Bible teaches us to meditate. But the practice of biblical meditation is nothing like the meditation taught by the gurus and religions of the Far East. In those religions, one is taught that meditation is the emptying of the mind. The Bible never tells us to empty our minds! Instead we are to fill them with His Word. Biblical *meditation* is the practice of focusing our minds on Jesus Christ, the wonderful promises He has made to us, and the teachings of the Bible. Where most non-Christian philosophies teach that meditation is a skill that takes years to master, the simple truth is that mediation is a practice that each of us *already does every day of our lives.*

Heart "Sounds"

Meditation is simply the practice of focused thinking. It comes from several Hebrew root words. In Psalm 19:14, the word *meditate* comes from the word *hig·gä·yōn*, which means to repeatedly strike the string of a harp so as to make a lasting sound. It is used in these other passages:

"Upon an instrument of ten strings, and upon the psaltery; upon the harp with *a solemn sound"* (Psalm 92:3 KJV; See also Psalm 9:16).

The word translated *heart* in Psalm 19:14 is *leb.* It is the Hebrew word for *the core of one's soul, thought, imagination, and memory.* These two words form a powerful image of what happens when we focus our innermost thoughts on a particular idea or thing. David was actually praying that the *sounds* of his *mind* would be acceptable in the sight of God.

When we think about anything for an extended period of time, we create a "sound" in our minds. This sound has a way of dominating our perspective of life, eventually making us sensitive to things that have the same "tone." Positive or negative, right or wrong, blessing or cursing, the focus of our meditations will begin to attract people, circumstances, and feelings that are tuned to that same pitch. And whatever we meditate on long enough will begin to control our thinking, impact the direction of our choices, and become our experience. *Whatever we think about over time, we begin to attract.* Our minds begin to draw associations and reinforce beliefs that cause us to fixate on the things we think. This is why it is so important to develop the right meditations. Whatever fills your mind will eventually fill your life!

As previously stated, each of us meditates every day. In our spare moments, while driving to work, or silently waiting in line, our minds drift towards the dominant patterns of thinking we have established. These are not empty thoughts! These meditations of our hearts are powerfully impacting the way we experience life and they are putting forth their particular sound—either attracting or repelling us from the promises of God. One of the best ways to see how we use the power of our minds to meditate every day is by looking at the things we *worry* about.

Defeating the Worry Habit

The Bible has a lot to say about the negative impact of worry in our lives. *Worry* is the practice of meditation in the negative realm. Note what Jesus and Paul taught about the worry habit:

> "Therefore I say to you, *do not worry about your life*" (Matthew 6:25a).

> "Therefore *do not worry*, saying, 'What shall we eat?' or 'What shall we drink?' or 'What shall we wear?'" (Matthew 6:31).

> "Therefore *do not worry about tomorrow*, for tomorrow will worry about its own things. Sufficient for the day is its own trouble" (Matthew 6:34).

Worrying is imagining the future in a negative way. We don't worry about things that have already happened—only things that we fear might happen. Worry pictures the bills going unpaid, the promotion at work passing us by, or the pain in our chest becoming a heart attack. When we worry, we yield the power of our minds to imagine the worst outcome possible in every situation. Worry destroys faith. We become focused on our fears instead of God's plans and the possibilities He offers for our lives. Worry keeps us trapped in fear and avoidance. It never solves or resolves anything! This is why the Bible tells us to exchange our worried imaginations with targeted prayer requests. Instead of letting our fears and problems marinate in our minds, we are to take action by bringing them to God in prayer. Only God has the power to change our circumstances. When we pray, God comes to our aid. He exchanges our fear and worry for His peace in our minds, and our weakness in the face of our trouble transforms into a strong and renewed faith in our hearts in God's sovereign plan for us.

For example, instead of worrying about an upcoming bill or a negative medical report, turn the problem into an opportunity to exercise your faith through prayer. God already knows the problem so make this a time in which you can speak His Word over your situation. As you do, ask God for wisdom, help, direction, or healing. Add a generous amount of heartfelt thanksgiving and your prayer will release the power of the Holy Spirit over your situation. Your faith has dislodged your fear. This very practical technique is a powerful way to break the negative thinking patterns that keep us locked in fear and keep us from changing. Paul gives us a powerful cure for the worry habit. He tells us to use the power of our minds to switch our focus from fearing the worst to expecting God's answer!

> "*Don't worry about anything*; instead, *pray about everything*. Tell God what you need, *and thank him* for all he has done. *Then you will experience God's peace,* which exceeds anything we can understand. His peace will guard your hearts and minds as you live in Christ Jesus" (Philippians 4:6-7 NLT).

The result of right thinking will always bring about God's perfect peace. In fact, one way to know whether or not your thought life is moving in the right direction is by checking your *peace level*. If your thoughts are fixed on God, His Word, and you trust Him with your problems, you will have real inner peace. This peace is not the result of everything in your life being perfect, or all your circumstances going well. It comes from relying on the Lord in your mind. In fact, this peace will stay the same, regardless of your circumstances. The Prophet Isaiah said,

> "You will guard him and keep him in perfect and constant peace whose mind [both its inclination and its character] is stayed on You, because he commits himself to You, leans on You, and hopes confidently in You" (Isaiah 26:3 AMP).

DAY 3 EXERCISES

1. What is the law of exchange?

_____

_____

_____

2. The life you are living today is largely the result of what?

_____

_____

3. What is a mindset?

_____

_____

_____

4. Whatever we meditate on long enough will begin to do what?

_____

_____

5. Apply prayer to every worry daily. Write Philippians 4:6-7 here.

_____

_____

_____

_____

_____

6. Think about the verse you just wrote. Mentally apply it to every circumstance and trouble you can imagine. As you meditate about how He is in control, ask the Lord to fill you with His peace. Picture in your mind what the benefits of that peace from God are: strength, security, relaxation in the face of stressful situations, and so on. Write down some of those benefits.

_____

_____

_____

_____

_____

DAY 4: A DIET FOR YOUR MIND

In the same way that your body takes on the character of the food you feed it, your mind and emotional health take on the character of the thoughts you feed them. It is vitally important that we are given a specific diet of God's Word for our minds. This diet may take some getting used to. It might be difficult to restrict your intake of mental junk food, unhealthy images, and high-calorie negativity at first. But if you will focus on the items on this list, and feed your mind with thoughts, images, and friendships that reinforce them, you can truly develop a fit and healthy mind. Here's the list:

> "And now, dear brothers and sisters, one final thing. *Fix your thoughts* on what is true, and honorable, and right, and pure, and lovely, and admirable. *Think about things* that are excellent and worthy of praise. Keep putting into practice all you learned and received from me—everything you heard from me and saw me doing. Then the God of peace will be with you" (Philippians 4:8-9 NLT).

Paul gives us eight categories of mind food on which to fix our thoughts. Everything we are tempted to think about needs to go through the filter of these eight categories. If the thoughts don't pass the test, reject them and replace them with thoughts that do qualify!

Paul's Mind Diet:

1. Truthful Things
Our minds need to be rooted in truth, or real facts. We need to test our thoughts to be sure they are accurate and grounded in Scripture. The opposite of truth is lies, deception, and fantasy.

2. Honorable Things
This means our thoughts need to respect God, others, and ourselves. We need to think honorably towards our spouses, children, parents, pastors, and employers.

3. Right or Righteous Things
Our minds need to feed on things that reflect righteousness, justice, and the kingdom of God.

4. Pure Things
We should allow no unclean or morally polluted things, including those that are sexually impure, to taint our minds.

5. Lovely Things
We need to feed on beautiful sights, sounds, and relationships. If something is ugly or unattractive to our flesh, we need to avoid it in our minds.

6. Admirable Things
To admire something or someone is to feel inspired by them. We need to find people and things that inspire admiration within us and focus our attention on them. We are drawn to what we admire—good or bad.

7. Excellent Things

Our minds need a quality diet. *Excellence* means beyond mediocre or average. We need to read books, associate with people, and be in environments that challenge us to rise above the status quo and reach our potential.

8. Praiseworthy Things

One way to defeat dark thinking habits is to focus on things for which you can thank and praise God. If your mind is drifting towards the negatives in your life, immediately imagine one thing for which you can sincerely thank and praise God. It can be ANYTHING. Begin to verbalize to God your praise and thanks, while allowing yourself to feel grateful. This one action alone has a powerful effect in resetting the mind, and breaking negative thinking cycles.

> *If we will change our minds, we can change our lives. If we can change our lives, God can change our world through us!*

Developing the Mind of Christ

> "And we have received God's Spirit (not the world's spirit), so we can know the wonderful things God has freely given us....But we understand these things, *for we have the mind of Christ*" (1 Corinthians 2:12, 16b NLT).

The Holy Spirit lives inside every believer to help them in the process of renewing their minds. Having the mind of Christ within us refers to the ongoing process of the Holy Spirit revealing the thoughts and plans of God to our hearts and minds. Jesus taught that the Holy Spirit would be our Helper. One of the primary ways He helps us is in revealing the mind or thinking of Christ to us.

> "When the Spirit of truth comes, he will guide you into all truth. He will not speak on his own *but will tell you what he has heard.* He will tell you about the future. He will bring me glory *by telling you whatever he receives from me*" (John 16:13-14 NLT).

Each believer can rely on the inner presence of the Holy Spirit to guide them. He lives inside us to tell us what Jesus and the Father want us to know. The primary way He speaks to us is through the Scriptures. We can ask Him to help us to understand God and His Word.

> "Open my eyes, that I may see wondrous things from Your law [Word]" (Psalm 119:18).

FEEDING ON THE WORD

By far, the most important tool we have to renew our minds is the Word of God. The Bible is filled with God's thoughts and ways (Isaiah 55:8-11). It has the power to heal our toxic thinking and deliver our minds from destructive patterns of believing and feeling.

"Humbly accept the word God has planted in your hearts, for it has the power
to save [heal and deliver] your souls [minds]" (James 1:21 NLT).

God's Word is a mirror of how God sees us in Christ. The New Testament letters written to the churches are filled with powerful images of what God has done for the believer in Jesus Christ. It describes over and over what we have become "in Christ." It tells us who we are in Christ, and reveals our true identity. The more we look into the mirror of God's Word, the more we will see ourselves as God really sees us—new creatures in Christ Jesus (2 Corinthians 5:17).

When we look at ourselves in a natural mirror, we see only our physical selves. We notice the imperfections, the mistakes, the realities we wish to change. But God's Word gives us the real picture of our true selves. As believers in Jesus, we have been made in God's image, and possess the love, peace, and wisdom of God. In our spirits we have been given His divine nature—the very life of God! He has made us to be more than conquerors, and given us authority over all the power of the enemy. This image is the one God longs for us to capture in our minds. He wants us to know in our heads what He has already made us to be in our hearts!

Ways to Feed on God's Word

Jesus said, "Man shall not live by bread alone, but by *every word that proceeds from the mouth of God"* (Matthew 4:4). Just as our bodies feed on natural bread to gain strength and nourishment, our spirits and souls need to feed on the spiritual food of God's Word. The Bible teaches that there are numerous ways to feed on God's Word, and each one is essential for our development as believers.

The Teaching of the Local Church
The first way we receive God's Word is by regularly listening to it taught in the local church. The earliest Christians could only feed on God's Word in this manner. It was centuries before full copies of the Bible could be found in most churches, and many centuries later before it was printed in smaller copies and available to everyone. God designed us to gather with other believers every week in local churches so we could be taught the Word of God under the leadership of His anointed preachers and teachers and allow His spiritual gifts to minister through us to the rest of the body. The local church pastor's primary responsibility is to feed the flock a balanced diet of God's Word. Notice in these passages that the pastors of God's church are responsible to teach God's people.

"Remember your leaders who *taught you the word of God*. Think of all the
good that has come from their lives, and follow the example of their faith"
(Hebrews 13:7 NLT).

"So guard yourselves and God's people. *Feed and shepherd God's flock—*
his church, purchased with his own blood—over which the Holy Spirit has
appointed you as elders" (Acts 20:28 NLT).

Personal Bible Reading and Group Study

Secondly, every believer should seek to study the Bible and good biblical teaching materials. This can be done individually or in groups. When we read and study the Bible by ourselves, we allow the Holy Spirit to speak through the Scripture into our lives using the stories, lessons, and teachings to help us think correctly. By joining a Bible study that is provided under the direction of the local church, we learn God's Word in an accelerated way. Often believers help one another to grow by learning from the insights that others are receiving from God's Word.

Memorizing Scripture

One of the most powerful ways to feed on God's Word is to spend time committing helpful Bible verses to memory. This may sound difficult, but the fact is the average person has already memorized thousands of lines and verses to songs, movies, and popular media. Memorizing the Bible may take a little discipline and focus, but there is not a song in the world that will benefit you more than God's Word. Psalm 119 is the longest chapter in the Bible and every verse is a celebration of the power of God's Word in the believer's heart and life. It teaches us to commit God's Word to memory. Take note of these selected verses:

> "I have *hidden your word in my heart,* that I might not sin against you....I will *study* your commandments *and reflect* on your ways. I will delight in your decrees *and not forget* [memorize] *your word*....I will *never forget* your commandments, for by them you give me life....Oh, how I love your instructions! I think about them all day long....Your laws are my treasure; they are my heart's delight....I have wandered away like a lost sheep; come and find me, for *I have not forgotten your commands"* (Psalm 119:11, 15-16, 93, 97, 111, 176 NLT).

Bible Teaching Materials, Conferences, and Media

There are many excellent resources for learning God's Word and enhancing your development available today. Look for books, e-books, podcasts, digital downloads, videos, and other media that focus on Bible teaching by reputable ministers who support learning that agrees with what you are experiencing and learning in your local church. Remember that supplemental teaching should always encourage you to be faithful to God and your local church. Any teaching that inspires division among fellow believers, or pulls you away from living your Christian life outside of a healthy local church community, is contrary to God's purpose for you and should be viewed with caution.

HEALING YOUR MEMORIES

One of the most important aspects of renewing your mind involves the healing of your past. Memory is a powerful component of the human mind, and has an enormous impact on the way we think and feel about our lives and our future. Because we live in a world that is filled with pain and brokenness, all of us grow up with experiences that scar our memories. Whether it is love and affirmation we failed to receive, or rejection and abuse we did not deserve, each of us develops thinking patterns that grow like scar tissue around these unhealed wounds. Often it is many years later—after we have reached physical adulthood—before we begin to face our painful memories and realize how they have impacted our thoughts, feelings, and decisions. In Psalm 23:1, 3, David said, "The Lord is my shepherd; I shall not want....*He restores my soul."*

As a born-again believer in Jesus, your spirit has been made new. The soul however contains these unhealed hurts, and patterns of thinking and feeling that are contrary to the love, joy, and peace that God has placed in your spirit. By following Christ and serving others in the local church, we begin a journey that, over time, will bring many of these wounds and past hurts to the surface. When this occurs, God's desire is to heal the soul and give us a new way to think about our past as well as our future.

Getting Unstuck

Sometimes we seem to stagnate in our spiritual growth. Our minds get locked into patterns of thinking and feeling that prevent us from moving forward. When this is the case, it is important to take the time to examine our thoughts and feelings. Often the real reason we are "stuck" is because God wants us to examine old patterns of thinking we picked up in our past that are hindering us.

The Importance of New Relationships

Building healthy relationships with other believers is an important part of growing up spiritually and renewing our minds. When we move in new directions, we need people who are traveling with us. Often this requires us to lay aside the relationships that tie us to our past ways of thinking. If you want to get to California, you can't stay on a bus that's going to Boston. God uses people who are heading in the direction of our purpose and destiny to help us arrive at the right places in life. When believers really care for each other, share their hearts and hurts with each other, and take the time to encourage and pray for each other, an environment for growth is created in our lives.

Christian Counseling

Sometimes our minds and feelings become so troublesome that we need help to heal. God works through His Word, His Spirit, His church, and through other people to help us grow. Trained professional ministers, counselors, and doctors have spent their lives learning how to help people heal in their minds and emotions. Sometimes part of God's plan for our growth includes time with wise and well-trained mature people who have been called to this type of ministry. If you, your family, or your spiritual leaders feel that you may need this kind of help, try to locate someone who has a Christian-based worldview.

When the Brain is Sick

The brain is the organ that contains the human soul and mind. Just like any other part of the body, it can become run down, over-stressed, imbalanced, or physically sick. But unlike most other parts of our bodies, when our brains become imbalanced or sick, we often don't realize it. The brain is a wonderfully complex network of chemical, hormonal, and electrical signals that can fall out of balance. When this occurs, it manifests in ways we don't often associate with brain health. Our thinking can become confused, our emotions depressed, our sleep patterns disturbed, or our weight can rise or fall. It can become difficult to think clearly and control our impulses.

When the brain is weak or sick due to stress, trauma, hormonal imbalance, or other imbalances, we need to give ourselves permission to find the help we need to heal. Once, when God's

Prophet Elijah had finished a very intense time of ministry, he became vulnerable to the threats of his enemies. Elijah was so weary, he lost his capacity to think and feel well. The Bible says he ran away and hid himself inside a cave on a mountain, eventually praying to die. But along the way, the Lord let him rest, had angels prepare food to restore him, and eventually helped him out of his depression by sending a personal assistant to help Elijah carry the load. This shows the great mercy of God for His people when they fall into places of exhaustion and toxic thinking.

In the fourth chapter of Jonah, we see that God's prophet became depressed and fixated on negative thinking. Things didn't work out the way he wanted, and he actually prayed for God to kill him. Instead, we find that God taught the prophet a valuable lesson by gently correcting his perspective. God shifted his thinking so Jonah could change how he was feeling!

Sometimes, part of healing the brain may involve changes in diet, sleep, stress levels, and even medication. A believer should not feel condemned if, in the process of renewing their minds, they discover that part of God's plan for their healing includes counseling or medical treatment. The most important thing is that we do whatever it takes to have healthy brains, healthy minds, and healed memories and emotions.

The renewing of the mind is the single most important factor in living the transformed life. If we will change our minds, we can change our lives. If we can change our lives, God can change our world through us!

DAY 4 EXERCISES

1. List the eight categories of Paul's mind diet.

    1. _____

    2. _____

    3. _____

    4. _____

    5. _____

    6. _____

    7. _____

    8. _____

2. Having the mind of Christ within us refers to what?

_____

_____

3. List four ways we can feed on the Word of God.

    1. _____

    2. _____

    3. _____

    4. _____

4. Name the two biblical figures mentioned in this chapter who dealt with mental trauma and depression.

    1. _____

    2. _____

5. Let's begin Paul's diet; look at the list in Philippians 4:8. Because of our fallen nature, those things may not seem interesting to us—and yet, it is these things which have the power to transform us. Choose one of them today. Give an example of a way you can practice thinking about the one you chose. Write it below.

_____

_____

_____

_____

_____

_____

CHAPTER SEVEN

THE TRANSFORMED BODY

CHAPTER SEVEN
The Transformed Body

DAY 1: OUR EARTH SUIT

You are *not* your body. As simple as that sounds, this fact is one of the most important truths you must master in the journey of living the transformed life. Failing to really distinguish between your *inner self* and your *outer or physical self* will result in confusion, frustration, and persistent feelings of condemnation. As a believer in Jesus Christ, your spirit has been reborn into the image and likeness of God. Yet as we have been learning, God has placed this new creation inside a physical body that has been largely unchanged. Just as the believer's *mind* must be "renewed as you learn to know your Creator and become like him" (Colossians 3:10 NLT), so also the believer's *body* must be trained to obey God by following the directions given by the born-again spirit.

In the meantime, your physical body is important to God—so important that the Bible devotes much of its teaching to understanding the nature of the body, the struggles of living in our bodies, and the promises God has made for the future of our bodies. God wants us to master the art of learning how to live in our own body. He wants us to learn how to use our bodies as vessels for our born-again spirits to accomplish His purpose for our lives.

> "I beseech you therefore, brethren, by the mercies of God, that you present your
> bodies a living sacrifice, holy, acceptable unto God, which is your reasonable
> service" (Romans 12:1).

The Nature of the Body: Our Earth Suit

When the first astronauts went into outer space, the scientists who sent them knew they would need vessels to both travel in, and to navigate within, the hostile and foreign environment of outer space. Scientists worked for years to develop ships that could escape the forces of gravity and eventually land on the moon. Scientists also knew that in order for humans to walk on the moon, they would need an outer suit that would be uniquely designed to the extremes of outer space. As long as our astronauts used the space suits they were given, they could explore the surface of the moon. But if for one moment that suit were to somehow become vulnerable to the outside atmosphere, the astronaut would die within seconds.

In the same way, you and I were created by God as spiritual beings. Our true home is our Father's house in heaven. In order to navigate and operate on this physical planet, God designed an "earth suit" for us. Understanding how to live in that suit is essential to mastering life on this planet. Someday, you will leave your body through the process known as physical death. What we call death is nothing more than stepping out of our earth suit and into our true spiritual home. Until then, you and I are going to need to learn how to live in our bodies if we hope to live the abundant life Jesus has promised.

> *We are not fighting ourselves; we are mastering the control of our bodies, and renewing our minds.*

Made in the Image of God

Out of everything God has created in the universe, there isn't an animal, angel, or object that may be said to resemble its Creator—except one.

> "Then God said, '*Let us make human beings in our image*, to be like us. They will reign over the fish in the sea, the birds in the sky, the livestock, all the wild animals on the earth, and the small animals that scurry along the ground.' So God created human beings in his own image. In the image of God he created them; male and female he created them" (Genesis 1:26-27 NLT).

As we have learned, only men and women have been made in God's own image. An image is a reflection of oneself. That means that only in examining human beings may we learn about the true nature and form of God. Human beings alone bear the unique responsibility of reflecting God. Just as God is Spirit, mankind's essential nature is spirit. God's intelligence is revealed in the human mind. Even the physical form of the human body teaches us that God has a form in heaven that may be seen and recognized. God has a face, eyes, ears, a mouth, arms, hands, and feet that someday we will behold. This is not to say that God is a man, or that He in any way limited to spatial dimensions like we are. Yet God is a person. He exists not just in His infinite expansiveness, but also in a personal form that the human body reflects. God designed men and women to mirror—in spirit, mind, and body—the essential image of Himself.

In Psalm 8, the prophet David said,

> "What are *mere mortals* that you should think about them, *human beings* that you should care for them? Yet you made them only *a little lower than God* and *crowned them with glory* and honor. You gave them charge of everything you made, putting all things under their authority" (Psalm 8:4-6 NLT).

Our first human parents were *crowned* with glory. The word translated "crowned" in this passage means to surround or clothe. The first man and woman were so majestic in their original form that they needed no natural clothing—the visible glory of God covered their nakedness. It was only after their fall that Adam and Eve became aware of their own nakedness because it was only then that the glory of God departed. Sin marred the image of God in mankind, and as a result, we are now like a broken mirror—reflecting God's image in a distorted fashion.

> "For all have sinned and *fall short of the glory* of God" (Romans 3:23).

This broken image is what Christ came to restore. Only in the human life of Jesus Christ do we capture a perfect image of God's intention for humankind. When we receive Jesus as our Lord, God begins the process of restoring His image in us. It begins in our born-again spirit, and then

His Spirit works to transform our minds and behaviors until our lives become restored mirrors of God's image in the world.

Connection to the Physical World

In Genesis chapter 2, the Bible gives us more detail on the process of our creation.

> "And Jehovah God *formed man of the dust of the ground*, and *breathed* into his nostrils *the breath of life*; and man became a *living soul*" (Genesis 2:7 ASV).

Scientists tell us that our physical bodies are composed of about one third water, and two thirds elements and minerals that are found in the crust or surface soil of the earth! This not only confirms what the Bible teaches, but gives us a powerful clue to the nature of our physical bodies, and why we often struggle with them as we seek to please God.

House of the Senses

Because our bodies are made from the dirt of the physical world, they were designed with capacities to connect us to the physical realities around us. We call these capacities *the physical senses*. Our senses are an intricate *communication system* that enable us to understand our life on earth. Through touch, sight, sound, taste, and smell, our bodies connect with the world around us. While our senses are very useful in navigating the natural world, they were never designed to control our thoughts and actions.

Our senses are attracted to pleasure and comfort, but recoil from whatever causes discomfort and pain. Because the physical senses do not distinguish between moral right and wrong, they are drawn to physical comforts and pleasures regardless of their source or safety. If we live by the senses alone, we will often choose to avoid things that may cause short-term discomfort but yield long-term benefits—like exercise, healthy eating, and resisting the pleasures of sin.

By the same token, our senses will often deceive us into choosing to indulge in things that appear beautiful, and feel pleasurable, but will be harmful to us and others in the long run. When Satan came to deceive Eve, he appealed to her senses of sight, smell, and taste. He enticed her to trust her physical senses and distrust the word of God.

> "And when the woman *saw* that the tree was good for food, and that it was a delight *to the eyes*, and that the tree was to be desired to make one wise, she took of the fruit thereof, and did eat; and she gave also unto her husband with her, and he did eat" (Genesis 3:6 ASV).

The Effects of the Fall on the Senses

The fall of the human race into sin resulted in severe consequences in the human body. Adam and Eve would have never known physical death, disease, poverty, aging, pain, grief, or addictive compulsions. Their bodies would have remained obedient vessels for their spirits to navigate the physical world. Their senses would not have gained the upper hand in guiding their thoughts and choices. It is hard to imagine a world like this—where the body would have remained as a reliable servant of the human spirit and soul. But the remnants of the fall have deadened our spiritual side and our bodies. Now our physical senses seek to dictate our choices and rule our lives.

Breaking the Horse

Understanding the way the body and the spirit relate to each other is very important to learning how to bring our bodies under the control of the spirit within us. One way to think of this relationship is by looking at the way a horse is trained by an experienced rider.

Before you were born again, your body was like a wild horse. It was used to going where it wanted and running without restraint. Wild horses are resistant to control. Likewise, our old spiritual nature was used to "riding" wherever it wanted to go. But one day, you were born again. You became a whole new person in your spirit—a new and purposeful rider. But the new rider has been stuck on the same wild horse. Naturally, when the "new you" endeavors to direct the horse, it bucks, fights, and resists control. The rider must become seriously focused on breaking the will of the horse in order to make it a fit vehicle to carry the rider on his journey.

The process of breaking a wild horse is difficult. It requires a combination of patient understanding and the use of a healthy amount of discomfort and distress upon the horse when it resists the training. But once the horse is taught who is boss and learns to obey its master, both the horse and rider can win in the contests of life. While the body can often feel like it has a mind of its own, in reality it is nothing more that the attraction of the physical senses to the pleasures that we feel.

> "Where do wars and fights come from among you? Do they not come from your *desires for pleasure that war in your members*?" (James 4:1).

The Greek word translated "members" here and elsewhere in the New Testament is the word *melos* which is best translated "body parts." Simply put, the different parts of our bodies crave comfort and pleasure. These desires are not evil in and of themselves, but they are indiscriminate. Once the body has experienced a certain pleasure, or been trained to react a certain way in a particular environment, the body and mind form an automatic connection with that experience. This is how habits form. It is also why breaking habits can be so difficult. The body and mind become fused to respond consistently with each other. So when the body feels stress, it craves pleasures to bring balance to the discomfort. It does not discriminate between healthy and unhealthy. It simply wants whatever is the quickest fix that has brought pleasure in the past. The problem is that many of these pleasures are sinful and have negative long-term effects on us, others, and our relationship with God. We must learn to break the horse and retrain the body.

Notice what the Bible says about our body's nature and our need to resist its cravings:

> "All athletes are disciplined in their training. They do it to win a prize that will fade away, but we do it for an eternal prize. So I run with purpose in every step. I am not just shadowboxing. *I discipline my body like an athlete, training it to do what it should*. Otherwise, I fear that after preaching to others I myself might be disqualified" (1 Corinthians 9:25-27 NLT).

WHY DO I WANT TO DO THINGS I HATE?

> "For what I am doing, I do not understand; for I am not practicing what I would like to do, but I am doing the very thing I hate" (Romans 7:15 NASB).

This verse describes the struggle that all people who want to please God face from time to time. While Paul was directly referring to his pre-Christian life of struggling to please God through religion, it can also be applied to the believer who is struggling with the battle to overcome their sinful desires. Note that Scriptures locate the source of our internal struggle: "in my flesh" (7:18), "sin which is in my members" (7:23), and "this body of death" (7:24). All these terms are different ways of describing the fact that our physical bodies are still impacted with the wild nature of sin and temptation.

The Flesh versus the Spirit

The New Testament has a term for describing the part of us that still fights against the will of God and our new nature. It is simply called "the flesh." The term *flesh* is translated from the Greek word *sarx*, which means "the soft substance of the living body, which covers the bones and is permeated with blood." Roughly, it is the word we use for meat. Flesh is used in Scripture to refer to either the physical body, or the sinful urges that reside in the body.

Are We Fighting Ourselves?

The Bible teaches that our bodies have been impacted by the fall and often war against the desires of our born-again spirits.

> "But I say, walk by the Spirit, and you will not carry out the desire of the flesh. For the flesh sets its desire against the Spirit, and the Spirit against the flesh; for these are in opposition to one another, so that you may not do the things that you please" (Galatians 5:16-17 NASB).

The word *spirit* is not just referring to the Holy Spirit. Since it is your human spirit that is born again by the Holy Spirit, the real battle is between your flesh and your spirit. It is the desires of this inner man versus the passions of the outer man that are at war with one another. This battle can only be won by focusing on the development of your new spiritual nature through a daily walk with God.

It is important to remember that these sinful passions do not come from your born-again spirit. You are a new creature in Christ. "Old things have passed away; behold, all things have become new" (2 Corinthians 5:17). The battle with the flesh is not a battle with two opposite natures inside of you. It is a battle between the born-again "inner" you and the unchanged "outer" you: your physical body. Some Bibles translate the term *flesh* as "sinful nature." The problem with this is that it can confuse the believer into thinking that they have two natures inside of themselves—sort of like Dr. Jekyll and Mr. Hyde.

This is why the word *flesh* is a better description of where the nature of sin still remains in the born-again Christian. The believer is not fighting two opposite natures within his or her spirit. Understanding this distinction makes all the difference in the world when dealing with our struggles against sin. We are not fighting ourselves; we are mastering the control of our bodies, and renewing our minds.

Your Body: Your Servant or Your Master?

> "That every one of you should know how to possess his vessel in sanctification and honour" (1 Thessalonians 4:4 KJV).

> "Where do wars and fights come from among you? Do they not come from *your desires for pleasure that war in your members*?" (James 4:1).

> "But each one is tempted when he is drawn away by his own desires and enticed" (James 1:14).

It is through the passions of the flesh that we become tempted to sin and break fellowship with God. While not every desire or passion of the flesh is sinful or wrong, our bodies cannot be relied upon to guide us into choices and lifestyles that will please God. It is through the body that Satan and the world offer temptations. God designed the body to be the servant of the spirit of man. However, since the fall of Adam and Eve, our bodies now long to be the masters of our thoughts and choices. The body makes an excellent servant, but a lousy master.

DAY 1 EXERCISES

1. Failing to do what will result in confusion?

   _____

2. What do our senses attract, and what do they recoil from?

   _____

   _____

   _____

3. In the Scriptures, the term *flesh* is used to describe what two things?

   1. _____

   2. _____

4. The battle every person faces is a battle between what two parts of themselves?

   1. _____

   2. _____

5. God designed the body to be the servant of _____.

6. Before we were saved, we were completely led by our senses, choosing what we wanted when we wanted it. Once we are saved, we no longer have to live that way. Through Jesus we have the power to overcome the desires of our flesh and live a life worthy of the Lord. Relate here one thing that you have changed about your life—something you chose to change that has had a positive impact on your life.

   _____

   _____

7. Why is it important that we understand that we are not "Jekyll and Hyde" Christians?

   _____

   _____

   _____

   _____

   _____

DAY 2: THE CARNAL CHRISTIAN

In 1 Corinthians, the Apostle Paul writes to a large church in the ancient city of Corinth. Paul had founded the church several years before he wrote this letter, and since its beginning it had grown to well over ten thousand members. The Corinthians loved Jesus, but they had never learned to control their flesh. As a result, they were constantly acting in ways that were hurtful to others and themselves. In this first letter, Paul has to correct them about things like jealousy, strife, sexual behaviors outside of marriage, divorce, suing each other, and getting drunk on the communion wine! Can you imagine? Paul never once doubted their salvation. In fact, He began his letter by affirming that they were saved, sealed, and belonged to Christ!

> "I am writing to God's church in Corinth, to you who have been called by God to be his own holy people. He made you holy by means of Christ Jesus, just as he did for all people everywhere who call on the name of our Lord Jesus Christ, their Lord and ours….I always thank my God for you and for the gracious gifts he has given you, now that you belong to Christ Jesus….He will keep you strong to the end so that you will be free from all blame on the day when our Lord Jesus Christ returns" (1 Corinthians 1:2, 4, 8 NLT).

Yet in spite of Paul's affirming their genuine salvation, he immediately began to correct their actions and behaviors. Paul begins by identifying the root of the Corinthians' struggle with their choices and behaviors:

> "And I, brethren, could not speak to you as to spiritual people but as to *carnal*, as to babes in Christ" (1 Corinthians 3:1).

Body-Ruled Believers

The word *carnal* literally means "body-ruled" or controlled by the flesh. He goes on to say,

> "I gave you milk to drink, not solid food; for you were not yet able to receive it. Indeed, even now you are not yet able, *for you are still fleshly*. For since there is jealousy and strife among you, *are you not fleshly*, and are you not walking like mere [unsaved] men?" (1 Corinthians 3:2-3 NASB).

If a believer never learns to control their flesh and its selfish impulses, they will look and act like the world. The only remedy for the carnal Christian is to strengthen their spirits and renew their minds with the solid food of God's Word. As we have been learning throughout *The Transformed Life*, feeding on God's Word is essential to every aspect of spiritual growth.

The truth is that we are all carnal from time to time in one way or another. Whenever we choose to allow the impulses of our bodies to sway our choices, we are "walking in the flesh" or acting carnally. In Galatians chapter 5, Paul gives a list of behaviors that are indicators of being body-ruled. He calls these actions the "works of the flesh" or the behaviors of the sinful nature in your body.

"When you follow the desires of your sinful nature [or flesh], the results are very clear: sexual immorality, impurity, lustful pleasures, idolatry, sorcery, hostility, quarreling, jealousy, outbursts of anger, selfish ambition, dissension, division, envy, drunkenness, wild parties, and other sins like these. Let me tell you again, as I have before, that anyone living that sort of life will not inherit the Kingdom of God" (Galatians 5:19-21 NLT).

In other words, there are serious consequences for allowing the sinful impulses of your flesh to govern your life. He says it is so serious that if your fleshly choices become a lifestyle, you will not experience the blessings of your inheritance of the kingdom that should be enjoyed by every child of God. This has two applications. First, Paul is reminding us that this kind of lifestyle belongs to the unsaved world. People will not enter God's kingdom now or in the future unless they receive Jesus. Secondly, Paul is warning carnal Christians that persistently allowing the flesh to govern your life will disqualify you from the privileges of God's kingdom in this life. Let's talk about the results of sin in the life of the believer and God's plan to help us bring our bodies under the control of the Holy Spirit and our new born-again nature.

> *If a believer never learns to control their flesh and its selfish impulses, they will look and act like the world. The only remedy for the carnal Christian is to strengthen their spirits and renew their minds with the solid food of God's Word.*

WHAT HAPPENS WHEN I FALL?

Three Important Facts

There are three important facts to remember when discussing how God deals with the sins and failures of His children when they walk in their flesh. Each of these is important to keep in mind because they keep our hearts in balance, and safeguard us against falling into either complacency or condemnation.

1. We Are Safe in God's Family

As a child of God, we enjoy the wonderful security that comes from being a part of His family. Because God is our Father, He has made promises to us as a parent. These promises give us assurance, in times of personal failure, that our place in the family is based upon His love—and not our performance. Our place in God's family is based upon our relationship with Him through being born again. When we received God's Son, Jesus Christ, we became born again as new beings in Christ. We are just as much the spiritual children of God as we are the biological children of our human parents. This relationship is eternal. Even though we are in the sanctification process with our minds and bodies, God has assured us in His Word that He will certainly finish what He began in us.

> "And I am certain that God, who began the good work within you, will continue his work until it is finally finished on the day when Christ Jesus returns" (Philippians 1:6 NLT).

He has declared that no one can remove us from His hand:

> "And I give them eternal life, and they shall never perish; neither shall anyone snatch them out of My hand. My Father, who has given them to Me, is greater than all; and no one is able to snatch them out of My Father's hand" (John 10:28-29).

Jesus has promised the Father that He would not lose anyone who put their trust in Him, and that He would raise us at the end of the age and present us to His Father as faultless, blameless, and holy.

> "Jesus replied, 'I am the bread of life. Whoever comes to me will *never* be hungry again. Whoever believes in me will *never* be thirsty….And this is the will of God, that *I should not lose even one* of all those he has given me, but that I should raise them up at the last day. For *it is my Father's will that all* who see his Son and believe in him should have *eternal* life. *I will raise them up at the last day"* (John 6:35, 39-40 NLT).

> "Now all glory to God, who is able to keep you from falling away and will bring you with great joy into his glorious presence without a single fault" (Jude 1:24 NLT).

> "He will keep you *strong to the end so that you will be free from all blame* on the day when our Lord Jesus Christ returns" (1 Corinthians 1:8 NLT).

When you were born again, God marked you with a special seal that guarantees you will receive the inheritance of His family.

> "And now you Gentiles have also heard the truth, the Good News that God saves you. And when you believed in Christ, he identified you as his own by giving you the Holy Spirit, whom he promised long ago. The Spirit is God's guarantee that he will give us the inheritance he promised and that he has purchased us to be his own people. He did this so we would praise and glorify him" (Ephesians 1:13-14 NLT).

Understanding your secure place in His family is the first step in learning to receive God's process of discipline and spiritual growth. Without an understanding of our position of love and acceptance by the Father, you will process His discipline as condemnation instead of love, and keep Him at a distance.

2. God Understands Our Weakness
God knows that we will stumble in sin after we become His children.

> "For *we all stumble in many things"* (James 3:2a).

> "*If we claim we have no sin, we are only fooling ourselves* and not living in the truth….*If we claim we have not sinned, we are calling God a liar* and showing that his word has no place in our hearts" (1 John 1:8, 10 NLT).

Jesus, having lived a human life, understands our struggles and is deeply compassionate in helping us overcome our faults and sins.

"Therefore, it was necessary for him to be made in every respect like us, his brothers and sisters, so that he could be our *merciful* and faithful High Priest before God....Since he himself has gone through suffering and testing, *he is able to help us when we are being tested*" (Hebrews 2:17-18 NLT).

"So then, since we have a great High Priest who has entered heaven, Jesus the Son of God, let us hold firmly to what we believe. This High Priest of ours *understands our weaknesses,* for he faced *all of the same testings we do*, yet he did not sin" (Hebrews 4:14-15 NLT).

Because God knows our human weaknesses, temptations, and struggles, He makes provision for us when we fall. There is not a thing we have ever done or mistake we will ever make that God has not foreseen in advance and provided grace so we could be forgiven, restored, and cleansed. The compassion and mercy of God has already been extended to us in Christ. God has chosen to make you His child and to never leave or forsake you—even in the midst of your worst failures and most shameful faults.

3. God Expects Us to Grow Up
Being secure in God's family, however, does not mean we are free to behave sinfully or irresponsibly. Being God's children does not liberate us from the consequences of the carnal or sinful choices we make. Our Father in heaven expects us to live in a way that honors His Son Jesus. He wants us to use our bodies and minds in ways that reflect His image in us! While we have been saved from the wrath of God and the fires of hell, we now have a heavenly Father who expects us to grow up and learn to overcome the flesh. He commands us to struggle against the flesh by relying on His grace and the indwelling presence of the Holy Spirit.

"Let us strip off every weight that slows us down, *especially the sin that so easily trips us up*. And let us run with endurance the race God has set before us. *We do this by keeping our eyes on Jesus,* the champion who initiates and perfects our faith....After all, you have not yet given your lives *in your struggle against sin*" (Hebrews 12:1-2a, 4 NLT).

THE EFFECTS OF SIN IN A BELIEVER'S LIFE

Far from giving the believer a free pass from the consequences of sinful behavior, our relationship with God as our Father actually places us in a position of great responsibility. We are supposed to gain the victory over our flesh. The unbeliever will face God as a judge, but the believer lives every day with God as their Father. A good father does not ignore the immaturities and poor choices of His son. A good father is actively involved in the discipline of his children.

"And you have forgotten the exhortation which is addressed to you as sons, 'My son, do not regard lightly the discipline of the Lord, nor faint when you are reproved by Him; for those whom the Lord loves He disciplines, and He scourges every son whom He receives.' It is for discipline that you endure; God deals with you as with sons; for what son is there whom his father does not discipline? But if you are without discipline, of which all have become partakers, then you are illegitimate children and not sons. Furthermore, we had earthly fathers to discipline us, and we respected them; shall we not much rather be subject to the Father of spirits, and live? For they disciplined us for a short time as seemed best to them, but He disciplines us for our good, so that we may share His holiness. All discipline for the moment seems not to be joyful, but sorrowful; yet to those who have been trained by it, afterwards it yields the peaceful fruit of righteousness" (Hebrews 12:5-11 NASB).

This passage shows that far from being a disengaged parent, our heavenly Father is intimately concerned with our growth and development as we learn to discipline our flesh. And, just as a good father provides both loving care and firm correction, God is faithful to do the same. Let's consider some of the effects that sin has in the life of the believer.

1. Broken Fellowship, Not Relationship

Sin is painful and destructive because of what it does to us and others, as well as how it impacts our intimacy with the Father. When a believer commits sin, it immediately causes us to break our fellowship with God. As a result, we lose our sense of *peace*.

There is a difference between fellowship and relationship. A child's disobedience does not change his or her relationship with his or her father. It does, however, impact the warm fellowship between the child and the father. Fellowship is that sense of pleasure and closeness that is shared between two people. When a believer sins, their spirit instantly knows that something wrong has occurred. The indwelling Holy Spirit convicts the believer that their thoughts or actions have broken the will of God. This sense of conviction is designed to draw us to the Father for mercy and forgiveness.

> "So let us come boldly to the throne of our gracious God. There we will receive his mercy, and we will find grace to help us when we need it most" (Hebrews 4:16 NLT).

2. Destroyed Confidence

> "In whatever our heart condemns us; for God is greater than our heart and knows all things. Beloved, if our heart does not condemn us, we have confidence before God; and whatever we ask we receive from Him, because we keep His commandments and do the things that are pleasing in His sight" (1 John 3:20-22 NASB).

Sin always affects the believer's confidence in prayer and therefore diminishes our spiritual effectiveness. When our flesh is governing our choices, it impacts our peace with God and erodes our assurance that God will answer our prayers. This is why we should always seek to get right with God when we have fallen into sinful behavior. Our spiritual confidence is important to following God and in helping others to know Him.

3. Loss of Testimony

"For 'the name of God is blasphemed among the Gentiles because of you,' as it is written" (Romans 2:24).

"But when you thus sin against the brethren, and wound their weak conscience, *you sin against Christ*" (1 Corinthians 8:12).

When a believer perpetually commits sin, it has the potential to ruin their influence to those in and outside of the family of God. Unbelievers will not see how the work of Christ has impacted your life. If we continue to act like the world, we will have no platform from which to share Christ with those who are still in the world and lost. It confuses the unbeliever, and diminishes the impact of the gospel.

4. Diminished Authority

The believer who continues in sinful behaviors loses their sense of spiritual authority over the work of the enemy. Scripture tells us to submit to God, resist the Devil, and he will flee from us (James 4:7). However, you cannot submit your body to the enemy through sin, and then expect him to submit to your spiritual authority in Christ.

5. Opening Doors to the Enemy

Perhaps one of the greatest reasons to conquer our flesh is because of how sin can open a door to the work of Satan in our lives. Peter teaches us that we must,

"Be sober, be vigilant; because *your adversary the devil* walks about like a roaring lion, *seeking whom he may devour. Resist him*, steadfast in the faith, knowing that the same sufferings are experienced by your brotherhood in the world" (1 Peter 5:8-9).

While Satan cannot take us out of God's hand or His family, the enemy can devour the blessing and goodness of God in our lives. The enemy is looking for believers he may attack. One of the surest ways to open a door for the Devil to attack your life is by knowingly allowing sin to continue in your life.

"We know that God's children do not make a practice of[20] sinning, for God's Son holds them securely, and the evil one cannot touch them" (1 John 5:18 NLT).

6. Spiritual Dullness and Insensitivity

"Speaking lies in hypocrisy, having their own conscience seared with a hot iron" (1 Timothy 4:2).

---

20. This passage reads "keeps himself" in the NKJV. The implication is that the one who is born of God is the believer, and in particular this refers to the spirit of the believer. As John teaches in John 3:6, through salvation, the Holy Spirit gives birth to the believer's spirit. It is in this essential core that a believer does not sin, because the spirit is a new creation and is one aspect of the believer that is perfectly and permanently righteous (1 John 3:9; Ephesians 4:24 NLT).

"To the pure all things are pure, but to those who are defiled and unbelieving nothing is pure; but even their mind and conscience are defiled" (Titus 1:15).

Every believer has a conscience. Your conscience is the voice of your born-again spirit. It is designed to give you a sense of peace when you are living in God's will, and to feel disturbed and troubled when you sin or are acting outside of God's will. When believers ignore the inner messages of their consciences and continue to act in sinful ways, they eventually numb themselves to that inner voice. It becomes more and more difficult to "feel" the Holy Spirit's conviction and leading. Eventually a person may become so acclimated to the sinful choices they continue to make that they fall into deception and actually begin to believe that their sin does not matter to God. They may try to justify their actions. This is a very dangerous place for a child of God to be in because it requires our Father to move us into a more severe form of discipline.

7. The Loss of Rewards

Perhaps the most disturbing effect that perpetual sin has in the life of the believer is that it can result in the loss of heavenly reward. We are only given so much time to live on the earth. The Bible says that,

"And as it is appointed for men to die once, but after this the judgment" (Hebrews 9:27).

When we waste our lives in sinful behaviors, we lose valuable time that we could have used to serve the Lord. Opportunities to share Christ are lost and our ability to impact the world is diminished.

THE BELIEVER'S JUDGMENT

The Judgments of God

God's Word teaches that every human being will one day be judged for their sin. God will hold every human accountable for their lives and will require payment for the sins they have committed. This fact is a frightening and inescapable reality that faces every man and woman who is born into this world. The *way* God deals with us will be according to what we do with the work of His Son. The New Testament speaks of two judgments for human sin.

1. The Judgment of the Unbeliever's Sin
The unbeliever will appear before God Himself. On this day God will hold the unbeliever accountable for their own sins and sentence them to be condemned for the rejection of His Son. This judgment will result in condemnation of the unbeliever and their removal from the presence of God. The Scripture refers to this as the day of the Lord's wrath. It is the approaching and horrible future for the human race outside of Jesus Christ.

"He who does not believe the Son shall not see life, *but the wrath of God abides on him*" (John 3:36).

"For *the wrath of God is revealed from heaven against all ungodliness and unrighteousness of men*" (Romans 1:18a).

"Because of these things *the wrath of God is coming upon the sons of disobedience*" (Colossians 3:6).

2. The Judgment of the Believer's Sin

The Father has provided a way of escape from this day of His wrath. He has made it possible for each of us to have our sins judged at the cross of His Son instead. On the cross Jesus bore the full measure of God's wrath for our sins (Isaiah 53:6). When we believe upon Him as our sin bearer, God considers the penalty for our sins fully paid through the blood of His Son. We are eternally pardoned. This is why the Scripture says that He who has received Jesus will never come under His eternal wrath. In this way, we escape eternal separation from God. The believer's sin is judged upon the cross of Christ once and for all time. Once we have received the judgment of the cross, we will never know the wrath of God for our sins. That is the wonderful news of the gospel!

"Most assuredly, I say to you, he who hears My word and believes in Him who sent Me has everlasting life, and shall not come into judgment, but has passed from death into life" (John 5:24).

"Much more then, having now been justified by His blood, *we shall be saved from wrath through Him*" (Romans 5:9).

"And to wait for His Son from heaven, whom He raised from the dead, even *Jesus who delivers us from the wrath to come*" (1 Thessalonians 1:10).

"For God *did not appoint us to wrath*, but to obtain salvation through our Lord Jesus Christ" (1 Thessalonians 5:9).

3. The Judgment of the Believer's Life

"For we shall all stand before the judgment seat of Christ. For it is written: 'As I live, says the Lord, Every knee shall bow to Me, and every tongue shall confess to God.' *So then each of us shall give account of himself* to God" (Romans 14:10b-12).

We Will All Stand before the Judgment Seat of Christ

The Bible teaches that someday we will stand before Jesus and have a discussion about our lives and how we lived in our earthly bodies. This meeting will occur after we physically die and enter heaven to meet the Lord. The way we used our bodies is actually the primary topic of this heavenly meeting with Jesus.

"We are confident, yes, well pleased rather to *be absent from the body and to be present with the Lord*….For we must all appear before the judgment seat of Christ, that each one *may receive the things done in the body,* according to what he has done, whether good or bad" (2 Corinthians 5:8, 10).

The word translated "judgment" in the passages above is the Greek word *bema*. It refers to the place in ancient Greek society where public announcements, awards, and rewards were given. It is used by Paul to refer to the place in the believer's future where we will be evaluated for the quality of our life and our service to God since the moment we became born again.

When we think of judgment, we often think of a courtroom. But the believer's judgment at the *bema* seat of Christ will be more of an examination. The Lord will evaluate the quality of our lives. Although the believer will never experience the eternal penalty for sin, they will be held accountable for choices made while living in their bodies since they were saved. Paul describes this moment in his warning to the carnal believers at Corinth.

> "For no man can lay a foundation other than the one which is laid, which is Jesus Christ. Now if any man builds upon the foundation with gold, silver, precious stones, wood, hay, straw, each man's work will become evident; for the day will show it because it is to be revealed with fire, and the fire itself will test the quality of each man's work. If any man's work which he has built upon it remains, he will receive a reward. If any man's work is burned up, he will suffer loss; but he himself will be saved, yet so as through fire" (1 Corinthians 3:11-15 NASB).

After a person is born again, they have a choice about how they will live the rest of their lives. Christ is the foundation of every believer's life. But the choices we make after we accept our salvation build upon that foundation for good or for ill. We can choose to live passionately for Christ, serve others, and enjoy the blessings of living for Him—or we may choose to live largely for ourselves, ignore opportunities to grow spiritually, and allow our flesh to dominate our thoughts and actions.

The Fire of Purity

Scripture says there is coming a day when every believer will stand face to face with Jesus. We will be examined and rewarded for eternity based on how we lived in our bodies. This examination of our works is described as a fire that will test the quality of what we have done with our lives (verse 13 quoted above). Scripture describes the spiritual believer as having built their lives with "gold, silver, and precious stones." The carnal or flesh-ruled believer has built their lives with "wood, hay, and straw." The obvious difference between these two sets of materials is that fire purifies the first, and consumes and eliminates the second.

Note that in verse 15, it says that this fire will consume the carnal believer's works, but "he himself shall be saved, yet so as through fire." In other words, the foundation of Jesus' saving grace will remain, but they will enter eternity without any reward or fruit from their lives. This may seem like a small thing, but at the judgment seat of Christ it will be the awakening to a terrible reality—missed opportunities.

The Place of Good Works

Our works do not earn us entry into heaven. Christ's blood alone qualifies us to spend eternity with God. But our works after our salvation matter because they speak of our love for Christ. Our good works are our way of saying thank you to our heavenly Father.

Someday we who have believed in Jesus are going to stand before Him and receive rewards we have earned in this life. One by one, each of us will hear the names and see the awards given out to every believer for the work they did for Jesus. We will also be evaluated for our carnal deeds.

There will be no day like it in our lives before or after. I believe each of us will feel some regret on that day. Truthfully, none of us lives life perfectly. Even the most diligent believer will realize on that day how much more they could have lived to honor Christ.

However, we can enter that day with as much or as little celebration as we choose. Saved by God's grace from the fires of hell, we will face in full the fire of truth about ourselves and the lives we have led. Only at this assembly, there will be no second chance at another year or a second life. We will face eternity with the fruit of our choices.

"It is appointed unto men once to die, but after this the judgment" (Hebrews 9:27).

Those who have built well will be rewarded generously. God knows how to bless and reward His children. He is the ultimate parent. He cannot be outdone. You can be certain of that. Unfortunately there will be many on that day who will enter heaven with nothing to show for their lives on earth.

"Watch yourselves, that you do not lose what we have accomplished, but that you *may receive a full reward*" (2 John 1:8 NASB).

"Look, I am coming soon, *bringing my reward with me* to repay all people according to their deeds" (Revelation 22:12 NLT).

"For he who comes to God must believe that He is, and *that He is a rewarder of those who diligently seek Him*" (Hebrews 11:6).

When Paul thought of this day he said, "Knowing, therefore, the terror of the Lord, we persuade men" (2 Corinthians 5:11a). Paul spoke of facing the Lord as a believer for an examination of one's life as a fearful thing. While the sins we have confessed and forsaken will never be brought up again, the opportunities we ignored, the selfishness we allowed to dominate our choices, and love we failed to show towards Christ and others will be fully exposed and our motives examined. Then Christ will award us "so that each one may be recompensed for his deeds in the body, according to what he has done, whether good or bad" (2 Corinthians 5:10 NASB).

DAY 2 EXERCISES

1. What is the definition of the word *carnal*?

_____

_____

2. When a believer falls, what are the three important facts to remember?

   1. _____

   2. _____

   3. _____

3. Sin has consequences in a Christian's life. Name three effects here and explain how they impact the believer.

   1. _____

_____

_____

   2. _____

_____

_____

   3. _____

_____

_____

4. What is judgment based on for the unbeliever?

_____

_____

_____

_____

5. Once we have received the judgment of the cross, we will never know _____.

DAY 3: POSSESSING YOUR BODY IN HONOR

JUDGING YOURSELF

Because God is a good parent, He is full of both grace and truth. He holds us in the palm of His hand, but is also willing to discipline us when necessary to make sure we stay there! God's grace and mercy means He will never let us go. His holiness and love also require that He teaches us to grow up and put away the sinful and destructive choices of the flesh.

> "Let a man examine himself...For if we would judge ourselves, we would not
> be judged" (1 Corinthians 11:28a, 31).

While the Lord does not want us to judge each other, He does command us to judge ourselves. Each of us is responsible to be honest with ourselves and God about our sins and daily struggles—with the way we live in our bodies. If we will allow the Holy Spirit and the Word of God to point out the areas of our lives that need to change, God will give us the grace to do so.

CHASTENING OF THE LORD

> "But when we are judged, we are *chastened by the Lord*, that we may not be
> condemned with the world" (1 Corinthians 11:32).

This passage may appear to be harsh at first glance. However a closer look reveals just how loving and good, God is to us. He loves us so much that instead of allowing us to continue in sinful and self-damaging behavior, he uses whatever measure of discipline we require to be corrected, healed, and delivered. His heart is intent on preventing us from continuing in sin so that "we may not be condemned with the world." In Hebrews 12, we learn that God's discipline is actually a sign that we are His children.

> "And have you forgotten the encouraging words God spoke to you as his children?
> He said, 'My child, don't make light of the Lord's discipline, and don't give up
> when he corrects you. For the Lord disciplines those he loves, and he punishes
> each one he accepts as his child" (Hebrews 12:5-6 NLT).

There are three stages in the process of the Lord's chastening. Each one is progressively more severe than the one before it. It is the Lord's desire for us to respond to the earliest stages, and only after we ignore these opportunities will He move to a more severe level.

1. He Speaks to Us

> "Now ye are *clean through the word which I have spoken* unto you"
> (John 15:3 KJV).

> "Sanctify them by Your truth. *Your word* is truth" (John 17:17).

> "Christ also loved the church and gave Himself up for her, so that He might
> sanctify her, having cleansed her by the washing of *water with the word"*
> (Ephesians 5:25-26 NASB).

Like a good father, God's first method of correcting us is with His voice. He speaks to us in a number of ways. First, when we do something wrong, our spirit convicts us of our error. This is one way God speaks—through the voice of our conscience. God also speaks to us through the voices of other believers who warn us. Additionally, He speaks to us when we attend church, read the Bible, listen to or watch teaching resources, pray or worship; He even convicts us through the voices of our own children. Sometimes God will warn us in a dream or through the gift of prophecy. When God wants to say something to us, He knows how to do it! This is always God's first and preferred method of correcting us. Often He will speak to us patiently for quite a while before moving to the second stage of His discipline.

2. He Allows Us to Experience Consequences

We sometimes call this the law of sowing and reaping. Paul told the Galatians church,

> "Do not be deceived, God is not mocked; for whatever a man sows, that he will
> also reap. For he who sows to his flesh will of the flesh reap corruption, but he
> who sows to the Spirit will of the Spirit reap everlasting life" (Galatians 6:7-8).

After some time, if we do not heed God's inner voice and the warnings he sends through our environment and others, He will allow us to begin to experience the consequences of our disobedience. Consequences can be relatively small—like getting caught in a lie—or great—like getting pulled over for driving under the influence, losing a job, a friendship, or possessions. In each case, the negative experience is not God doing something hurtful to us, but rather it is God allowing us to experience the results of our own choices. When we enter this stage of God's discipline, His purpose is to allow us to learn from our mistakes by experiencing some of the pain of our choices. At every moment, He stands ready to forgive, cleanse, and restore us when we turn to Him. A believer may move back and forth between stages one and two for months or even years, depending on the willingness of their hearts to learn and remain humble toward God. However, if we will not learn from this stage of God's discipline, He can move us towards a third, and even more severe, stage of His grace.

3. Severe Grace: Physical Discipline

> "Deliver such a one to Satan for the destruction of the flesh, that his spirit may
> be saved in the day of the Lord Jesus" (1 Corinthians 5:5).

> "Of them are Hymenaeus and Alexander, whom I delivered to Satan that they
> may learn not to blaspheme" (1 Timothy 1:20).

> "For this reason many among you are weak and sick, and a number sleep. But if
> we judged ourselves rightly, we would not be judged. But when we are judged,
> we are disciplined by the Lord so that we will not be condemned along with the
> world" (1 Corinthians 11:30-32 NASB).

As frightening as this may sound, each one of these verses is referring to believers who were unwilling to judge the sin in their lives. While this stage of God's discipline is very severe from a human standpoint, it is actually an act of mercy by a loving Father. If God's child continues to ignore their own sin, God can permit us to open doors to Satan to attack our bodies with weakness, sickness, and even early death. It is better to have a shortened life and go to heaven, than to continue in sin until we become so hardened that we deny Christ and become condemned with the world. This is part of God's system for keeping the true believer in Christ. This means that as born-again believers, we are responsible to deal with our flesh. Nowhere in the Bible are we told to ask God to control our bodies for us. He expects us to learn who we are in Christ and exercise our own authority over our physical temptations, all while relying upon Him for the strength and the strategy to do so.

Learning to "Possess Your Vessel"

"For this is the will of God, your sanctification [separated and set apart for pure and holy living]: that you should abstain from sexual immorality; that each of you should know how to possess [*control, manage*] his own vessel in sanctification [purity, separated from things profane] and honor" (1 Thessalonians 4:3-4).

In other words we must *learn* how to control our bodies. Learning is a process. It is not enough to learn *what* is right and wrong in God's sight. We must learn *how* to do what is right. Thankfully, God has called us to learn how to master sin and take control of our bodies in the Word of God.

> *When tempted, we need to remember our born-again spirit does not desire to sin. Your new nature is the true you.*

FACING TEMPTATION

"No temptation has overtaken you except *such as is common to man;* but God is faithful, who will not allow you to be tempted beyond what you are able, but with the temptation will also make the way of escape, that you may be able to bear it" (1 Corinthians 10:13).

Everyone is Tempted. Period.

You are either tempted or dead. Temptation is common to all humans. So don't feel personally persecuted. Even the most gifted pastor or anointed prophet struggles with temptation. While we cannot escape temptation, we can learn to successfully resist and overcome our weaknesses so that our flesh no longer has the same power over our lives.

"Beloved, do not be surprised at the fiery ordeal among you, which comes upon you for your testing, as though some strange thing were happening to you" (1 Peter 4:12 NASB).

God is Not the One Tempting You

"Let no one say when he is tempted, 'I am tempted by God'; for God cannot be tempted by evil, nor does He Himself tempt anyone" (James 1:13).

> "But each one is tempted when he is drawn *away by his own desires* and enticed" (James 1:14).

God is not the one responsible for your temptations. He is actually working inside the believer to help us overcome temptation, identify our weaknesses, and teach us how to live in victory. Do not confuse what God allows in your life with what God wants for your life. He permits us to struggle so that we learn to grow in our faith and become strong. Just like our bodies are developed through diet and physical exercise, our spirits are strengthened through learning to resist the impulses of the flesh. God rewards us greatly when we overcome temptation. Look what James says:

> "Blessed is the man who endures temptation; for when he has been approved, he will receive the crown of life which the Lord has promised to those who love Him" (James 1:12).

Satan is the Author of Temptation and He is Persistent

> "Now when the devil had ended every temptation, he departed from Him *until an opportune time*" (Luke 4:13).

Even when we successfully resist temptation, the enemy departs only for a season. The enemy is always looking for *an opportunity* to entice our flesh. Paul calls the Devil "the tempter" in 1 Thessalonians 3:5. While we are not to be afraid of the Devil and his demons, we are to be aware of their presence in our world and their efforts to entice our flesh to sin. This is why Jesus taught us to pray, "And don't let us yield to temptation, but rescue us from the evil one" (Matthew 6:13 NLT).

We Are Not All Tempted by the Same Things

> "Therefore…let us lay aside every weight, and the sin which so easily ensnares us, and let us run with endurance the race that is set before us" (Hebrews 12:1).

The truth is that in our flesh, each of us has been broken somewhat *differently* by the sin principle that is in the world and in our flesh. Each of us not only deals with common temptations, but we also have *particular* things that tempt us. These temptations are not equally present and do not carry the same allure in each individual. Sin has broken our human nature in different ways. One person may struggle with addictions to substance abuse. Others battle different kinds of lusts, like promiscuity, adultery, same-sex attraction, or other forms of sexual sin. Some believers struggle with anger, gossip, pride, envy, compulsive and unhealthy eating, or being negative and critical.

You Are Not What Tempts You

It is critical to our spiritual growth that we understand this. We live in a world that teaches us to identify ourselves by things that appeal to our flesh. This is living from the outside in. Our bodies and their appearance or passions is not who we are. Each of us will experience strong passions for things that God calls sin. Those passions are not who we are. They are nothing more than our senses wanting pleasure. And as we are learning, there are many things that may please our flesh momentarily, but damage our lives in the long run.

The thing we need to remember is that our temptations do not define us. Those things do not form our true identity. We are not what tempts us! As born-again believers, we are all new creations in Christ. Our flesh, not our *spirits,* is the source of our temptations.

> "Where do wars and fights come from among you? Do they not come from your *desires for pleasure that war in your members*?" (James 4:1).

> "For I joyfully concur with the law of God in the inner man, but I see a different law in the members of my body, waging war against the law of my mind and making me a prisoner of the law of sin which is in my members" (Romans 7:22-23 NASB).

This means that a believer is not to define themselves by what tempts their flesh. We shouldn't identify ourselves by any particular characteristic of our flesh. It is better to say, "I am a born-again child of God. I am learning to overcome lust, alcohol, lying, anger, addiction, or sexual sin." Some often question whether a Christian can overcome the struggles of their flesh in such life-controlling matters. But hear what Paul wrote to the believers in Corinth:

> "Do you not know that the unrighteous will not inherit the kingdom of God? Do not be deceived. Neither fornicators, nor idolaters, nor adulterers, nor homosexuals, nor sodomites, nor thieves, nor covetous, nor drunkards, nor revilers, nor extortioners will inherit the kingdom of God. *And such were some of you.* But you were washed, but you were sanctified, but you were justified in the name of the Lord Jesus and by the Spirit of our God" (1 Corinthians 6:9-11).

Paul acknowledged that these believers were still struggling with the desires of their old life— the things that identified them before they were made righteous in Christ. But he goes on to remind them that although they struggled with the temptations of the old life, they were not to be identified by these things. "And such *were* some of you" (1 Corinthians 6:11). That means they were delivered from these life-controlling behaviors. It is possible to change our identity and overcome our flesh.

Even though you may yet continue to struggle with the flesh nature, if you have been born again by faith in Jesus, you are no longer that old person. When tempted, we need to remember our born-again spirit does not desire to sin. Your new nature is the *true* you. "You were washed, but you were sanctified, but you were justified in the name of the Lord Jesus Christ and by the Spirit of our God" (1 Corinthians 6:11). Knowing this is half the battle in defeating temptation in your flesh.

Your Spirit is Stronger than Your Flesh

> "Watch and pray, lest you enter into temptation. The spirit indeed is willing, but the flesh is weak" (Mark 14:38).

When we are praying, we are allowing our new nature to fellowship with God. We are forcing our bodies to focus on Jesus. The body and the spirit are often at odds with each other. The body will often fight prayer at first. The flesh is weak. It wants to eat, sleep, be entertained, or experience some momentary pleasure. Prayer is a function of your spirit. Our hearts desire to pray, even though our bodies often do not. But because you are not your body, you and I can bring our bodies into subjection to our hearts. Prayer is one way we strengthen our spirits and weaken our flesh.

God Has Provided a Way of Escape

"For in that He Himself has suffered, being tempted, He is able to aid those who are tempted" (Hebrews 2:18).

"No temptation has overtaken you except *such as is common to man;* but God is faithful, who *will not allow you to be tempted beyond what you are able*, but with the temptation will also *make the way of escape*, that you may be able to bear it" (1 Corinthians 10:13).

Because Jesus lived a real human life in a genuine physical body like ours, he experienced every kind and form of temptation we experience. He knows what it's like! And He is faithful to make a way for us to escape temptation. The word *escape* means "to evade or to get away from." God will not allow the enemy to tempt us in such a way that we are without either the strength to endure it, or a path to get away from it. Time and again I have helped struggling Christians to really evaluate what happens when they stumble into sin. Often people feel overwhelmed by their temptations—as if they were not responsible for their choices. But the Bible says God is faithful. He will provide paths to escape the heat of the battle. The problem is that we often don't realize what these paths are. Consequently, we stumble into sin again and again. Let's look at some of the ways God provides for us to achieve victory over our flesh.

DAY 3 EXERCISES

1. In what three ways does the Lord chasten us?

    1. _____

    2. _____

    3. _____

2. 1 Thessalonians 4:3-4 tells us that we must learn how to do what?

_____

_____

_____

_____

3. Do not confuse what God _____ in your life with what God _____ for your life.

4. What is the thing we need to remember regarding our temptations?

_____

_____

5. According to Mark 14:38, what should we do to avoid temptation?

_____

_____

6. For every temptation, God provides a way of escape. Take a moment to think of a time when that happened for you and relate it here.

_____

_____

_____

_____

_____

_____

7. Do not allow the enemy to trap you with regret. Don't give him the satisfaction. Instead of looking at your failures in despair, accept them as learning experiences and be thankful to God for what He has revealed to you through them. Write below some of the lessons you have learned from your past failures.

_____

_____

_____

_____

_____

DAY 4: GAINING VICTORY OVER THE FLESH

You Can Change!

God does not want His children to struggle continually with their flesh. While it is true that as long as we live we will have to control our bodies with the grace of God and by the power of the Holy Spirit, it is possible to see habits change, old temptations die off, and a powerful new life emerge! But it does involve the discomfort of change.

All change requires us to leave our comfort zone. But whether it's physical change through diet and exercise, intellectual change through study and learning, or economic change through disciplined saving and spending, all change for the better requires the "discomfort" of short-term pain. It has been said that there are two pains in life: the pain of discipline and the pain of regret. Each day we choose one or the other. If you fail to choose the pain of positive change through personal discipline, you will experience the pain of regret later. And the pain of regret is always greater than the pain of discipline.

> *God is more confident in the power of His redeeming love and grace in your life than He is in the power of Satan to tempt you or the power of your temptations.*

BIBLICAL STEPS TO GAINING VICTORY OVER YOUR FLESH

Here are some important steps revealed in God's Word to help you gain victory over your flesh and live in your body in a way that pleases God.

Present Your Body to God

"I beseech you therefore, brethren, by the mercies of God, to *present your bodies a living sacrifice*, holy, acceptable to God, which is your spiritual service. And be not fashioned according to this world" (Romans 12:1-2a ASV).

"Therefore do not let sin reign *in your mortal body*, that you should obey it in its lusts. And do not present your members as instruments of unrighteousness to sin, *but present yourselves to God as being alive from the dead*, and your members as instruments of righteousness to God. For sin shall not have dominion over you, for you are not under law but under grace" (Romans 6:12-14).

As a Christian, God has become the rightful owner of your body. The Bible actually teaches that He purchased you as His own when you received Christ. God expects us to confront the passions of our flesh by presenting our bodies to God as "instruments of righteousness" (vs. 13). That means we need to think of our bodies as vessels to be used for serving Jesus, not just self-serving and empty pleasures. Paul calls this a "living sacrifice." In other words, we should daily remember that we are born-again children of God living in bodies that we are responsible to use for God's purposes.

"Or are you not conscious that your body is a house for the Holy Spirit which is in you, and which has been given to you by God? And *you are not the owners of yourselves; for a payment has been made for you*: let God be honoured in your body" (1 Corinthians 6:19-20 BBE).

You can begin each day with a simple prayer:

Father, I worship You this day. I acknowledge that I am Your child. You have made me a new creation. My spirit is willing to serve You today. Father, I present my body to You for Your glory. You own my body because You purchased it with the blood of Jesus. Lord Jesus, You know the struggles I have in my flesh; You experienced the same temptations. Help me to make choices to use my body, my mind, and my voice in ways that honor You. Go before me and prepare ways of escape from the temptation of the enemy. I believe Your Holy Spirit lives in me and will provide the strength I need to resist sin today. Help me to reach out to You and others for help when I am weak. I will glorify You with the body You have given me. In Jesus' name.

Confess and Claim Victory by Faith

Faith is the force that enables us to receive God's promises. In fact, faith is the only thing that fully pleases God. By faith we must boldly claim for ourselves what God has said about us in His Word. As we have learned in chapters one and six, the Word of God is powerful. We release that power into our lives when we speak the Scriptures in faith. Listen to what Paul said about how he lived in body:

"My old self has been crucified with Christ. It is no longer I who live, but Christ lives in me. So I live in this earthly body by trusting in the Son of God, who loved me and gave himself for me" (Galatians 2:20 NLT).

Paul boldly declared that he was alive in Christ, and that he lived in his body by faith in Jesus and His work on the cross.

Remember that you are not your body. You are not a feeling. You are an eternal spirit! You have feelings and you live in a body. The things God's Word says about you are eternally true whether they appear to be true or not and regardless of how you feel about them. We can trust the Word of God to express the real truth about who we really are.

Call Yourself Dead to Sin and Alive to God

"Even so consider yourselves also dead to sin and your relation to it broken, but alive to God [living in unbroken fellowship with Him] in Christ Jesus" (Romans 6:11 AMP).

The words translated "consider" in the passage above is a term that means "to imagine, think of, and declare something to be so." There is not an exact English word that fully explains this powerful way to combat sin. The term was often used in a legal sense to make a formal declaration. When a judge considers a case and makes a decision, he or she will formally announce their judgment in a court of law and then bang their gavel. The moment the gavel is struck, the judgment is considered true and legally binding. When a judge announces a "not guilty" verdict in court, the person on trial may still be in prison clothes, handcuffed, and even believed to be guilty by others who are present, but the verdict is final. It means that from that time forth, the accused is to be "considered, imagined, and legally thought of" as innocent, because the judge declared it to be so.

There are things we struggle within our flesh that God has already legally declared to be dead to us. He judged them at the cross of His Son. Now it is our responsibility to consider ourselves to be dead to sin. We are to imagine it to be the case—regardless of how we feel, or the temptations that still persist in our lives. The Bible teaches that the Lord calls those things that do not yet exist as though they did exist (Romans 4:17). We too must learn to agree with Romans 6:11, and call ourselves dead to sin and alive to God.

James said our mouths control our bodies.

> "Indeed, we all make many mistakes. *For if we could control our tongues*, we would be perfect and could also control ourselves in every other way"
> (James 3:2 NLT).

You will never gain control of your flesh until you get control of your tongue. Use your mouth to speak positive things—don't just talk about the things you are tempted to do. Start talking about the direction you want to go in. Speak about what you want, not about what you don't want. Whatever you talk about in faith, you will draw into your life!

> "A man's stomach shall be satisfied from *the fruit of his mouth*; from *the produce of his lips he shall be filled.* Death and life are in the power of the tongue, and those who love it will eat its fruit" (Proverbs 18:20-21).

As you feel temptation throughout the day, speak to your body and tell it, "I am dead to that desire. I am dead to sin. I declare myself alive to God, to His desires and to His truth. Body, you are dead to that temptation. That is not who I am anymore." Saying this will release the Holy Spirit into that area because you are verbally agreeing with God's Word over your life, and taking a stand against sin.

Remove Things That Offend

> "*Abstain from* all appearance of evil" (1 Thessalonians 5:22 KJV).

> "*Remove* from me the way of lying" (Psalm 119:29a).

> "And if your right hand causes you to sin, *cut it off and cast it from you*" (Matthew 5:30a).

In that last verse, Jesus was not actually recommending we take a saw to our bodies. What Jesus is teaching is that you have to remove from you the particular thing that causes you to sin. If your temptation involves substance abuse, get the substances you abuse out of your house and life. If it is some form of lust, remove the materials or block the portals that allow you to access the images, places, and people that entice you. This can be difficult at first. We often think that since we are believers and are filled with the Spirit, we should be strong enough to resist temptation alone. Yet if you find yourself continuing to stumble, then you need to remove the obvious things in your life that cause you stumble. Sometimes this means giving up cable television for a while, or driving a different way to and from work. Whatever it takes, remove the things that cause you to be tempted.

Make No Provision for the Flesh

"But put on the Lord Jesus Christ, and make no provision for the flesh, to fulfill its lusts" (Romans 13:14).

Not only do we need to close the obvious "front door" to sin, we need to close the "back doors" as well. Sometimes we make little accommodations for our flesh just in case we feel we really need an escape under pressure. Back doors are bridges to our past life, and sooner or later we will use them if we don't lock them and throw away the key. If you know a particular party, event, place, or entertainment medium, like books, movies, music, concerts, social media, or television programs, are going to feed your flesh and strengthen temptation in your life, remove your access to them. The word *provision* means "to see and prepare for something in advance." Instead of making provision for our flesh and its desires, we should make godly provision for a successful Christian life by closing off those areas in which we are weak in our flesh.

Once, a few years ago, I came home from a meeting at church to discover a mangy, flea-ridden old cat screaming outside my garage. I am fascinated by animals, and was simultaneously annoyed and intrigued by this cat. As soon as I got out of the car, it came right over to me and began rubbing its body in circles around my legs, still making that awful screeching sound. Now I must confess that I love animals.

As such, I started paying attention to that old cat. I surmised she might be hungry so I thought I would feed her and she would go on her way. I poured her milk, gave her sliced ham and turkey, and even some cereal. She loved it. She ate it all. About an hour later the cat started screaming again. All day long I fed her. The more I fed her, the more she hung around. Finally I thought I would pick her up and pet her. The moment I did, she attacked me and bit me several times. Shocked and bleeding, I dropped the cat and went in to tell my wife. She promptly called 911; the animal was removed, and I had to undergo rabies testing. Thankfully, neither of us were infected with the disease.

You see, my curiosity led me to believe I could just feed that mangy cat and she would go on her way. But the more I fed her, the more she hung around. Eventually she became strong enough and bold enough to attack me. My wife later pointed out that if I wanted to get rid of the screaming cat, the best thing to do would have been to *not* feed it.

Our flesh is the same way. Sometimes it screams for attention, for food, for sinful indulgences, promising to shut up if we just feed it a little. But the more we feed our flesh, the stronger it gets. Sooner or later our "back doors" of little indulgences and "pressure relievers" end up biting us. That's why we must stop feeding our flesh and make no provision for its demands.

Run!

"*Run from anything that stimulates youthful lusts.* Instead, pursue righteous living, faithfulness, love, and peace. Enjoy the companionship of those who call on the Lord with pure hearts" (2 Timothy 2:22 NLT).

"But you, Timothy, are a man of God; *so run from all these evil things*. Pursue righteousness and a godly life, along with faith, love, perseverance, and gentleness" (1 Timothy 6:11 NLT).

"*Run from sexual sin!* No other sin so clearly affects the body as this one does. For sexual immorality is a sin against your own body. Don't you realize that your body is the temple of the Holy Spirit, who lives in you and was given to you by God? You do not belong to yourself" (1 Corinthians 6:18-19 NLT).

This may sound weak, silly, and pitiful, but the Bible tells us to run from evil. So often we think we can just look the other way, but still be around people, places, and things that tempt us. The truth is that if you are still learning to gain victory, you have to get away from the sources of temptation as quickly as possible. There is a story in the Bible about Joseph, who was living as a slave in the house of a wealthy Egyptian lord. This ruler's wife was a beautiful and unfaithful seductress.

"And Potiphar's wife soon began to look at him lustfully. 'Come and sleep with me,' she demanded. But Joseph refused. 'Look,' he told her, 'my master trusts me with everything in his entire household.'…She kept putting pressure on Joseph day after day, but he refused to sleep with her, and he kept out of her way as much as possible. One day, however, no one else was around when he went in to do his work. She came and grabbed him by his cloak, demanding, 'Come on, sleep with me!' Joseph tore himself away, but he left his cloak in her hand *as he ran from the house*" (Genesis 39:7-8, 10-12 NLT).

Joseph paid a price for resisting the temptations of his master's wife. But God rewarded him for doing what was right. Eventually, Joseph was given rule over the entire land of Egypt, including this woman! It may appear like you are being weak, but the moment you start feeling yourself going down the wrong path, turn and run. If your conversations on social media drift into inappropriate dialogue with people that are enticing you to sin, delete the account, put down the technology, and get away immediately. Run. It's simple, but it's effective!

Replace Old Habits with New Ones

Simply avoiding old habits will not be enough to defeat the weaknesses of our flesh. The fact is that God made us to be creatures of habit. Our bodies and brains work together in a complex system run by hormonal, chemical, and electrical signals and systems. Whatever we do repeatedly, our brains and bodies mark, remember, and root within the operating system. Our bodies can be trained to desire almost anything if we expose them to it enough. The first time a person drinks alcohol or smokes a cigarette, the body typically resists. But if we continue to expose ourselves to these things, our bodies will signal that we need them and they will become habits. Most of what we do every day, we do subconsciously. We are constantly making choices based on our long forged habits—both good and bad. Those choices become entrenched in us.

In the same way, there are habits that are good for us that our body will initially resist, but can be trained to enjoy, even desire. Exercise is one of them. Healthy eating is another. Praise and worship, Bible reading, prayer, and healthy pleasures can all be programmed into habits that our body will eventually stop resisting and can even begin to crave.

The Bible says, "Do not be overcome by evil, but overcome evil with good" (Romans 12:21). The law of exchange teaches that the way to remove something you don't want is to replace it with something you *do want.* Replace wasted time in excessive TV watching with reading, working on a hobby or project, or taking a class that will improve your mind. Replace old weekend habits with new activities and new people. Focus more on what you want to do rather than what you want to stop doing. Over time, your body and brain will create chemical and electrical bonds that will "wire" you to habits that will pull you in new and better directions.

Use the Power of Association (Relationship)

One of the most powerful spiritual laws we can ever learn is the *law of association.* Simply stated, this law teaches that whatever and whomever we choose to associate with will eventually determine our direction. Our destiny is tied to our relationships. We almost never achieve anything, receive anything, or experience anything new except through a relationship with someone. Most people work in jobs that they received through a connection with someone else. All great successes are achieved through a network of relationships. In fact, most people will never rise above the intellectual, financial, physical, relational, or spiritual level of the five people that are closest to them at any given time.

It has been said, if you are the smartest person in your group, it's time to get a new group! This is true in Scripture as well. Elisha's destiny was tied to Elijah. Joshua's destiny was tied to Moses. Timothy's destiny was tied to Paul. Your destiny is tied to the people you choose to associate with—for good or ill! Note these passages:

> "Walk with the wise and become wise; associate with fools and get in trouble" (Proverbs 13:20 NLT).

> "He who walks with wise men will be wise, but the companion of fools will be destroyed" (Proverbs 13:20).

> "Don't team up with those who are unbelievers. How can righteousness be a partner with wickedness? How can light live with darkness? What harmony can there be between Christ and the devil? *How can a believer be a partner with an unbeliever?* And what union can there be between God's temple and idols? For we are the temple of the living God. As God said: 'I will live in them and walk among them. I will be their God, and they will be my people. Therefore*, come out from among unbelievers, and separate yourselves from them,* says the Lord. *Don't touch their filthy things,* and I will welcome you. And I will be your Father, and you will be my sons and daughters, says the Lord Almighty'" (2 Corinthians 6:14 NLT).

When we begin our walk with Christ, we are to find new relationships in His family in the local church. Believers in Christ are commanded to live their Christian lives in a community. The local church is that community. God has placed others in the church who are there to help us gain victory over our flesh. Our pastors teach us God's Word. Other believers are given spiritual gifts to help us in our journey of transformation. The local church is God's community of spiritual growth and victory. When we stumble and struggle, we are to go to other believers for prayer, counsel, comfort, and accountability.

Accountability in the Family

"Dear brothers and sisters, if another believer is overcome by some sin, you who are godly should gently and humbly help that person back onto the right path. And be careful not to fall into the same temptation yourself. Share each other's burdens, and in this way obey the law of Christ" (Galatians 6:1-2 NLT).

God wants us to rely on one another for accountability and support as we struggle to gain victory over our flesh. Opening up to one or two other spiritual believers can be a powerful force in finding strength to overcome our sinful and negative habits. Many good churches today have small groups that meet confidentially for the purpose of providing mutual support to one another in gaining victory over problems like depression, compulsive gambling, spending, addiction, lust, eating disorders, divorce or separation, and life-controlling behaviors. When we open our lives and are honest with others about the struggles of our flesh, we can find forgiveness, restoration, strength, accountability, and hope.

When You Fall Down, GET UP!

The steps of a good man are ordered by the Lord, and He delights in his way. *Though he fall, he shall not be utterly cast down;* for the Lord upholds him with His hand" (Psalm 37:23-24).

As simple as this may sound, the only appropriate thing to do when you fall down is get back up. Satan is not only our tempter, he is also our accuser. He entices us to sin. Then after we sin he endeavors to tell us how worthless we are, how disappointed God is with our behavior, and how we will never change. But Satan is a liar. And Jesus has defeated him!

"Then I heard a loud voice saying in heaven, 'Now salvation, and strength, and the kingdom of our God, and the power of His Christ have come, for the accuser of our brethren, who accused them before our God day and night, has been cast down'" (Revelation 12:10).

The Holy Spirit will always lead us to confess our sins to our heavenly Father—not run from Him. He has been given to help us when we fail. Scripture says that when we fall, we are to go to God and receive His mercy, grace, and forgiveness.

"If we say that we have no sin, we deceive ourselves, and the truth is not in us. If we confess our sins, He is faithful and just to forgive us our sins and to cleanse us from all unrighteousness" (1 John 1:8-9).

"The Lord *upholds all who fall, and raises up all* who are bowed down" (Psalm 145:14).

"For a righteous man *may fall seven times and rise again*" (Proverbs 24:16a).

"Do not gloat over me, my enemies! *For though I fall, I will rise again.* Though I sit in darkness, the Lord will be my light" (Micah 7:8 NLT).

Don't allow Satan the pleasure of condemning you when you stumble. Remember, that God knew you before you became His child. He knew all your struggles and shameful secrets. Yet He saved you anyway. He is more confident in the power of His redeeming love and grace in your life than He is in the power of Satan to tempt you or the power of your temptations. He is greater, and He loves you. You can change!

We Have an Advocate

"My dear children, I am writing this to you so that you will not sin. *But if anyone does sin, we have an advocate who pleads our case before the Father.* He is Jesus Christ, the one who is truly righteous. He himself is the sacrifice that atones for our sins—and not only our sins but the sins of all the world" (1 John 2:1-2 NLT).

Jesus has a present ministry before our heavenly Father. It is to be our advocate and intercede on our behalf. An *advocate* is someone who promotes the cause of another. In a court proceeding, an advocate looks out to get every advantage for his client. As our advocate, Jesus talks to the Father on our behalf. He reminds the Father that His blood has paid the price for all our sins—past, present, and future! Because He is the beloved Son of God, He knows His Father well, and has never lost a case before Him.

Jesus is also advocating for us before we sin. He is always present to provide the way of escape, and if we rely upon Him, He will give us the strength to resist.

It is not the end when a believer sins. No matter how long you may have been struggling in your life with the same habit, Jesus has made provision for you to be both forgiven and free. No matter how bad you feel after you fall, do not allow the accuser to condemn you. Run to your Advocate, Jesus Christ. Ask for His grace. Confess your failure to Him. He already knows all about it. And He is waiting not only to forgive you, but, if you will ask Him, He will teach you why you fell and how to make a different choice the next time. Remember no matter how persistent sin may be in your flesh, God will never give up on you. He may discipline you, may let you experience consequences, but it is all part of His loving grace—so you may grow up and partake of His holiness.

> *Jesus is also advocating for us before we sin. He is always present to provide the way of escape, and if we rely upon Him, He will give us the strength to resist.*

The Future of the Body

"But we are citizens of heaven, where the Lord Jesus Christ lives. And we are eagerly waiting for him to return as our Savior. *He will take our weak mortal bodies and change them into glorious bodies like his own,* using the same power with which he will bring everything under his control" (Philippians 3:20-21 NLT).

The Christian faith teaches that while our physical bodies are fallen, God's love for humanity includes a marvelous plan for their redemption as well. Jesus did not just intend to defeat sin in our spirits and souls. Jesus' work on the cross includes the ultimate achievement of redemption—the salvation of our bodies!

"Yet what we suffer now is nothing compared to the glory he will reveal to us later….And we believers also groan, even though we have the Holy Spirit within us as a foretaste of future glory, *for we long for our bodies to be released from sin and suffering.* We, too, wait with eager hope for the day when God will give us our full rights as his adopted children, *including the new bodies he has promised us*" (Romans 8:18, 23 NLT).

At death we leave our earthly homes and enter the presence of Jesus.

> "So we are always confident, knowing that while we are at home in the body we are absent from the Lord….We are confident…to be absent from the body and to be present with the Lord" (2 Corinthians 5:6, 8).

But someday Christ will return and actually reconstruct our physical bodies from the "dust of the ground," restoring to them the glory we lost in the garden long ago. At that moment, our spirits shall reenter our resurrected bodies, which will no longer have the nature of sin or the effects of the fall of Adam. The Scripture says our bodies are buried as mortal and corruptible, but will be raised immortal and incorruptible. No longer will we have to struggle against the "law of sin and death" (Romans 8:2) at work in us. Our bodies shall actually be replicas of the resurrected body of Jesus Christ Himself!

> "We know that when He is revealed, we shall be like Him, for we shall see Him as He is " (1 John 3:2b).

> "Who will transform our lowly body that it may be conformed to His glorious body, according to the working by which He is able even to subdue all things to Himself" (Philippians 3:21).

As remarkable as this sounds, this is the promise that awaits the born-again believer in Jesus Christ. On this day, Christ will finish in us the good work that He began (Philippians 1:6). The Bible says that all of creation is awaiting this day as the glorious revealing (or full liberation) of the children of God.

> "For all creation is waiting eagerly for that future day when God will reveal who his children really are….The creation looks forward to the day when it will join God's children in glorious freedom from death and decay" (Romans 8:19, 21 NLT).

What happens next for both the earth and God's children is wonderful beyond imagination. The Scripture says, "Eye has not seen, nor ear heard, nor have entered into the heart of man the things which God has prepared for those who love Him" (1 Corinthians 2:9). While Scripture tells us much about what follows, the Apostle Paul sums it up by stating that "in the ages to come He might show the exceeding riches of His grace in His kindness toward us in Christ" (Ephesians 2:7).

What a great salvation we have received! What a future God has planned for us! What more reason could we have to live in our bodies on earth in a way that brings glory to God?

> "It is the same way with the resurrection of the dead. Our earthly bodies are planted in the ground when we die, but they will be raised to live forever. Our bodies are buried in brokenness, but they will be raised in glory. They are buried in weakness, but they will be raised in strength. They are buried as natural human bodies, but they will be raised as spiritual bodies. For just as there are natural bodies, there are also spiritual bodies….Just as we are now like the earthly man, we will someday be like the heavenly man….But let me reveal to you a wonderful

secret. We will not all die, but we will all be transformed! It will happen in a moment, in the blink of an eye, when the last trumpet is blown. For when the trumpet sounds, those who have died will be raised to live forever. And we who are living will also be transformed. For our dying bodies must be transformed into bodies that will never die; our mortal bodies must be transformed into immortal bodies. Then, when our dying bodies have been transformed into bodies that will never die, this Scripture will be fulfilled: 'Death is swallowed up in victory.'… But thank God! He gives us victory over sin and death through our Lord Jesus Christ" (1 Corinthians 15:42-44, 49, 51-54, 57 NLT).

DAY 4 EXERCISES

1. Faith is a force that does what for us?

_____

_____

_____

_____

2. What does the word *provision* mean?

_____

_____

_____

_____

3. Explain the law of association.

_____

_____

_____

_____

4. As an advocate, Jesus paid the price for our sins _____, _____,
   and _____.

5. What does Philippians 3:20-21 tell us will happen to our mortal bodies?

_____

_____

_____

_____

6. When you fall down, _____ _____! Just do it!

CHAPTER EIGHT

THE PLACE OF TRANSFORMATION

CHAPTER EIGHT
The Place of Transformation

DAY 1: CREATED FOR RELATIONSHIP

Y ou cannot do it on your own. In fact, God never intended for you to try. God designed you for a *family*.

> "For this reason I bow my knees to *the Father* of our Lord Jesus Christ, from whom *the whole family* in *heaven* and *earth* is named" (Ephesians 3:14-15).

In the passage above, God is called the Father of the *whole family in heaven and earth*. The family in heaven are those believers throughout history who have finished their earthly lives and are now with the Father. As we learned in chapter seven, when the physical body wears out and dies, the eternal spirit that is the *true* you departs to be with Christ (Philippians 1:23). In God's presence, we will be consciously united with our loved ones who know the Lord and every other believer who has left the earth.

The question then is, "Exactly who is my family *on earth?*" In this chapter we are going to learn that when you were born again, you were joined to the Father *and His family*. Understanding the nature of God's family on earth is absolutely essential to living the transformed life.

> *While times of fasting and private devotion are essential to spiritual growth, they are not in themselves the path to spiritual maturity.*

THE FATHER AND HIS FAMILY

You Were Created for Relationship

One of the first things we have learned about our Father is that He is a *relational* being. You and I were made in His image, and therefore we are relational beings too. However, we were not designed to be in a relationship with God alone. In His wisdom, God made us to also live in loving connection with one another.

You cannot reach your full potential in Christ by developing your personal relationship with God privately. Some believers consider their faith a private affair between themselves and God and have no interest in sharing their spirituality with others. Sometimes you may hear sincere believers say things like, "All I need is Jesus. I have no interest in having a relationship with people." They imagine that true spirituality is achieved by withdrawing from others and going "inside themselves" to find God. While times of fasting and private devotion are essential to spiritual growth, *they are not in themselves* the path to spiritual maturity. In fact, personal isolation is a sign of spiritual weakness and immaturity.

After God created and established a relationship with Adam, He said an amazing thing: "It is not good that man should be alone; I will make him a helper comparable to him" (Genesis 2:18). As astounding as this may sound, it was not enough for Adam to have a personal relationship with God alone! In order for Adam to fully bear the image of God, he needed to experience human relationship. By creating Eve as Adam's partner, the Lord was "redesigning" man to need both a *vertical* relationship with God and *horizontal* relationships with others. There is something in each human heart that longs for this connection with others.

The Impact of Sin on Human Relationships

When sin entered the world, it immediately destroyed our relationship with God and our capacity to have healthy connections with one another. Adam and Eve had the first fight in their marriage, each blaming the other for what had happened (Genesis 3:12-13). Love and trust were replaced by fear and selfishness. Their first child had such anger in his heart that he killed their second child (Genesis 4:8). By the time Noah arrived on the scene, the entire human race was so filled with violence and hatred for one another that God determined to remove them from the planet. Noah's family was the only group of humans left whose relationships were not thoroughly corrupted by violence and evil (Genesis 6:5-13). After God restored the earth, He gave Noah strict instructions about how humans were to live and govern their relationships (Genesis 9:6-7). This is known as the covenant of Noah, and it contained the first laws that God gave to humanity after the garden.

This demonstrates how important our human relationships are to God. The Bible teaches that there are seven things God actually hates. Each of them has to do with how we injure and hurt one another.

> These six things the Lord hates, yes, seven are an abomination to Him: A proud look, a lying tongue, hands that shed innocent blood, a heart that devises wicked plans, feet that are swift in running to evil, a false witness who speaks lies, and one who sows discord among brethren" (Proverbs 6:16-19).

GOD'S PLAN TO RESTORE THE HUMAN FAMILY

God chose to restore us to Himself through a family. This concept is so important that the Bible cannot be fully understood without it. After the story of Noah and his family, the rest of Genesis is the story of how Abraham's descendants developed into a great nation known as Israel. Israel was the name the Lord gave to Abraham's grandson, Jacob, from whom the Jewish people descended.

The Family of Abraham

In Genesis 12, God spoke to a man named Abraham. He said to him,

> "I will make you *a great nation*; I will bless you and make your name great; and you shall be a blessing. I will bless those who bless you, and I will curse him who curses you; and in you *all the families of the earth* shall be blessed" (Genesis 12:2-3).

This promise made to Abraham indicated that God would use a single human family to bring His blessing to all the people of the earth!

The Family of Israel—God's Old Testament Church

The Old Testament tells how God established this family as a nation, and how He used that nation to deal with the rest of the world. While the Bible is filled with stories of how God dealt with individuals, they are told within the larger framework of the story of the family of Israel.

By the time God delivered the people of Israel out of slavery in Egypt, Abraham's family had grown into well over a million people. God saved them as a family—*together*. It was to this family that the Lord gave the Ten Commandments and the rest of the Old Testament. He led them to the Promised Land *together*, under the guidance of one man, Moses, who had been both a prince of Egypt and a shepherd.

Moses became the first "pastor" of the Lord's "congregation" (Acts 7:38). Israel was God's first church—an example of how His future church would be built. Through this powerful picture, we see that God saves individuals in the context of a community. The Lord made a way for the Gentiles (non-Jewish people) to be saved by joining the community and faith of Israel (Leviticus 19:34).

The Family of Jesus—The New Testament Church

God's Son came to save the entire world by stepping into this single human family—Israel. Jesus lived His life in the Jewish community, even as He ministered to the Gentiles as well (Matthew 8:5; Mark 7:26; John 4:9). The true mission of Jesus was hidden from His disciples, who often thought He had come as a prophet or political leader who would restore Israel to national greatness (Acts 1:6). It wasn't until several years into ministry that Jesus finally revealed who He was, and the real reason He had come into the world.

> "Then he asked them, 'But who do you say I am?' Simon Peter answered, 'You are the Messiah, the Son of the living God.'…Now I say to you that you are Peter (which means "rock"), and upon this rock *I will build my church, and all the powers of hell will not conquer it.* And I will give you the keys of the Kingdom of Heaven. Whatever you forbid on earth will be forbidden in heaven, and whatever you permit on earth will be permitted in heaven"
> (Matthew 16:15-16, 18-19 NLT).

Jesus came for *one* primary purpose. Everything He did in His earthly ministry, everything He did for us on the cross and resurrection, and everything He has done for us ever since, has been for this purpose: to *build His church*. Everything Christ does on the earth today is for the purpose of building His church. The church is the New Testament family of God. Just as salvation in the Old Testament joined you to the family of Israel, salvation in the New Testament joins you to the family of Jesus: His church.

Jesus said that He would give His church the keys of the kingdom of heaven—keys that would carry the authority of Jesus to carry out God's will on earth. These keys are given not just to individual believers, but to the church collectively. This is why it is essential to understand that when you are born again, you enter a relationship with God *and* His church.

Saved Together

It is impossible to read the New Testament letters and not see that everything Christ did for us *personally*, He also achieved for us *collectively*. Most of the time when Paul or Peter spoke of Christ's work in their writings, they used the plural pronouns "we," "our," and "us." They understood that our individual salvation was accomplished as part of something Christ was doing collectively. Just as God saved Israel as one related community from the bondage of Egypt, so Jesus secured us individually and collectively through His finished work on the cross.

Did Jesus Really Die "Just for You"?

Becoming a Christian is a very personal experience. Because we come to Christ as individuals, each of us has a testimony or story of how and when we received Jesus as our *personal* Savior. Our self-worth soars when we hear that Jesus died for us individually. Sometimes people say, "If you were the only person on the planet, Christ still would have died just for you." We say such things to emphasize the personal love God has for each of us.

> *Jesus did not die for us one by one. He redeemed us as a community—purchasing salvation for all of us at once. We were saved together.*

It *is* true that Jesus knows each of His sheep by name, loves us individually, and calls each of us to Himself personally (John 10:3). The Bible, however, almost never refers to salvation in this manner. In nearly *every instance* where the New Testament speaks of Christ's work on the cross, it uses the language of *community*. We are saved *together* with others. We are not just a group of individual believers. We are a *team* of faith.

Jesus did not die for us one by one. He redeemed us as a community—purchasing salvation for all of us at once. We were saved together. When writing to the churches about salvation, the apostles almost always used the term *you* in reference to the entire community of the local church. It was not unlike the common expression found in the southern United States today, "y'all." Notice how the word *you* in the following verses speak to the entire local church collectively:

> "But God, who is rich in mercy, because of His great love with which He loved *us*, even when *we* were dead in trespasses, made *us* alive *together* with Christ (by grace you have been saved), and raised *us* up together, and made *us* sit *together* in the heavenly places in Christ Jesus, that in the ages to come He might show the exceeding riches of His grace in His kindness toward *us* in Christ Jesus. For by grace *you* have been saved through faith, and that not of *yourselves*; it is the gift of God" (Ephesians 2:4-8).

> "*To the saints* and faithful brethren in Christ who are in Colosse: Grace *to you* and peace from God our Father and the Lord Jesus Christ. We give thanks to the God and Father of our Lord Jesus Christ, praying always *for you*" (Colossians 1:2-3).

> "For this reason we also, since the day we heard it, do not cease to pray for *you*, and to ask that *you* may be filled with the knowledge of His will in all wisdom and spiritual understanding; that *you* may walk worthy of the Lord, fully pleasing Him, being fruitful in every good work and increasing in the

knowledge of God;…giving thanks to the Father who has qualified *us* to be partakers of the inheritance of the saints in the light. He has delivered *us* from the power of darkness and conveyed *us* into the kingdom of the Son of His love, in whom *we* have redemption through His blood, the forgiveness of sins" (Colossians 1:9-10, 12-14).

Jesus died for us together. We were raised with Christ together. We are called to live our Christian faith together.

You Are Not Alone!

There is a joy in knowing, embracing, and understanding our collective salvation. This joy is found in the wonderful comfort of realizing that we are *never* alone! Jesus designed you for a family, and a family for you. Embracing Jesus means embracing His family. No matter what you or I face in life, both the Lord *and His church* are there to help. As Peter taught, "You are a chosen generation…His own special people, that you may proclaim the praises of Him who called you out of darkness into His marvelous light; who once were not a people but are now the people of God" (1 Peter 2:9-10a).

In fact, many of the things God has planned for you as an individual, He designed for you to receive through a relationship with His church. The church of Jesus Christ is the only environment God has given for us to experience the transformed life. That's why we need to study and develop a loving relationship with Jesus and His church.

DAY 1 EXERCISES

1. We were created for _____ relationship with God and _____ relationship with each other.

2. Who was the first pastor of God's congregation on earth? _____

3. What was the primary purpose that Jesus came?

_____

_____

_____

4. What Christ did for us _____, He also achieved for us _____.

5. How do you receive many of the things that God has planned for you as an individual?

_____

_____

_____

DAY 2: OUR FAMILY—SEEN AND UNSEEN

THE TWO DIMENSIONS OF THE CHURCH: VISIBLE AND INVISIBLE

The word *church* is used in two ways in the New Testament. It is important to remember that the church is God's family in *two locations*. He is called "*the Father*…from whom *the whole family* in *heaven* and *earth* is named" (Ephesians 3:14-15). This means that part of our spiritual family is invisible and part is visible.

The Invisible or Universal Church

The invisible church may not be seen with your physical eyes, but is real nonetheless. It has several important characteristics:

The Invisible Church is *Universal*
When you are born again, you are joined invisibly to every other believer in heaven and earth throughout time. While we will never meet most of our fellow Christians in this life, through Christ we are one family.

The Invisible Church is *Physically Separated*
The barriers of time, geography, culture, language, life, and death separate us from having interaction directly with our invisible family. These distances mean that we cannot currently have a conscious relationship with our family that lives on the other side of these divides.

The Invisible Church is *Spiritually Connected*
Even though we are physically separated from our invisible family, we are spiritually united to them through our relationship with our Father in Jesus Christ. Because we have the same Father, we are genuinely related. Scripture even indicates that our family in heaven may witness in some measure our spiritual progress on earth.

> "Therefore, since *we are surrounded* by such a *huge crowd of witnesses* to the life of faith, let us strip off every weight that slows us down" (Hebrews 12:1a NLT).

The Invisible Church Will Be *United*
Someday our whole family will be united in one place. The barriers that have separated us will be completely removed. That will be a day like no other! We will see our loved ones in heaven and meet every other member of the incredible family of God!

> "God has now revealed to us his mysterious plan regarding Christ, a plan to fulfill his own good pleasure. And this is the plan: At the right time he will bring everything together under the authority of Christ—*everything in heaven and on earth*" (Ephesians 1:9-10 NLT).

The Visible Church

The second dimension of God's family is the present church on earth. It is the church that you can see, touch, and connect with physically. Consider this: *Most New Testament teaching about the church refers to the visible church.* The word *church* is used 118 times in the Greek

New Testament. Only 14 times is it used to describe the universal and *invisible* church. *All* of the other 104 references are speaking of the visible, or *local*, church. Just as Israel was God's visible family in the Old Testament, the local church is His visible family in the earth today. When Jesus said He would build His church, He indicated that He would give the keys to the kingdom of heaven to the church. He said we were to use them on earth (Matthew 16:19). Therefore, Jesus was talking about building the *visible* church.

SEVEN CHARACTERISTICS OF THE VISIBLE CHURCH

1. The Visible Church is Local

The first fact about the visible church is that you can see it. That means it is near to where you live. For this reason we speak of the church as being *local*. The word *local* comes from the Latin word *locus*, which means "place." A *location* is a particular place. A locomotive is a vehicle that moves you from place *to* place. The local church is a place. It exists in a geographic area. Because the church is a place where you actively participate, it needs to be in the region in which you live. Every believer needs to discover the place near them where they can participate in God's church (Acts 4:23 NLT; 15:22).

2. The Visible Church is a Community of Regenerated People

The local church is more than property, buildings, and a parking lot. It is not a social club, an educational center, a non-profit corporation, or a relief agency. *The church is a community of people who have been born again by faith in Jesus and called together into loving relationship.* Simply attending church does not make you a part of this community. You must have had the genuine work of the Holy Spirit creating a new heart inside you in order to authentically belong to the local church.

The word *community* comes from the Latin word *communis* which means "to share a place intimately with others." God has called the church to be a community who follow Jesus and experience his transforming life *together.* Members of our Father's family need to commune and share their lives with one another. This requires that we develop a genuine personal relationship with both Jesus Christ *and* His church.

The local church is also a community of faith within a community of darkness. Every church is to be a witness to the world around them. Jesus referred to His people as a "city that is set on a hill" and a "lamp" that gives light to those in the darkness (Matthew 5:14-16). As believers grow in the local church, their faith becomes a witness to the greater community in which they live. He also said, "Your love for one another will prove to the world that you are my disciples" (John 13:35 NLT). The local church evangelizes the world by loving each other. It is impossible to show the world your love for other believers unless you are in a *visible,* genuine relationship together.

3. The Visible Church is a Gathering

> "Not forsaking the *assembling of ourselves together*, as is the manner of some, but exhorting one another, and so much the more as you see the Day approaching" (Hebrews 10:25).

The word *church* in ancient Greek was used to describe a special assembly of people called out of their homes to a public meeting or council. In fact, the word *church* could be translated "those called to meet together." This is the word Jesus chose to describe the new family of God He had come to establish. That tells us something essential about God's ideal purpose for the church. Of all the things the church might be and do, it is first and foremost a physical gathering of people. In other words, *every* believer is supposed to go to church.

> *The church describes both a people and an event. It is both a group and a gathering.*

From the very beginning of Christianity, believers understood that being a church meant regularly meeting together. The first church meetings were on the Sunday of Christ's resurrection (John 20:19), and the Sunday of Pentecost, seven weeks later (Acts 2:1). From that time forward, Christians would gather each weekend to worship God and hear the teaching of His Word (Acts 20:7; 1 Corinthians 16:2).

There are some Christians who do not understand the importance of being physically present with their fellow believers each week. Some think that because they have a personal relationship with the Father, they have no need for commitment to a particular local church. They have failed to understand that many of the things God has designed for their lives can only be received *through* a living connection with others in the local church.

The church describes both a people and an event. It is both a group and a gathering. When you become a part of the group, you are supposed to gather. By coming each week to the event of local church worship, you build real connections with the people God has given to be your spiritual family. In this environment, there are special gifts that are exercised, practices that we participate in, and ministry we receive. When we go to church, we are not going to a building, but rather going to a part of the body. Where we gather is not as important as the fact that we gather.

4. The Visible Church Has a Creed

A *creed* is a set of beliefs that are designed to guide one's actions and shape one's thinking. While we may have our own ideas about music, movies, politics, and food, to be a part of the church, the members must be committed to a set of beliefs that are non-negotiable. There is room in the Christian faith for differences about many things, but each local church must decide what is essential for their individual community.

For a local church to be effective, it must be unified around a set of core doctrines, beliefs, and key values that guide its mission. The *Transformed Life* has been developed to help local churches teach powerful truths that will instruct believers and cause local churches to grow into transformational communities *together*.

5. The Visible Church is Organized

Heaven is an organized place. God is not just figuring things out as He goes. The angels don't just do whatever they want, whenever they feel like doing it. Through the eyes of God's prophets, the Bible allows us to capture a glimpse of what heaven is like. In each case, we see that our Father lives in a place that is highly organized. Every detail is planned and its beauty and order is overwhelming. There are specific numbers of angels that surround God's throne—

each executing specific details in perfect harmony. When the Prophet Isaiah saw this, he was "undone" (Isaiah 6:5). God showed Moses a vision of heaven and he built a replica of what he saw (Hebrews 8:1-5). The details of God's sanctuary, and its furnishings and dimensions as described by Moses, reveals that our Father's home is a place of unmatched beauty and exquisite detail. Why would His church on earth operate otherwise?

> *God actually commands us to worship and do everything in the local church with planning, organization, and excellent execution.*

Today many people have rejected "organized religion" because of the elaborate rituals and controlling structures of some church denominations. In many cases, these Christians have imagined that following Jesus is purely a personal matter. But the New Testament commands believers to worship God in organized local churches.

> "For He…is not a God of confusion and disorder but of peace and order. As [is the practice] in *all the churches* of the saints (God's people),…But all things should be done with regard to decency and propriety and in an orderly fashion"
> (1 Corinthians 14:33, 40 AMP).

The Greek word translated "decency" comes from two root words. The first is the word *eu* which means "of good quality." The second word is *schema* from which we get the word "scheme" or "well-formed plan." The Lord is telling us that all things in the local church are supposed to be developed according to a well-formed plan of high quality.

The word *orderly* in verse 40 is the Greek word *tasso* which was a military term that means "to systematically organize people according to rank and file." It also means "to arrange in order and according to a fixed time." This verse could be read like this,

> "Let everything in the local church be developed according to a well-formed plan and with attention to a process of quality organization."

In other words, the local church is not supposed to be a loose, unplanned environment. God actually commands us to worship and do everything in the local church with planning, organization, and excellent execution. While each local church may have its own particular flavor, approach, and methods, all local churches are called to be well-planned and organized.

Organization does not mean stuffy and predictable. Good organization enables the local church to maximize its creativity by increasing its quality.

6. The Visible Church Has a Structure of Authority

There is no such thing as a biblical church without biblical leadership. We are going to study this in depth in the next chapter, but the principle of church leadership was established by Jesus Himself. He chose twelve men and trained them as leaders. It is clear from the book of Acts that wherever people responded to the gospel, these apostles appointed leaders for the local churches. The earliest word that was used to describe the role of the *pastor* was "elder."

"So when they had *appointed elders* in *every* church, and prayed with fasting, they commended them to the Lord in whom they had believed" (Acts 14:23).

"For this reason I left you in Crete, that you should set in order the things that are lacking, and *appoint elders* in every city as I commanded you" (Titus 1:5).

There is not a single example in the New Testament of a church that was without authorized spiritual leadership. There are *no exceptions in Scripture*. That means a group of Christians meeting in a living room does not constitute a local church unless it is meeting under qualified spiritual leadership. Believers may gather in kitchens, public places, coffee shops, rented auditoriums, or elaborate cathedrals for prayer, Bible study, sharing, and testimony. These fellowships are expressions *of* the church. But if there is not a qualified, God-appointed pastor or minister present to lead, it is not a complete expression of the New Testament local church. The New Testament knows no spiritual ministry outside of local church authority. It is the primary agency of God's work on earth today. All scriptural Christian ministry is either under the covering, or in service *of,* the visible local church.

7. The Visible Church Pursues the Mission and Purposes Given by Jesus

Every local church has particular purposes and assignments that are unique to their mission in the community. But all churches share the responsibility to pursue the *main mission* given to us by Jesus Christ. We call this the *Great Commission.*

"'Go therefore and *make disciples of all the nations*, baptizing them in the name of the Father and of the Son and of the Holy Spirit, *teaching them* to observe all things that I have commanded you; and lo, I am with you always, even to the end of the age.' Amen" (Matthew 28:19-20).

The mission that God has called the church to perform above all others is to reproduce ourselves by sharing the life and teaching of Jesus Christ in our generation. All local churches are called to expand by sharing the gospel with the world, baptizing those who believe, and turning them into passionate disciples (Christ-followers) through teaching and instruction.

DIFFERENT BRANCHES, COMMON ROOTS

There are some beliefs that are common to all genuine Christians, regardless of their denomination. We call these beliefs the "orthodox" or essential truths of the Christian faith. These truths include the authority of Scripture, the Trinity, humanity's need for salvation, and the bodily death and resurrection of the Lord Jesus Christ.

Other doctrines or teachings of the Christian faith are viewed differently by sincere believers. As the gospel spread over the centuries throughout various cultures, new branches of the church formed and different perspectives developed. These differences typically involve the way in which the orthodox doctrines are to be understood and carried out by the church. For example, some churches baptize by sprinkling water on the head. Others baptize by complete submersion in water. The different perspectives about these things are *real and important*. They affect the way you think and how you will live as a Christian. Some branches of the church were formed in protest to alarming abuses and corruption that had entered the historic church. Others came about because God was restoring a forgotten truth that the existing church did not want to embrace.

But there is room in the Christian faith for genuine disagreement. Some think the different churches are a sign that Christianity is not true. Instead, it is evidence of the adaptability and enduring quality of the church. From it, we learn how the gospel inspires people of all cultures to follow Jesus and that God's church is greater than the weakness of men. Jesus actually prophesied that this would occur.

> "Then He said, 'To what shall we liken the kingdom of God?...It is like a mustard seed which, when it is sown on the ground, is smaller than all the seeds on earth; but when it is sown, it grows up and becomes greater than all herbs, and *shoots out large branche*s, so that the birds of the air may nest under its shade'" (Mark 4:30-32).

The kingdom of God on the earth today is the church of Jesus Christ. As the church grew throughout the ages, it put forth various branches, just as Jesus indicated it would. It is important to remember that these branches, while different, *are all connected to the same trunk* and have common roots.

DAY 2 EXERCISES

1. What Scripture reference tells us that the church is both visible and invisible at the same time? _____

2. What are the four main characteristics of the invisible church?
   1. _____
   2. _____
   3. _____
   4. _____

3. How often is the Greek word for "church" used in reference to the visible local church in the New Testament? _____ How many times for the invisible church? _____

4. Name the seven characteristics of the local church and why they are important.
   1. _____
   2. _____
   3. _____
   4. _____
   5. _____
   6. _____
   7. _____

5. According to 1 Corinthians 14:33, 40, what does the Bible say about organization in the practice of our faith?

   _____
   _____
   _____

6. It is hard for us to imagine an "invisible" church. Although we can't see it, it is there. When all the barriers are gone, we will be part of a very large family! Thank Jesus for your adoption today.

DAY 3: PURPOSES OF THE LOCAL CHURCH

The church is also purposeful. There are special purposes that God has designed for your life through the local church. In the rest of this chapter we are going to look at these purposes.

> *The reason some Christians neglect the local church is because they really don't understand its purpose in their lives.*

PURPOSES OF THE LOCAL CHURCH

A *purpose* is a reason for being. Everything God does has a purpose. Everything God has made has a reason for existing. There are specific purposes Jesus intended for His church to accomplish. Knowing those purposes is important for every believer. The *law of purpose* states that unless you know the purpose of a thing, you will be likely to either neglect, misuse, or abuse it. The reason some Christians neglect the local church is because they really don't understand its purpose in their lives.

> "And *let us not neglect our meeting together*, as some people do, but encourage one another, especially now that the day of his return is drawing near" (Hebrews 10:25 NLT).

There are many people today who have received God as their Father, love Jesus, and mistakenly think that they can grow spiritually without having to make any formal connection with the local church. Because of technology, it is possible to watch church meetings online, listen to great teaching through electronic means, and interact with others on the internet. While all of these things are wonderful tools that can supplement our spiritual development, none of them can replace God's purpose for the local church.

The Lord designed the church as a *distribution* system. There are many things that Jesus distributes to His people exclusively through the local church. The Lord intended for us to live the transformed life in community together. Knowing the purposes God intends for us in the local church enables us to receive them. Let's look at these purposes.

1. Experiencing the Special Presence of Jesus

When Jesus began teaching about the purpose of His church, He made this statement:

> "For where two or three are gathered together in My name, I am there in the midst of them" (Matthew 18:20).

Throughout the Scripture, whenever God's people would gather to worship, God promised a special manifestation of His presence. This is known as the *corporate presence of God*. While the Lord is present inside of each of His children, when we come together to worship as the church, He is present in an even greater way. Throughout the Bible, when God's people came together in His name, powerful things occurred. Whether it was the dedication of Solomon's Temple (1 Kings 8:10), the miraculous outpouring of the Holy Spirit on the day of Pentecost (Acts 2:1-4), or the sudden healing of a lame man (Acts 14:8-10), the record shows that the Lord longs to manifest special blessings on His gathered people.

When you come to church, expect the Lord to manifest His presence. Know that regardless of what you may feel emotionally or physically, Jesus is there in a special way. Often it is your presence in church and participation in worship by faith that sets the environment for the Holy Spirit to move in the service. He is present to minister to the needs of His family, so attending worship services is a selfless way in which your presence helps to create the environment God uses to move in the lives of *others*.

> "*Together*, we are his *house*…We are *carefully joined together* in him, *becoming a holy temple* for the Lord…being made part of this dwelling where God lives by his Spirit" (Ephesians 2:20-22 NLT).

2. To Make Disciples by Teaching and Preaching God's Word

> "All the believers devoted themselves to the apostles' teaching" (Acts 2:42a NLT).

> "'Go therefore *and make disciples of all the nations*, baptizing them in the name of the Father and of the Son and of the Holy Spirit, *teaching them to observe* all things that I have commanded you; and lo, I am with you always, even to the end of the age.' Amen" (Matthew 28:19-20).

Every believer needs to regularly hear the teaching and preaching of God's Word in order to develop in faith and grow to spiritual maturity. Paul told us to be "transformed by the renewing of your mind" (Romans 12:2). Anointed preaching in the local church is the cornerstone of this transformation.

When the Lord Jesus left the earth, He appointed ministers to lead His church. "And He himself gave some to be apostles, some prophets, some evangelists, and some pastors and teachers, for the equipping of the saints for the work of ministry, for the edifying of the body of Christ" (Ephesians 4:11-12). They are referred to as the *ministry gifts* because Jesus personally chose, called, equipped, and sent them as gifts to minister to the local church.

The primary way these ministers lead the church is through anointed preaching and teaching. If the ministers of the church are Christ's gifts to us, then we need to receive them in order to reach our potential and fulfill our purpose! There is a difference between reading the Bible on your own and hearing the anointed teaching of God's Word through the pastors and ministers of the church. When the church gathers to hear God's Word, the Holy Spirit speaks through the pastor to equip God's people to transform their lives. The teaching of God's Word is the most important aspect of the weekly worship event. No matter how long one has been a Christian, we never outgrow our need to be fed by our spiritual shepherd(s) by the living Word of God. The Bible tells us to "remember your leaders who taught you the word of God" (Hebrews 13:7a NLT).

> *There is a difference between reading the Bible on your own and hearing the anointed teaching of God's Word through the pastors and ministers of the church.*

From the beginning, the church met weekly to hear the teaching of God's Word (Acts 2:42; 20:7). Because most believers did not have personal copies of the available Scriptures, church meetings involved lots of Bible reading and teaching. The local church was the place the Lord's "flock" came to be "fed" (1 Peter 5:2). One of the first Christian historians who lived less than one hundred years after the resurrection of Christ was Justin Martyr (AD 100-165). He wrote about the practices of the first believers:

> "And on the day called Sunday, all who live in cities or in the country gather together to one place and memoirs [letters and gospels] of the apostles or the writings of the prophets [Old Testament Scriptures] are read, as long as time permits. Then, when the reader has ceased, the president [pastor] verbally instructs and exhorts to the imitation of these good things."[21]

Purposes of Local Church Preaching and Teaching

Increases Our Faith
Paul taught that "faith comes by hearing, and hearing by the word of God" (Romans 10:17). The Greek term translated "word" in this verse is the word *rhema* which means "that which is spoken in the moment." Paul was teaching that we need to be present to hear the inspired message of the preacher (Romans 10:14-15). When we gather to hear a sermon each week, the Holy Spirit works through the gifts in the pastor to inspire our faith. Strong faith is essential to pleasing God (Hebrews 11:6), receiving answers to our prayers (James 1:6-7), and living a victorious Christian life (1 John 5:4).

Enables Spiritual Growth
> "As newborn babes, desire the pure milk of the word, that you may grow thereby" (1 Peter 2:2).

Just like a newborn requires the proper diet in order to grow physically, our spirits need the "milk" of God's Word in order to develop into maturity.

Renews Our Minds
Anointed teaching and preaching can often help us to change our thinking and renew our minds faster than private Bible study alone. The Holy Spirit anoints the pastor to minister God's word in such a way that it takes deep root in our hearts and minds. The more we hear the preaching of the Word, the more our minds are strengthened in new and better patterns of thinking. Preaching and teaching uproots worldly thinking and replaces wrong and self-destructive thoughts with the inspired revelation of God's Word. Paul told the Corinthians that when he arrived to preach he was going to "cast down" their unhealthy mental strongholds and take every wrong thought into "captivity to the obedience of Christ" (2 Corinthians 10:5). This process is critical to our growth.

---

21. Justin Martyr, First Apology 67, Public Domain.

Corrects and Protects Us

Timothy was a young pastor of the enormous local church in Ephesus. Paul wrote Timothy two letters instructing him how to lead the church effectively. Much of what Paul told Timothy had to do with His teaching and preaching ministry. Paul wrote: "Preach the Word! Keep your sense of urgency [stand by, be at hand and ready], whether the opportunity seems to be favorable or unfavorable. [Whether it is convenient or inconvenient, whether it is welcome or unwelcome, you as preacher of the Word are to show people in what way their lives are wrong.] And convince them, rebuking and correcting, warning and urging and encouraging them, being unflagging and inexhaustible in patience and teaching" (2 Timothy 4:2 AMP).

The pastor needs to do more than encourage us. It is also the pastor's responsibility to correct and warn us. When God speaks correction through the pastor, He is actually protecting us from error and deception (Ephesians 4:14).

Provides Prophetic Guidance and Needed Inspiration

In the Spirit-filled local church, God often speaks through the pastor's message to address hidden problems or prepare the church for future events. Sometimes the pastor will find himself saying something he did not plan to say. Often the pastor will not know why he is being directed to say things in his message. Later it becomes clear that the Holy Spirit was using the pastor to speak to issues in the congregation or future events that are beyond the scope of the pastor's knowledge. This is a sign that God loves His people enough to speak personally to a room full of different people at the same time!

As a pastor, I have had several very unusual experiences along these lines. On Mother's Day, May 13th, 2001, I was a guest at my pastor's church, Christian Cultural Center in New York City. During the worship service, I had a vision in my spirit. When the senior pastor, Dr. A.R. Bernard sensed the Holy Spirit was speaking to me, he asked me to share what I was seeing in my heart with the congregation. Some of it I shared publicly, and the rest I shared privately after the service with Dr. Bernard. I remember saying, "I see dark clouds rising over the southern end of Manhattan—a great darkness that spreads out over the city and beyond. It feels like a disaster of some sort." I went on to share that I felt the Lord was going to use Dr. Bernard and the congregation to be a light and help to the city when this event occurred.

Naturally, I felt somewhat strange afterwards because I had no idea what I had seen or whether I was accurate or appropriate in sharing it. The pastor was very gracious and assured me that he had sensed they were preparing for something important as a church— to be a great witness to the city. On September 11th when the planes plunged into the World Trade Center, the congregation remembered the things I had shared and were instantly energized to bring relief. Dr. Bernard was asked by the churches of New York to coordinate a massive relief and recovery plan—helping thousands of New Yorkers rebuild their lives. His sensitivity to the Holy Spirit in recognizing I had a message from the Lord—combined with his great wisdom in leadership—set the stage for the thousands of members of that church to be prepared to bring Christ's love to a hurting city.

Not every pastor is used in the same way. However, every pastor called by the Lord will be inspired to teach and preach God's Word in a way that will apply to the needs of the moment, while often preparing the church for things to come as well. By faithfully attending church and listening carefully to the messages that are preached, you will often discover that God is speaking into your life and preparing you for the challenges that lie just ahead. Many times we leave church thinking the message was probably for someone else, only to discover later that week that God was speaking directly to us! Thank God for the supernatural ministry of the Holy Spirit through the preaching of the Word of God!

> "Then said Jesus to those Jews which believed on him, If ye continue in my word, then are ye my disciples indeed; and ye shall know the truth, and the truth shall make you free" (John 8:31-32 KJV).

3. United Worship

A powerful celebration takes place when believers gather and begin to worship and praise God together. United worship has a transforming effect on those who experience it. Throughout Scripture, we are told to praise and worship God *together* in His assembly.

> "I will give You thanks in the great assembly; I will praise You among many people" (Psalm 35:18).

> "Praise the Lord! I will praise the Lord with my whole heart, in the assembly of the upright and in the congregation" (Psalm 111:1).

> "Lift up your hands in the sanctuary, and bless the Lord" (Psalm 134:2).

> "I will declare Your name to My brethren; in the midst of the assembly I will sing praise to You" (Hebrews 2:12).

There is nothing quite like the experience of openly participating in united worship in the local church. As believers lay aside their personal struggles and focus on God through music and song, God's special presence begins to manifest in the church. The Bible says that God inhabits and "sits within" the praises of His people (Psalm 22:3). He often speaks to our hearts and reminds us of His love through His presence. Healing, deliverance, and the gifts of the Holy Spirit may begin to operate in the church as the Lord responds to His people in worship.

United worship is the part of the local church experience that is completely selfless. In true worship, we focus on Christ and His work, giving unrestrained thanks to God. The less we focus on those around us and the more intent we are on fully expressing our hearts to God, the greater our worship experience will be. While any believer may offer praise to God privately, there is something altogether different that happens in us when we openly worship God together in the local church.

Here are some biblical expressions of praise that God instructs us to perform in united worship:

- Singing together (Psalm 84:4; 100:2; Acts 16:25; Ephesians 5:19).

- Shouting and loud praise (Psalm 47:1; 84:2; 95:1; 2 Chronicles 20:19; Matthew 21:15).

- Lifting up of hands (Nehemiah 8:6; Psalm 28:2; 63:4; 134:2, 141:2; 1 Timothy 2:8).

- Playing various instruments, including strings and trumpets (Psalm 149; 150).

- Use of percussion and cymbals (2 Chronicles 5:13; Psalm 150:5).

- Moments of quiet and silent reflection (Psalm 46:10; Habakkuk 2:20).

- Dancing, jumping, and clapping (Psalm 47:1; 149:3; 150:4).

- Kneeling and laying down before the Lord (Nehemiah 8:6; Psalm 95:6; Ezra 10:1).

- Praising and singing in other tongues (Acts 2:11; 10:46; 1 Corinthians 14:14-18).

When you first visit a church that openly expresses their worship in some of these ways, it can be an overwhelming experience. While we are typically used to open and expressive "praise" in sports arenas and concert events, it can seem strange in a church environment. For many centuries, churches had abandoned many of the forms of worship taught in the Bible, focusing more on pre-written hymns and quiet reflection. While these are valid and respectful methods of united worship, the Scripture says much more about worship that is openly and outwardly expressive.

Today, many of the largest and fastest-growing churches have incorporated contemporary music, joyful praise, and the lifting up of hands in their united worship.

When you gather with others for worship, make a decision to participate, not just watch. Don't be a spectator! It helps to close your eyes and visualize allowing your born-again spirit to *use your body* in the worship of God. Try lifting up your voice as you sing, while filling your mind with thoughts of God's love and goodness in your life. Imagine that there is no one else looking at you, but God alone. You are worshipping for an audience of One. Then, try lifting up your hands as you sing and thank Him. As you give yourself over to Him, you will begin to sense His presence with you, and the Holy Spirit will begin to minister to you. Expect God to be present in your times of united praise and worship, and you will experience Him! He dwells in the praises of His people.

> "But You are holy, enthroned in the praises of Israel" (Psalm 22:3).

4. United Prayer

There is something powerful that occurs when believers gather to pray. Each of us need prayer. It is our living source of communication with our Father. The Bible teaches that we should pray both privately and with others. When the church prays together, there is a multiplication of our power in prayer. The Scriptures teach this principle in the Old Testament (Ecclesiastes 4:9; Deuteronomy 32:30). When Jesus was teaching about the church, He said:

> "Again I say to you that if two of you agree on earth concerning anything that they ask, it will be done for them by My Father in heaven. For where *two* or *three* are gathered together in My name, I am there in the midst of them"
> (Matthew 18:19-20).

When the church gathers to pray, Jesus Himself is present and the Father has promised to do whatever is asked of Him. This is an astounding promise for the local church. In the book of Acts, we see that the Holy Spirit was poured out as the church gathered on Sunday to pray in *one accord* (Acts 2:1-4). Then after the church leaders had been threatened, the church gathered to pray, and something supernatural occurred:

> "And when they had prayed, the place where they were assembled together was shaken; and they were all filled with the Holy Spirit, and they spoke the word of God with boldness" (Acts 4:31).

Paul told Timothy, pastor of the Ephesian church, "I urge you, first of all, to pray for all people. Ask God to help them; intercede on their behalf, and give thanks for them" (1 Timothy 2:1 NLT). In the New Testament, we see that some of the most powerful miracles occurred when the church gathered to pray about the needs of the moment. God does not hear our prayers because of our tone of voice or the special vocabulary we use. He knows how we talk every day. He longs for us to communicate with Him as a Father. It is the faith we offer in prayer that moves the heart of God to work on our behalf (Hebrews 11:6; 2 Corinthians 5:7; James 5:14-15; Mark 11:24).

United prayer may occur in general church meetings, small group prayer sessions, or in homes with just one or two others. Praying with others can inspire you to believe God and help you to become more skillful in communication with Him.

The next time you are in a church meeting, pay attention to the opportunities that are given for prayer. Participate in your heart as others lead in prayer. Expect God to perform miracles and answer the things that the church asks God to do. United prayer is an exciting way to experience the power of God for transformation!

> "Until now you have asked nothing in My name. Ask, and you will receive, that your joy may be full" (John 16:24).

5. Fellowship

> "All the believers devoted themselves to the apostles' teaching, *and to fellowship, and to sharing in meals* (including the Lord's Supper), and to prayer....And all the believers *met together* in one place *and shared everything they had*....They *worshiped together* at the Temple each day, *met in homes* for the Lord's Supper, and *shared their meals with great joy and generosity*" (Acts 2:42, 44, 46 NLT).

The word translated "fellowship" in this passage means to share or experience something with others or to have an intimate relationship with someone. One of the most important purposes of a healthy local church is to connect believers to one another in fellowship. In the verses above, we see that they did not just attend services to hear teaching. They opened their homes, shared their possessions, and ate together with *great joy*. Nearly every change that occurs in our lives for the better or worse comes by way of relationships. People have gravity. That means that they have a certain spiritual, emotional, and natural force of influence. Whether we intend it or not, the people we habitually associate with have gravitational influence on our feelings, thinking, and behavior. The people we associate with will either pull us upwards towards positive transformation or pull us downwards towards negative or distracting patterns of thinking and behaving.

> *When a person becomes a believer in Jesus, they need to build genuine relationships with others who love Jesus and are hungry for personal transformation.*

I told my sons as they grew up, "show me your friends and I'll show you your future." We become like the people we spend time with. If we are going to transform our lives, we need to discover people who are going in the direction of change we want to establish in our own lives. When a person becomes a believer in Jesus, they need to build genuine relationships with others who love Jesus and are hungry for personal transformation. While we may have many relationships with non-Christians who can help and advise us in natural things, our deepest intimacy needs to be forged with other believers in the local church who are seeking to follow Jesus. Choosing friends and building fellowship in the church is a choice that you must make. Because the church is made up of people from all walks of life, it is important to build quality relationships with different people and open your heart to the diversity of age, race, gender, and social status that make up the body of Christ, the members of the church.

Churches usually have programs, groups, classes, and events that are designed to build community. Ask the Lord to help you find others in the church who will inspire you to grow and reach your potential in spirit, mind, and body.

6. Sacred Unions and Passings (Marriage and Funeral)

The local church is the place where believers enter into the sacred covenant of marriage. Today marriage is thought of more as a legal contract issued by secular government. But human governments did not invent marriage. Neither can they change its definition. Christian marriage is a union of one man and one woman through vows of love and commitment made before the families and believers of the local church. The Bible calls marriage such a holy gift from God that everyone is to hold it in high respect (Hebrews 13:4). The Apostle Paul said that marriage was so sacred that it was the closest thing on earth to the special relationship the Jesus has with His people, the church. Marriage is the place that God designed for us to express and enjoy our sexual passions. God's church is the place where believers can enter into marriage and learn to enjoy this sacred gift from God.

Naturally, everyone will eventually leave this earth through the passage of physical death. As we learned in chapter seven, the physical body is still mortal, and therefore ages and wears out. Sometimes death occurs unexpectedly, prematurely, or painfully. While God has promised us an abundant life (John 10:10), sooner or later this life will be over for us, as well as for everyone we know and love. This is a sacred passage for the believer as they prepare to enter the presence of God and their heavenly home.

It is also a time of great emotion, as surviving family, friends, and coworkers endeavor to make the difficult adjustments of living their lives without their loved one. It is in these moments that the local church should be at her very best—a place believers go for comfort, counsel, as well as natural and spiritual support. The ministers of the church conduct special services for the families and friends of those who die, and offer perspective and hope to the living. At these moments, we need the body of Christ. We need living relationships with a visible community of faith to mark life's passages with dignity and meaning.

All of these passages of life—birth, marriage, raising families, facing tribulation, and physical death—are events for which God has provided the local church as a means of celebration, support, healing, and restoration.

7. Exercise of Spiritual Gifts

> "God has given each of you a gift from his great variety of spiritual gifts. Use them well to serve one another" (1 Peter 4:10 NLT).

When you were born again, you received at least one spiritual gift from the Lord. That gift was designed to be used in the local church. Some people imagine that their spiritual gifts are the same as their natural talents. We all have natural abilities that we may use to help others and serve the church. But the gifts spoken of here are given to the believer for ministry to others in the local church. They are spiritual in nature and come from the Holy Spirit. Every place in the New Testament where spiritual gifts are mentioned, they are always mentioned for use within the local church between believers. Not a single time in Scripture are our spiritual gifts given for ministry to the unbeliever. Not once.

> "A spiritual gift is given to each of us *so we can help each other*....It is the one and only Spirit who distributes all these gifts. He alone decides which gift each person should have....All *of you together are Christ's body*, and each of you is a part of it" (1 Corinthians 12:7, 11, 27 NLT).

> "Just as our bodies have many parts and each part has a special function, so it is with Christ's body. We are many parts of one body, and *we all belong to each other*. In his grace, God has given us different gifts for doing certain things well" (Romans 12:4-6a NLT).

One of the most important purposes of the local church is to discover and learn about spiritual gifts so that you can use the one or two that God has given you. He gives these gifts for use in the local church body. Someday we will have to give an account for what we did with our spiritual gifts as "good stewards of the manifold grace of God" (1 Peter 4:10b).

8. Evangelism: A Visible Witness of the Kingdom of God

When Jesus introduced the church, He said, "I will build my church...And I will give you *the keys of the kingdom of heaven,* and whatever you bind *on earth* will be bound in heaven, and whatever you loose *on earth* will be loosed in heaven" (Matthew 16:18-19). He was indicating that the church would have authority on earth to manifest God's kingdom to the world. Jesus was not just giving the keys of God's kingdom to Peter or the first disciples. He was giving these keys to the church! He was stating that God's invisible kingdom would be "unlocked" on earth through the ministry of the visible church.

When Jesus ascended to heaven He left a visible "body" on earth to carry on His work—the church. The local church stands in Jesus' place as the visible representation of the invisible God and His eternal kingdom. Every genuine church congregation in each generation throughout the world is a visible witness to the unsaved community of God's love and salvation through Jesus Christ. As we gather together to joyously worship, attentively learn, powerfully pray, participate in sacred events, and lovingly serve one another, God's kingdom becomes manifest as a witness to the world.

The local church should also organize to meet the needs of their generation in a practical way. No religious group in history has been more creative, more generous, or more effective in sharing its message. The first schools, hospitals, orphanages, elder care facilities, and disaster relief agencies were started by, or in the name of, the church of Jesus Christ. Modern science was a result of Christian thinkers seeking to explore the physical world as an act of worship to God. No religious faith has spent more of its own resources on relieving the suffering of humankind—particularly the suffering of those who are outside its faith. Christians have been on the cutting edge of technology throughout the ages to spread the message of Jesus. Massive public preaching events, books, radio, television, movies, internet, and every form of creative arts have been used to share Jesus with the world. Some of the finest paintings, sculptures, architectural marvels, songs, operas, and musical genres, have been inspired by a love for Jesus and His church.

While it is the responsibility of every believer to share their faith with others through personal testimony, it is our collective witness of mutual love and worship that is the greatest force for evangelism in the world. Jesus said, "By this all will know that you are My disciples, if you have love for one another" (John 13:35).

9. Spiritual Covering and Accountability

We all need a roof over our heads. That is true physically and spiritually. The local church provides *spiritual covering* for the people of God. A covering is not for the purpose of controlling or caging the people in its care. It is designed for protection, safety, and securing an environment for healthy personal growth. The local church is a community of believers who are living transparently with one another under the oversight and covering of spiritual leaders. The pastor, elders, and leaders of the church are responsible "for…constantly keeping watch over your souls and guarding your spiritual welfare, as men who will have to render an account" (Hebrews 13:17a AMP).

Every member of the body of Christ needs the spiritual covering of the local church and pastor. This "covering" is like a shelter in the midst of a world that is filled with deception, temptation, and demonic activity. There is a supernatural grace that connects members of the church to each other and their pastor(s) and leaders. Regardless of how long you have been a Christian or how gifted you may be, a believer should never exempt themselves from active membership in a local church.

DAY 3 EXERCISES

1. What is the law of purpose?

_____

_____

2. Everything under heaven has a purpose. This day's instruction outlines five of the purposes of the local church. Write them here and explain their significance.

    1. _____

    2. _____

    3. _____

    4. _____

    5. _____

3. List the five ways we benefit from the teaching of the Word of God in the local church.

    1. _____

    2. _____

    3. _____

    4. _____

    5. _____

4. What are the ministry gifts described in Ephesians 4:11-12?

_____

_____

5. What did the author tell his sons when they were growing up about their friends? What do you think this means for your life?

_____

_____

_____

_____

DAY 4: WATER BAPTISM, HOLY COMMUNION, AND OTHER CHURCH PRACTICES

10. Participation in Sacred Events (Sacraments and Ordinances)

Last, but certainly not least, of the ten purposes for the local church is that believers can participate in sacraments and ordinances. The word *sacrament* comes from a Latin word that means a "sacred or holy practice." The word *ordinance* means a "commandment or sacred ritual." Church groups sometimes use these words differently to describe various practices within their church communities. However, there are two special events that Christians agree should take a special place in the life of the local church: water baptism and Holy Communion, or the Lord's Supper as it is sometimes called. Additionally, the Bible teaches there is a special ordinance of the church called *the laying on of hands*. Each of these three holy experiences are given to the local church for the purpose of experiencing and building the transformed life.

> *There are two special events that Christians agree should take a special place in the life of the local church: water baptism and Holy Communion.*

WATER BAPTISM

Water baptism is a sacred rite of initiation into the body of Christ. While the event in itself does not save us, the Lord never intended for us to be saved without experiencing it. Baptism is designed to accompany our faith as an outward expression of our love for Jesus Christ. Throughout the book of Acts, whenever anyone believed in Jesus Christ they were immediately baptized in water. Baptism is the doorway into participation in the local church community.

Jesus began His earthly ministry by being baptized by John at the age of thirty. This event marked the moment the Holy Spirit anointed Jesus with power to preach, teach, heal, and perform miracles. Later, when Jesus had been raised from the dead, He told the apostles to "Go therefore and make disciples of all the nations, baptizing them in the name of the Father and of the Son and of the Holy Spirit" (Matthew 28:19). He said that, "He who believes and is baptized will be saved" (Mark 16:16a). When the church began on the day of Pentecost, over three thousand people were born again and water baptized *that same day.*

> "Then Peter said to them, 'Repent, and let every one of you be baptized in the name of Jesus Christ for the remission of sins; and you shall receive the gift of the Holy Spirit.'…Then those who gladly received his word *were baptized; and that day about three thousand souls were added to them*" (Acts 2:38, 41).

Some churches baptize infants, believing with the parents that these children will grow up in the church community and know the Lord. While this practice is not mentioned in Scripture, it is nonetheless a very ancient tradition. What the Bible directly teaches and commands us to practice is the baptism of believers. When a person is mature enough to understand the gospel message, sense the conviction of the Holy Spirit for their sin, and believe for themselves in Jesus Christ, the church is to baptize them in water as soon as possible.

The word *baptize* comes from the Greek word *baptizo* which means to "submerge into or under water." The Bible says that when we are baptized, we are experiencing a symbol of the death, burial, and resurrection of Jesus. Paul taught that believers are "buried with Him in baptism" (Colossians 2:12; Romans 6:4). Therefore, in many churches today and throughout history, believers are baptized by being fully submerged in water. The pastor or appointed church leaders carefully dip or immerse the believer into the water for a few brief moments, just as Jesus was "submerged" into the grave when He was buried. During this special moment, the believer declares they are separated from sin, Satan, evil spirits, and every curse that was a part of their past life. God's Spirit is present in baptism to sever the claims of darkness and the past. The love of God enfolds the believer through the experience, bringing comfort and assurance that they have died to sin and been raised with Jesus to a new life.

IMPORTANT TRUTHS ABOUT BELIEVER'S BAPTISM

1. Baptism Follows Believing

> "And He said to them, 'Go into all the world and preach the gospel to every creature. *He who believes and is baptized will be saved*; but he who does not believe will be condemned'" (Mark 16:15-16).

> "But *when they believed* Philip as he preached the things concerning the kingdom of God and the name of Jesus Christ, both men and women *were baptized*" (Acts 8:12).

> "Then Simon himself *also believed; and when he was baptized* he continued with Philip, and was amazed, seeing the miracles and signs which were done" (Acts 8:13).

> "Then Crispus, the ruler of the synagogue, *believed* on the Lord with all his household. And many of the Corinthians, hearing, *believed and were baptized*" (Acts 18:8).

2. Baptism is the First Step in Becoming a Disciple of Jesus Christ

> "And Jesus came and spoke to them, saying, 'All authority has been given to Me in heaven and on earth. Go therefore and make disciples of all the nations, *baptizing them in the name of the Father and of the Son and of the Holy Spirit*, teaching them to observe all things that I have commanded you; and lo, I am with you always, even to the end of the age.' Amen" (Matthew 28:18-20).

3. Baptism Claims the Forgiveness of Sins

> "Peter replied, 'Each of you must repent of your sins and turn to God, *and be baptized in the name of Jesus Christ for the forgiveness of your sins*. Then you will receive the gift of the Holy Spirit" (Acts 2:38 NLT).

"Then they *that gladly received his word were baptized*: and the same day there were added unto them about three thousand souls" (Acts 2:41 KJV).

"And now why are you waiting? Arise and be baptized, and wash away your sins, calling on the name of the Lord" (Acts 22:16).

4. Baptism May Precede or Follow the Gift of the Holy Spirit

"While Peter was still speaking these words, the Holy Spirit fell upon all those who heard the word. And those of the circumcision who believed were astonished, as many as came with Peter, because the gift of the Holy Spirit had been poured out on the Gentiles also. For they heard them speak with tongues and magnify God. Then Peter answered, '*Can anyone forbid water, that these should not be baptized who have received the Holy Spirit just as we have?*' And *he commanded them to be baptized in the name of the Lord*. Then they asked him to stay a few days" (Acts 10:44-48).

5. Baptism Connects Us to the Work of the Cross

"Or do you not know that as many of us as were baptized into Christ Jesus were baptized into His death?" (Romans 6:3).

6. Baptism Initiates Us into the Church (Body) of Christ

"For by one Spirit we were *all baptized into one body*" (1 Corinthians 12:13a).

7. Through Baptism We Claim Our Sonship and Inheritance

"For you are all sons of God through faith in Christ Jesus. For as many of you as were baptized into Christ have put on Christ....And if you are Christ's, then you are Abraham's seed, and *heirs* according to the promise" (Galatians 3:26-27, 29).

HOLY COMMUNION

Jesus began His earthly ministry by receiving *water baptism*, and ended His earthly ministry by introducing a new practice called *Holy Communion*.

Communion is a sacred event that demonstrates our ongoing fellowship and intimate connection with the *body* of Christ. It is a celebration of our relationship with Jesus and His family—the church. While there is nothing in Scripture that forbids believers from receiving the Lord's Supper in private devotion, the biblical purpose of communion is to commune with Christ *and* His assembled family. The word *commune* means to share intimately with another. It is the basis of the word *community*. Therefore, Holy Communion is a sacred event that should be experienced *with* the full community of believers in the local church.

Jesus: Our Passover Lamb

At Jesus' baptism, John prophesied, "Behold! The Lamb of God who takes away the sin of the world!" (John 1:29b). In this moment, God was declaring through John *how* His Son had come to deal with the problem of human sin—as a *lamb*. There is one Jewish feast that involves the sacrifice of a lamb. It is known as the Feast of the Passover.

Every spring, the nation of Israel would celebrate the Feast of the Passover in memory of the last night they spent as slaves in Egypt. God had warned the Pharaoh that if he did not let His people leave Egypt, terrible plagues would come upon the land. Pharaoh resisted God's command, and plague after plague came upon the Egyptians. The final plague was the most severe. Unless Pharaoh released His "firstborn son," *Israel*, God would send an angel to take the lives of all the firstborn of Egypt (Exodus 4:22-23).

God told Moses to instruct the people to sacrifice a spotless lamb and spread its blood over the lintel and side frames of their homes—forming the endpoints of a cross. As the Jews feasted in their homes that night, the angel of death *passed over* every house that was covered by the blood of the Passover lamb. This terrible judgment was what it took to let the people of Israel go. Afterward, God commanded the Jewish people to have an annual feast to remember how they were delivered from bondage through the blood of His Passover (Exodus 12:2-14).

On the night before His crucifixion, Jesus sat with His disciples to share the Jewish Feast of the Passover. As Jesus broke the unleavened bread of the traditional Passover meal, He said, "This is My body which is given for you; do this in remembrance of Me." After they had eaten, He took the cup that traditionally was filled with red wine, and said, "This cup is the new covenant in My blood, which is shed for you." (Luke 22:19, 20). With these simple words, Jesus was proclaiming that a new era had come—a new covenant between God and man was being forged. The Lord was declaring Himself as the final Passover Lamb who would be sacrificed. His body and blood would fulfill the prophecy of John the Baptist and "take away the sin of the world."

The first Christians regularly met together to receive the Lord's Supper. Different churches practice the communion event in different ways. Some Christians receive it weekly—others monthly, quarterly, or annually during the Feast of the Passover. The Bible does not tell us how often to receive the Lord's Supper, but the practice of weekly or monthly communion goes back to the earliest histories of the church.

Three Necessary Elements in Holy Communion

1. The Bread
Following the Lord's example during the Feast of the Passover, the communion bread is consecrated in prayer and broken into pieces and distributed to each believer. The breaking of the bread shows that Jesus' body was broken in death upon the cross. It also demonstrates that the local church is one loaf—made up of many members (1 Corinthians 10:17).

2. The Cup
The fruit of the grape is lifted and consecrated in prayer and then distributed to each believer. The cup represents the blood of Jesus that cleanses us from all sin and has given us eternal life. Just as Jesus' blood is necessary for each believer to be forgiven and transformed, each believer drinks from the cup to show that Jesus' one life was given for many (1 Corinthians 10:16).

3. The Gathered Church
After the Last Supper, the only direct instructions given in the Bible for Holy Communion is in 1 Corinthians. Here we learn that communion is a special event that is to occur when

you come together as a church in one place (1 Corinthians 11:17-34). The gathered church represents many believers as parts of one unified body of Christ. In communion, we are declaring our union with Christ *and* one another. As Paul indicates,

> "For we, though many, *are one bread* and one body; for *we all partake of that one bread*" (1 Corinthians 10:17).

FIVE PURPOSES OF HOLY COMMUNION

1. Partaking in the Benefits of the Body and Blood of Christ

The body and blood of Jesus have a physical and spiritual reality. The physical body of Jesus was broken upon the cross, raised from the dead, and ascended to heaven. The physical body of Jesus exists today at the right hand of God. Jesus is seated in heaven next to His Father in the same body that purchased our redemption (Hebrews 1:3; 12:2).

The blood of Jesus was poured out upon the cross, and later taken by Jesus into heaven. Jesus presented His blood to our Father as a continual reminder of the price that was paid for our sin (Hebrews 9:11-14; 20-24). When we consecrate the bread and cup in Holy Communion, we identify them as earthly symbols of the actual body and blood of Jesus in heaven. As we eat and drink together, we *commune* (or intimately connect) *by faith* with the real body and blood of Jesus and all of its benefits. Whatever we need is made available to us in that holy moment.

> "The cup of blessing which we bless, *is it not the communion of the blood of Christ*? The bread which we break, *is it not the communion of the body of Christ*?" (1 Corinthians 10:16).

In this way, Holy Communion enables the believer—through the local church—to connect to the living benefits of Jesus' sacrifice. Together, as a believing community, we receive the forgiveness of sins, deliverance from evil, healing for our body and soul, protection from the enemy, and every other good thing that belongs to us in Christ Jesus. The bread and the cup are like earthly extension cords that the church collectively places a hand upon and uses to plug into the power that flows from the presence of Christ's body and blood in heaven!

It is important to note that every believer may claim and experience the benefits of Jesus' body and blood as individuals at any time. After all, we each have received a direct personal relationship with our heavenly Father and can access His love and grace whenever we need to by faith (Hebrews 4:16). In Holy Communion, however, we are accessing these benefits collectively and therefore we receive God's grace as a community. We are believing for God's blessing for our entire local church family, not just for ourselves, when we participate in this sacred time.

2. A Declaration of Jesus' Death, Resurrection, and Future Return

Jesus taught the disciples, "do this in remembrance of Me" (Luke 22:19). Paul added that "For as often as you eat this bread and drink this cup, you proclaim the Lord's death till He comes" (1 Corinthians 11:26). As we take part in Holy Communion, we actively remember that Jesus paid the highest possible price for our redemption. We publicly declare together our living faith in Jesus; He died for us. We also express our expectation that Jesus is alive and coming again!

There is something powerful that happens when God's people release their faith together in a public gathering. It is a testimony to the world that Jesus is alive.

3. Opportunity for Personal Cleansing

The Scripture says, "So anyone who eats this bread or drinks this cup of the Lord unworthily is guilty of sinning against the body and blood of the Lord. That is why you should examine yourself before eating the bread and drinking the cup" (1 Corinthians 11:27-28 NLT). Because this event is sacred, God expects us to examine our lives and confess any personal sin or unforgiveness we may have towards others before eating and drinking. It is better not to partake of Holy Communion than to do so without getting our hearts right with God. In this way, communion is an opportunity for the entire church to be cleansed of the errors and sins that we all commit as we live in this world.

4. Connecting with Our Spiritual Family

Through Holy Communion, we become aware of our real supernatural connection with others in the local church. "For we, though many, are one bread and one body; for we all partake of that one bread" (1 Corinthians 10:17). We are not designed to live out our faith in isolation from others. Communion is important because it reminds us of this fact, humbles our pride and independence, and supernaturally strengthens us by connecting us to our spiritual family.

5. Healing and Restoration of the Weak and Sick

Paul went on to indicate that when believers continue in personal sin while receiving Holy Communion, the sacred event actually becomes a time for the Father's judgment and discipline. The Corinthian church was behaving so carnally that they often fought with each other, sued each other, divorced and remarried each other, practiced sexual sin, and *then* behaved as if there was nothing wrong with their choices. They continued to come to church, operate in spiritual gifts, and take Holy Communion—without examining their behaviors and judging themselves. Paul said, "For he who eats and drinks in an unworthy manner eats and drinks judgment to himself, not discerning the Lord's body" (1 Corinthians 11:29). He then explained, "That is why many of you are weak and sick and some have even died" (1 Corinthians 11:30 NLT).

While this may seem severe, the truth is that this judgment at the communion table is an act of loving discipline by our Father. He is allowing us to experience the consequences of our own sins physically through weakness, sickness, and premature death, so that we may avoid the ultimate judgment that will come upon the unbelieving world. "But when we are judged, we are chastened [or disciplined] by the Lord, that we *may not be condemned* with the world" (1 Corinthians 11:32).

The great news is that the same event that opens the door to judgment can close that door as well. When we examine ourselves and confess our sins, the communion table becomes a place of mercy, healing, and restoration. "For if we would judge ourselves, we would not be judged" (1 Corinthians 11:31).

OTHER CHURCH PRACTICES

The Laying on of Hands

One of the foundational teachings of the church is called the "laying on of hands" (Hebrews 6:2). This truth is often neglected, but it is an essential part of the ministry of the local church. Once again because it involves physical contact between at least two individuals, we can know with certainty that this special ordinance is designed for the visible local church. The Scripture teaches that there are four primary purposes for this practice:

1. Healing of the Sick and Oppressed

One of the most important ordinances of the local church is the healing of the sick. After His resurrection, Jesus instructed the apostles to preach the gospel to everyone. Then He said, "And these signs will follow those who believe…they will lay hands on the sick, and they will recover" (Mark 16:17-18). The Lord has placed a special healing ministry upon the elders of the local church.

> "Is anyone among you sick? Let him call for the *elders of the church*, and let them pray over him, anointing him with oil in the name of the Lord. And the prayer of faith will save the sick, and the Lord will raise him up. And if he has committed sins, he will be forgiven. Confess your trespasses to one another, and pray for one another, that you may be healed" (James 5:14-16a).

This is another reason we need to be committed members of a local church. You cannot call for the church elders to pray for your healing if you don't have any elders to call on! In many churches today, this ordinance is neglected. Sometimes a ritual of praying for the sick is practiced, but no one expects anything to really happen. That is why it is important to be a part of a local church that teaches the Bible, believes in the healing power of God, and has a pastor and elders that know how to pray the prayer of faith!

You cannot call for the church elders to pray for your healing if you don't have any elders to call on!

---

2. Dedication of Infants and Children

Jesus Himself was dedicated as an infant in the Lord's temple. During this Jewish ceremony, hands were laid upon Jesus and words of faith were spoken.

> "Now when the days of her purification according to the law of Moses were completed, they brought Him to Jerusalem to present Him to the Lord…And behold, there was a man in Jerusalem whose name was Simeon…and the Holy Spirit was upon him….So he came by the Spirit into the temple. And when the parents brought in the Child Jesus, to do for Him according to the custom of the law, he took Him up in his arms and blessed God…And Joseph and His mother marveled at those things which were spoken of Him" (Luke 2:22, 25, 27-28, 33).

Later, Jesus made it a practice to lay His hands upon children and babies to bless them:

> "Then little children were brought to Him that He might put His hands on them
> and pray" (Matthew 19:13).

> "And He took them up in His arms, laid His hands on them, and blessed them"
> (Mark 10:16).

Believers should follow this example and bring their newborns and young children to receive prayers and blessings by the elders of the church.

3. Appointing Church Leaders

Whenever people are set in places of ministry in the church, the laying on of hands is used. This serves as both a symbol of the transfer of authority and an actual impartation of God's grace to lead. Sometimes when church authorities lay hands on new leaders, God speaks through the gift of prophecy, giving encouragement and guidance to their lives.

> "Therefore, brethren, seek out from among you seven men of good reputation,
> full of the Holy Spirit and wisdom, whom we may appoint over this business…
> whom they set before the apostles; and when they had prayed, they laid hands
> on them" (Acts 6:3, 6).

> "As they ministered to the Lord and fasted, the Holy Spirit said, 'Now
> separate to Me Barnabas and Saul for the work to which I have called them.'
> Then, having fasted and prayed, and laid hands on them, they sent them
> away" (Acts 13:2-3).

> "Do not neglect the gift that is in you, which was given to you by prophecy with
> the laying on of the hands of the eldership" (1 Timothy 4:14).

4. Imparting Spiritual Gifts and Blessings

Spiritual gifts can be activated, prophesies given, and blessings imparted when believers minister to one another in prayer. There are also special gifts of the Holy Spirit that can operate through the ministers of the church. It is important to see that God has placed spiritual gifts in church leaders for the benefit of the members of the body.

> "Then they laid hands on them, and they received the Holy Spirit" (Acts 8:17).

> "And when Paul had laid hands on them, the Holy Spirit came upon them, and
> they spoke with tongues and prophesied" (Acts 19:6).

> "Therefore I remind you to stir up the gift of God which is in you through the
> laying on of my hands" (2 Timothy 1:6).

In the next chapter we are going to learn about taking our place in the local church. We are going to see how the church provides a covering for the believer through spiritual leadership. Together, we will discover God's plan for our personal transformation, which requires us to make a personal commitment to God's visible church.

DAY 4 EXERCISES

1. Water baptism is an outward sign of an inward work. Without the inward work, all you do when you get baptized is get wet! Explain in your own words, what the inward work is and what water baptism is all about.

_____

_____

_____

_____

2. What are the seven important truths about baptism?

    1. _____
    2. _____
    3. _____
    4. _____
    5. _____
    6. _____
    7. _____

3. What are the three elements of Holy Communion and what is their significance to the believer?

    1. _____
    2. _____
    3. _____

4. What Jewish feast involves the sacrifice of a lamb? _____

5. List the reasons we lay hands on people and pray for them in the local church.

_____

_____

_____

_____

_____

CHAPTER NINE

THE TRANSFORMED COMMUNITY

CHAPTER NINE
The Transformed Community

DAY 1: GOD'S APPOINTED LEADERS

God Has a Place for You

God has a place for you to experience transformation. It is not located in a distant land or an isolated wilderness mountaintop. It is not somewhere you go when this life is over. It is not a perfect place, because it is a human place. But it is a place where He will meet with you, challenge you, teach you, and change you. It is a place where you will meet with others who will need you. It may take you some time to find your place. It may require you to drive farther than you'd prefer, rearrange your work schedule, prioritize your life, and stretch you far past your comfort zone. It will certainly require you to give your time, talents, and treasure. But it's a wonderful place—one Jesus prepared for you. That place is His church.

> "God sets the solitary *in families*; He brings out those who are bound into prosperity" (Psalm 68:6).

> "My foot stands in an even *place; in the congregations* I will bless the Lord" (Psalm 26:12).

> "But now God has set the members, each one of them, in the body just as He pleased" (1 Corinthians 12:18).

> *It is popular today to confess being "spiritual," but not be connected to any "organized religion." But the entire New Testament was written to believers who were committed, identifiable members of visible and organized local churches.*

You cannot love Jesus and reject the local church. Go ahead, take a deep breath, swallow hard, and read that last sentence again. That sounds radical to many who have found a personal relationship with Christ outside of the local church. Some people attended church their whole life and never became born again until they dropped *out* of church. Many churches have developed so much tradition that the true gospel of Jesus is hidden behind a religious veil of recitations and rituals that were never really explained.

How can we say that loving Jesus *requires us* to love His church, especially with so many negative examples in history of abusive church systems and Christians? For one thing, those instances in history are not examples of real Christians and true churches, but of false Christians and corrupt churches. Secondly, the real church of Jesus Christ with all of its human faults is still the church *of* Jesus Christ! *It is His* to cleanse, to judge, and to preserve. In spite of all its mistakes and imperfections, Jesus has claimed the church *as His own*, and promised that "the gates of [hell] shall not prevail against it" (Matthew 16:18).

The main reason, however, that loving Jesus ultimately requires us to love the local church is that *nearly every commandment* given to believers in the New Testament involves the way we treat others in the visible local church. In fact, it is *not possible* to obey most of the New Testament unless you are in a genuine relationship with a community of believers. The Bible has more to say about how believers treat each other in the local church than how we should behave towards unbelievers in the world. In fact, nearly everything written in the epistles has to do with how believers are to live with and behave towards one another. The sheer volume of these passages is astounding.

> "By this all will know that you are My disciples, if you *have love for one another*" (John 13:35).

It is popular today to confess being "spiritual," but not be connected to any organized religion. But the entire New Testament was written to believers who were committed, identifiable members of visible and organized local churches. Independent spirituality sounds appealing, particularly to contemporary western believers who typically place a high value on personal liberty. But in this chapter we are going to see that our freedom in Christ is a freedom *from* selfish independence *through a living connection* to Jesus and His family. If you confess that you love Jesus, He expects you to demonstrate your love for Him by taking your place in the local church.

In this chapter, we are going to see how the local church is structured to enable the kind of relationships that produce genuine personal transformation. This requires that we take our place under godly leadership. It also means that we are to take our place of responsibility as members of His family. God has a place for you in the local church. He is waiting for you to take it.

The local church is a dynamic community of believers in Jesus Christ who have entered into a *committed relationship with one another* to worship, grow, serve, witness, and live transformational lives together *under spiritual leadership.*

Jesus Gave Us—Leaders!

When Jesus rose from the dead and ascended into heaven, He did a wonderful thing for His future church. He gave His church some very special presents. That is why the Scriptures say,

> "'When he ascended to the heights, he led a crowd of captives *and gave gifts to his people.*'...Now these are the gifts Christ gave to the church: the apostles, the prophets, the evangelists, and the pastors and teachers. *Their responsibility is to equip God's people to do his work and build up the church*, the body of Christ" (Ephesians 4:8, 11-12 NLT).

The Greek word translated "gifts" in verse 11 is the word *doma,* which means "presents"—like birthday or Christmas presents. These presents were given by Jesus at the time of His ascension into heaven. This means they were known, chosen, and appointed by Him for every church that He would call throughout all of time. These special presents are actually *people.* They are "apostles, prophets, evangelists, pastors, and teachers." In other words, they are leaders. If Jesus gave leaders to His church, then it must be His will for believers in the church to understand, appreciate, and receive them.

The Purpose of Spiritual Leadership

Most of us are naturally resistant to authority. Especially those who live in the western world. We prize our individuality, and put high value on freedom, independence, and self-sufficiency. While these things are not evil in and of themselves, there is something in our flesh that resists other important concepts like honor, self-denial, and yielding to others—especially those in authority. We like to get our own way. And most people don't want others to tell them what to do.

God's kingdom, however, is not designed around accommodating our rebellious natures. The Bible teaches that true freedom and individual fulfillment is found through an entirely different process altogether.

What Does It Mean to Be "Free"?

What most people call freedom is really a desire to live without any restrictions on their behavior and accountability for their actions. The Scripture says these ideas about freedom are in error and not true definitions of freedom at all. They are the basis for Satan's lies and designed to deceptively imprison humans to serving him instead of God. Living this way is living in bondage. *Christian freedom* is actually a freedom *from* sin and a life of submission to the authority of God.

> "Don't you realize that you become the slave of whatever you choose to obey? You can be a slave to sin, which leads to death, or you can choose to obey God, which leads to righteous living. Thank God! Once you were slaves of sin, but now you wholeheartedly obey this teaching we have given you. Now you are free from your slavery to sin, and you have become slaves to righteous living. Because of the weakness of your human nature, I am using the illustration of slavery to help you understand all this. Previously, you let yourselves be slaves to impurity and lawlessness, which led ever deeper into sin. Now you must give yourselves to be slaves to righteous living so that you will become holy.... But now you are free from the power of sin and *have become slaves of God"*
> (Romans 6:16-19, 22a NLT).

Contrary to the world's ideas about freedom, true liberty is having the power to choose what is right. The transformed life is a life that takes your *self* off the "throne," and bows its knee to God and His ideas of what is right and wrong. Our freedom comes from our choosing which master we will spend our lives serving.

> "For you have been called to live in freedom, my brothers and sisters. But don't use your freedom to satisfy your sinful nature [flesh]. Instead, *use your freedom to serve one another* in love" (Galatians 5:13 NLT).

> "Act as free men, and do not use your freedom as a covering for evil, but use it as bondslaves of God" (1 Peter 2:16 NASB).

Jesus—Our Servant-King

Jesus came into this world as an example of the kind of human life God wants us to live. He came as a *servant* of His Father, and of you and I.

> "For I have come down from heaven, not to do My own will, but the will of Him who sent Me" (John 6:38).

> "For even the Son of Man came not to be served *but to serve others* and to give his life as a ransom for many" (Matthew 20:28 NLT).

Being a servant did not make Jesus weak. He commanded storms to be stilled, and cast out demons. He healed the sick and powerfully confronted people who oppressed others. That is far from living a weak and powerless life. Jesus never gave up His place in the Trinity. He never ceased to be God. The key to Jesus' strength and power was in His constant obedience to His Father. By stepping out of eternity into a single human life, Jesus taught us that true freedom and real power came from living under God's authority. Now our Father wants us to be like Jesus. That means that our strength will also come from living in submission to God.

> "Let this mind be in you which was also in Christ Jesus, who, being in the form of God, did not consider it robbery to be equal with God, but made Himself of no reputation, *taking the form of a bondservant*, and coming in the likeness of men. And being found in appearance as a man, He humbled Himself and became obedient to the point of death, even the death of the cross" (Philippians 2:5-8).

Serving Jesus also means that we choose a life of serving others.

Jesus Appointed Human Leaders for His Church

There are some who teach today that in God's church everyone has equal authority. It is true that every believer has an equal standing before God as a son or daughter, and each of us has equal access to the Father directly through Jesus Christ. However, some believe that every person is called to ministry equally and that Christians do not need to be "under" any special spiritual leader to please God. This idea is inspired by human wisdom and is not grounded in the Scripture from which we must get our direction. As we've discovered on our journey, following the standard of the Bible is VERY important if we are to live lives that please and glorify God.

From the beginning of time, God has called particular people to represent Him as spiritual leaders to the human race. These men and women were given messages from God and special abilities to communicate them. Along with these gifts and responsibilities, God also gave them the authority to lead His people. Known by various names and titles in Scripture such as prophets, preachers, teachers, apostles, and pastors, these leaders were chosen, called, and appointed by God even before they were born (Jeremiah 1:5; Isaiah 49:1). The first ministers mentioned in Scripture are Enoch (Genesis 5:22; Jude 1:14), and Noah (Genesis 6:9; 2 Peter 2:5). Later, God chose Moses to lead His people to the land He had promised them. Known as the "congregation" (Acts 7:38) in the wilderness, the Lord instructed him to appoint assistant ministers, elders, teachers, and priests (Exodus 4:14-16; 7:1; 18:1ff; Leviticus 10:11; Numbers 1:50), to assist in leading. Throughout the Old Testament period, God called ministers and gave them authority to lead and speak to His people (Jeremiah 26:5).

Jesus Chose Apostles and Authorized Them to Lead

When Jesus came into the world and began His ministry, one of the first things He did was select leaders to train. They were given special responsibilities, heard Him teach different and more in-depth messages, and were given messages and authority He did not give to most of His followers.

"Then He appointed twelve, that they might be with Him and that He might send them out *to preach*, and *to have power* to heal sicknesses and to cast out demons" (Mark 3:14-15; See also: Luke 10:1).

The leaders Jesus chose were trained to use their positions to serve the people. Once when the disciples were arguing over who should be the highest ranking leader, Jesus said, "In this world the kings and great men lord it over their people…But among you it will be different. Those who are the greatest among you should take the lowest rank, and *the leader should be like a servant*" (Luke 22:25-26, NLT).

Receiving Whom Jesus Sends

Near the end of His life, Jesus did not disband His team or change their status of authority. In fact, when He spoke of their ministry in the future church, He made some astounding statements about the special role of His chosen leaders:

"So Jesus said to them again, 'Peace to you! *As the Father has sent Me*, I also send *you*'" (John 20:21).

"Most assuredly, I say to you, he who receives *whomever I send* receives *Me*; and he who receives Me receives Him who sent Me" (John 13:20).

These statements were not made to everyone to whom Jesus ministered. They were given in private teaching sessions to the disciples He had chosen for leadership. While all Christians are "sent" to be witnesses for Jesus, the Lord was originally referring to the sending of His ministers. In other words, Jesus *continued* the pattern of calling and sending leaders to His people. The title given to the first church leaders was *apostle*. The Greek word translated apostle means "one who is sent by another." This is why it is so important to receive and honor the leaders of the local church. They have been sent by Jesus, and carry His anointing. When you receive those God sends to lead you, it is like receiving Jesus Christ Himself!

Church Leaders Make Decisions for the Church

It was *the leaders* of the churches that met to decide matters that were authoritative for all the *believers* in the local churches. Individual Christians were expected to submit to the wisdom and the authority of the leaders of the church. In Acts 15 there was debate about what new believers should be required to do when they joined the church. Many of the Jewish believers wanted the Gentile (non-Jewish) converts to keep the Old Testament law that they had known all their lives. In order to settle this dispute, the pastors sent a delegation to the church in Jerusalem to decide the matter. It was the apostles and elders (pastors) who met to debate and ultimately resolve the issue.

"Therefore, when Paul and Barnabas had no small dissension and dispute with them, they determined that Paul and Barnabas and certain others of them should go up to Jerusalem, to *the apostles* and *elders*, about this question….And when they had come to Jerusalem, they were received by *the church* and *the apostles* and *the elders*; and they reported all things that God had done with them….Now *the apostles and elders* came together to consider this matter" (Acts 15:2, 4, 6).

"And as they went through the cities, they delivered to them the decrees to keep, which were *determined by* the apostles and elders at Jerusalem" (Acts 16:4).

In verse 4, three groups are mentioned: the church (believers), the apostles (founders of the church), and the elders (the pastors of the church). Here we see a hierarchy of spiritual authority. The apostles presided over the elders, and the elders over the people. These ministers of the church worked as a team to resolve the questions and problems faced by the churches. The final decisions were made *by the leaders*, and followed by the members of the local churches.

What's with All These Titles?

Admittedly, it can be confusing when reading about all the positions and titles given to spiritual leaders throughout the Bible. It's important to remember that, much like progressing through grade school, God's Word builds upon itself from the Old to the New Testaments. Because the cultures and languages changed over that 1500 year period, God introduced different words and new concepts to each passing generation. This does not mean that God was confused or changing His mind. It actually demonstrates the brilliance, wisdom, and love God has for us. In Scripture, we see the Lord guiding His prophets to carefully choose language that would be relevant to the culture of their time, while simultaneously containing truths that would apply to all people throughout time!

Each title given to God's leaders describes in some way the kinds of things they were called to do for Him. For example the word *prophet* in the Old Testament referred to a leader who was speaking for God. Some prophets were simply preachers of truth. Others had visions and made predictions about the future. Some were called to work in government and speak to the secular leaders or kings of their day.

The term *elder* is used in different ways as well. In the earliest times, the older men who were the leaders of their families were called "elders." It was a term of respect. When Moses needed help in caring for the people of Israel, the Lord directed him to select the most effective family leaders and gave them the title "elders." Their job was to help Moses care for the needs of the "flock." They were given authority to counsel the people, solve problems, and care for individual needs, so that Moses could hear from God, teach the people, write, and only deal with the more serious matters (Exodus 18:21-27). Later, God chose seventy of these elders to rise to an even higher level of leadership as the challenges Moses faced increased (Numbers 11:16-17).

There were levels of leadership and authority, known as a *hierarchy.* Just like in any well run company, government, or organization, God's kingdom operates in a hierarchy, or through a multi-layered structure of leadership:

Elders
In the New Testament, the apostles first used the term *elder* to refer to themselves (1 Peter 5:1) and the pastors of the local churches. Just as in Moses' day, as the churches grew, the pastors selected mature believers to help them care for the flock. These were called elders as well. Some of these elders were teaching ministers, while others were not (1 Timothy 5:17). This shows that there are levels of eldership in the church. As time passed, the term *pastor* was used to distinguish the leading teaching ministers of the churches from those that assisted them. Therefore while all pastors are elders, not all elders are pastors.

Pastors
The word *pastor* comes from the Greek word *poimen*, which means "shepherd." By using this term to refer to the highest leaders of the local churches, God gives us a

beautiful description of His heart for His people. Like a father in a family and a shepherd of a flock, a local church pastor and his team are to care for God's people gently—with loving authority and humble hearts of service to God.

Deacons

Another New Testament word used for leaders in the local church is the term *deacon*. While this word may sound stuffy and outdated to some, the role of deacon is very important in the local church. The word *deacon* simply means "servant." The first example of local church deacons occurs in Acts 6. Because of problems in a particular outreach program, the apostles needed a leadership solution that would come from among the people themselves. They needed help in serving the practical needs of the poor widows in the church. After receiving suggestions from the people who were struggling with this problem, the apostles prayerfully appointed seven men to lead the department. They became known as deacons, or servants, because their leadership involved serving the people in a particular department of ministry.

Later, the Apostle Paul gave a detailed list of qualifications to guide the pastors in developing local church deacons; he described it as an "office" (or formal position) of leadership (1 Timothy 3:8-12). Some churches no longer use the biblical term *deacon*. However, any believer in a local church that has been trained and appointed by the pastor(s) to oversee a department or specific task of ministry is doing the work of a deacon.

DAY 1 EXERCISES

1. You cannot love Jesus and _____ the local church.

2. What is Christian freedom?

_____

_____

_____

3. Who are the first ministers mentioned in Scripture?

_____

_____

4. What was one of the first things Jesus did when He came into the world and began His ministry?

_____

_____

5. What are the three groups that make up the hierarchy of spiritual authority?

   1. _____

   2. _____

   3. _____

DAY 2: WHO'S OVER THE LOCAL CHURCH?

After Paul started the church in Ephesus, he called the leaders of the church to a special meeting (Acts 20:17) where he gave them these instructions:

> "Therefore take heed to yourselves and to all the flock, among which the Holy Spirit *has made you overseers*, to shepherd [or 'pastor'] the church of God which He purchased with His own blood" (Acts 20:28).

These pastors were given the responsibility and the authority to *watch over* the local churches. The only way one can oversee another is if one person is "over" the other. Notice that the pastors of the local church receive their authority to lead from the Holy Spirit. Only He can call and equip the leaders of the church.

Receiving Spiritual Leadership

Later, the apostles wrote to the believers in the churches and gave them instructions on how to treat their leaders. It is important in reading these directions to keep in mind that the way we relate to the leaders God has sent to the church impacts our relationship with God. Jesus taught us that the way we treat those He sends to lead us is the way we treat Jesus Himself (John 13:20).

Honor Your Leaders

One of the earliest records of the early church gives instructions to believers about how they are to live and serve Christ in the local church. It says,

> "My child, him that speaks to thee the word of God remember night and day, and thou shalt honor him as the Lord; for where that which pertaineth to the Lord is spoken, there the Lord is."[22]

This principle is taught clearly in the New Testament as well. Believers are to see their pastors, elders, and church leaders as gifts from Jesus.

> "And we urge you, brethren, to *recognize* those who labor among you, *and are over you* in the Lord and admonish you, and to *esteem them* very highly in love for their work's sake" (1 Thessalonians 5:12-13a).

> "Obey your spiritual leaders, and do what they say. Their work is to watch over your souls, and they are accountable to God. Give them reason to do this with joy and not with sorrow. That would certainly not be for your benefit" (Hebrews 13:17 NLT).

The only way you or I can do what these verses teach is to be an active member of a local church and *follow the leader* (Hebrews 13:17). Notice in 1 Thessalonians 5:13 that we are called to recognize and esteem our spiritual leaders with a good attitude! Once you are born again into

---

22. The Didache, Chapter IV, line one, written sometime between AD 75-150, Public Domain.

266 | THE TRANSFORMED LIFE

the family of God, it is the responsibility of the believer to find a local church and pastor. The Lord expects us to live our Christian life in a committed relationship to the local church and grow under the example and teaching of a pastor. One of the reasons many Christians today continue to struggle in their walk with God is because they have not really committed in their hearts to a local church and do not receive the ministers that Jesus has sent to help them grow.

The Difference between Teachers and Fathers

In our development as Christians, we may be taught and helped by many different ministers and believers over the years. Some teachers come into our lives through small group Bible studies. Others teach us through various forms like books, television, podcasts, digital media, and online ministry tools. Conferences, seminars, workshops, and other events may also enhance our growth and develop our knowledge. However there is a difference between a teacher and a spiritual father.

> "I am not writing these things to shame you, but to warn you *as my beloved children*. For even if you had ten thousand others to teach you about Christ, you have *only one spiritual father*. For I became your father in Christ Jesus when I preached the Good News to you. So I urge you to imitate me" (1 Corinthians 4:14-16 NLT).

Paul was writing to the church at Corinth and reminding them that he enjoyed a special relationship with them. By using the term *father* he was obviously not referring to a physical relationship. He was their father *in the gospel*, or *spiritually.* In no way was Paul suggesting his role in their life was replacing their relationship with the Father in heaven. No human leader can ever insert themselves in between the believer and God. Instead he was showing that by founding the Corinthian church, and pastoring them for nearly two years, he held a place of spiritual leadership in their lives that was like the role a father has in a family. Later, in 2 Corinthians, he indicated that his role in their lives granted him a place of authority to develop and (when necessary) correct them.

> "For even if I boast somewhat further about our authority, which the Lord gave for building you up and not for destroying you, I shall not be put to shame" (2 Corinthians 10:8 NASB).

> "But we will not boast beyond our measure, but within the measure of the sphere which God apportioned to us as a measure, to reach even as far as you" (2 Corinthians 10:13 NASB).

The local church is like a family, and the lead pastor of the church is like a father. His role is to provide teaching, vision, and leadership to the local church, while endeavoring to live a godly life that is an example the members of the church can follow. When first hearing the doctrine of spiritual leadership in the local church, it can be intimidating and even scary. Important and necessary questions arise for most believers—"What is the limit of my pastor's authority in my life," "*How* does my pastor lead me," and "What is the pastor's role in overseeing the church family?" These questions require answers. Let's see what Scripture teaches about these areas.

> *One of the reasons many Christians today continue to struggle in their walk with God is because they have not really committed in their hearts to a local church and do not receive the ministers that Jesus has sent to help them grow.*

The Responsibilities of the Local Church Pastor

If you were to ask ten different people what a local church pastor's job should look like, you would likely get ten different answers. Many Christians think that pastors are supposed to do anything that anyone asks them to do—like a doctor who is on call for them. They want the pastor to visit their homes, care for the sick, provide counseling services at will, know the answers to all their questions, and have a perfect family life. But this is not the job of a pastor. God's Word gives us the job description of the pastor. Read this section in 1 Peter 5. You will notice there are three things mentioned.

> "And now, a word to you who are elders in the churches....*Care for the flock* that God has entrusted to you. *Watch over it willingly*, not grudgingly—not for what you will get out of it, but because you are eager to serve God. Don't *lord it over the people assigned to your care*, but *lead them by your own good example*" (1 Peter 5:1-3 NLT).

> "I warn and counsel the elders among you (the pastors and spiritual guides of the church) as a fellow elder and as an eyewitness [called to testify] of the sufferings of Christ, as well as a sharer in the glory (the honor and splendor) that is to be revealed (disclosed, unfolded): Tend (nurture, guard, guide, and fold) the flock of God that is [your responsibility], not by coercion or constraint, but willingly; not dishonorably motivated by the advantages and profits [belonging to the office], but eagerly and cheerfully; Not domineering [as arrogant, dictatorial, and overbearing persons] over those in your charge, but being examples (patterns and models of Christian living) to the flock (the congregation)" (1 Peter 5:1-3 AMP).

In this Scripture, special instructions are given regarding the motivation of a pastor's work. He is to model the Christian life to those around him and willingly oversee and guide the flock of God. This is the picture of a tender shepherd who compassionately leads his flock. He's not focused on the profit he can make on their wool; he isn't fleecing the sheep. His focus is on feeding, nurturing, and guarding the flock instead.

1. Feed the Flock

The Greek word translated "care for" in verse 2 is *poimaino*, which means "to feed and nourish a flock of sheep." The number one job of the pastor is to feed the flock through the preaching and teaching of God's Word. "Remember those who rule over you, who have spoken the word of God to you" (Hebrews 13:7a). The most important thing the local church offers its members is excellent teaching and preaching. If the pastor does not do this well, *you* will not grow. Spiritual growth requires spiritual food (Matthew 4:4). Everything else the local church provides is secondary to this fact. A church can have great music, facilities, children's and youth programs, and outreaches—but if the teaching and preaching does not feed you spiritually, you are missing the most important facet of the local church. This must be in place for a church to truly complete its mission before God.

When seeking a church home, look for a place that teaches God's Word in a way that feeds and challenges you to grow. Some Christians will remain for years in a church that does not feed them with anointed teaching. When you have found the shepherd that feeds you best, typically that means you have found *your church*.

2. Oversee the Flock
The second responsibility of the pastor is to oversee the vision, ministries, and work of the church. This requires the pastor to have some administrative gifting or organizational leadership skills. Pastors need to watch over the ministry and keep it on track with God's plan. An overseer inspects the work of the church and insures the quality of its ministry. The pastor also has the responsibility to correct, discipline, and remove members and leaders who are causing injury to others in the body. This kind of oversight is to be done in humility and gentleness (2 Timothy 2:25) with a heart of love and, when possible, restoration.

3. Be an Example to the Flock
"Lead them by your own good example" (1 Peter 5:3 NLT). The third responsibility of the pastor is to live as a proper example before the people. When Paul lists the qualities of an overseer in 1 Timothy 3, nearly everything on the list has to do with the pastor's character, family life, marriage, and reputation. No pastor is perfect. In fact, pastors struggle with their flesh like all believers. Sometimes pastors fail and go through seasons of conflict in their marriage and in raising their children. It is not the absence of these things that qualify a pastor to lead. Instead it is *the example that is set* by how the pastor faces, endures, and overcomes these challenges.

Paul instructed the young pastor Timothy to *"be an example to the believers in word, in conduct, in love, in spirit, in faith, in purity"* (1 Timothy 4:12). This means that our pastors should live lives like that of King David. When he failed or made mistakes, David repented and asked God for help. Our pastors should follow this same lifestyle—living humbly and walking in forgiveness as a living example of right relationship before God and His people—teaching those in their charge to do as they do.

Limits of Local Church Authority
Remember our definition: The local church is a dynamic community of believers in Jesus Christ who have entered into a committed relationship with one another to worship, grow, serve, witness, and live transformational lives together under spiritual leadership.

Jesus is the True Head and Great Shepherd of every local church (1 Peter 5:4). The pastors are to represent Jesus as *under-shepherds* (1 Peter 5:2). An under-shepherd is one who works for the Chief Shepherd. All spiritual leaders are ultimately called to be *servants* to the body. They are not to "lord it over God's inheritance" (1 Peter 5:3 NLT). The pastor's role is not to tell you who to marry, where to work, or dictate your decisions in life. They serve as guides, teachers, advisors, and coaches. While church leaders may advise you on personal matters and warn you when they feel it is necessary, they are never to take the place of Jesus or the Holy Spirit in your heart and life.

Pastors set the vision for the church, and coordinate its mission. The senior or lead pastor is like the "head coach" of all the other coaches, assistants, and team captains on the local church "team." The senior pastor and his appointed leaders have the primary authority over the direction and programs of the church and need to lead with diligence, passion, and transparency. Pastors need to be accountable to other pastors who help them in church decisions, and in dealing with personal challenges and failures.

Avoiding Spiritual Abuse

Spiritual abuse is a term that refers to the problem of spiritual leaders who overstep their role of authority in the lives of believers. While it is the pastor's job to lead the operations of the church and its ministries and services, it is not right for the pastors and elders to abuse their authority in any way.

Additionally, membership in the local church should be voluntary and never maintained by either threatening or manipulative methods. When a believer feels this is happening, it is important to speak to the church leaders truthfully and respectfully, with the hope of resolving the issues. If such problems are not resolved, it is best to withdraw your membership without causing disruption and seek another church family and reengage as soon as possible.

On this point, it is also important to note that while spiritual abuse does exist in some churches, *the majority of Bible teaching and Spirit-led churches are led by imperfect, but decent, men and women who desire to please God*. We must not use the existence of spiritual abuse in *some* churches as an excuse to avoid membership in *all* churches. If you are a believer, God has a church and a pastor for you. It will be an imperfect place full of other imperfect humans who are joined together with one common purpose—loving and trusting God in their lives. Jesus loves us and is faithful to place us in the family in which we belong. Make sure the one you choose teaches the Bible, joyfully worships, and practices the sacraments of baptism and Holy Communion—and then attend *faithfully*. Jesus will bless you.

A Word to Believers in the Persecuted Church

It is a sad and troubling fact that in many places in the world it is dangerous to publicly live as a Christian. In some nations, there are either written or unspoken laws that prohibit the assembly of Christians and punish anyone who converts. Many of these believers have paid a great price to receive Jesus into their lives. Some have been rejected by their families and shunned by their neighbors. They risk beatings, imprisonment, and in some cases, torture and death. Open preaching is forbidden. Often they come to Christ in secret through the private witnessing of a neighbor, or even through personal dreams and visions of Jesus. These believers belong to the persecuted church.

For our brothers and sisters in these lands, the dream of openly worshipping Christ in a regular church community is beyond their reality. For those precious believers who may be reading this book, please be assured that we love you and will continue to pray for you! Jesus sees and knows your hearts. If you are the only believer in your community, it is just because you are the *first* believer in your community. There will be others. Jesus always saves people in *community* with others. Ask Christ to lead you to others who may be saved or to whom you can witness. The Holy Spirit lives in you and will guide you! If even *two* believers are gathered in Jesus' name, He is present in your midst! If you pray, He will either raise up a pastor from among you, or send a pastor to feed you. Remember that you are a part of the invisible church, and you have brothers and sisters all over the earth. We are praying for you and for the light of Christ to break through the darkness wherever you live in the world. Jesus sees and knows your suffering, and He will strengthen, keep, and reward you.

> "God blesses those who patiently endure testing and temptation. Afterward they will receive the crown of life that God has promised to those who love him" (James 1:12 NLT).

> "We give great honor to those who endure under suffering. For instance, you know about Job, a man of great endurance. You can see how the Lord was kind to him at the end, for the Lord is full of tenderness and mercy" (James 5:11 NLT).

> "So be truly glad. There is wonderful joy ahead, even though you have to endure many trials for a little while" (1 Peter 1:6 NLT).

DAY 2 EXERCISES

1. The Bible teaches that Jesus sends ministers to lead His church. According to John 13:20, what happens when we receive these ministers?

_____

_____

2. In 1 Corinthians 4:14-16, what did Paul say was the key difference between a teacher and a spiritual father?

_____

_____

3. What are the three main jobs of a pastor?

1._____

2._____

3._____

4. What does the term *spiritual abuse* refer to, and how should you handle it?

_____

_____

_____

_____

5. Jesus has designed a safe place for you and your family where you can grow and prosper and be a blessing to others. Ask for His help in finding the place where you fit—a balanced, Bible-centered local church. And once you find that place, be patient as He fits you into it and you grow in relationship with others. Relationships take time and commitment to build. Spend some time in prayer asking God to help you to be open to the people He wants you to be close to and learn from in the church body. Write your prayer here.

_____

_____

_____

_____

_____

_____

DAY 3: TAKING YOUR PLACE

Not *every* church is for every believer, but there is *a* church for every believer. Once you have been born again, it is your responsibility to find, commit to, and connect with a biblical local church that is pursuing the mission and purposes of Jesus.

There are some good keys that you can use in locating a local church. As you begin your search, it is important to keep in mind that no pastor or leader can order you to be a part of their church. A good pastor will respect the Holy Spirit's role in guiding the believer to the pastor and church family to whom He is calling them. "But now *God has set the members,* each one of them, in the body *just as He pleased*" (1 Corinthians 12:18).

> *It is the responsibility of every believer to grow up, spiritually. That means we need to deal with our flesh, renew our minds, change our sinful behaviors, and take our place in the family.*

IDENTIFYING YOUR SPIRITUAL FAMILY

Here are some guidelines to help you discover and take your place in the local church family:

Discern the Season of Growth in Your Life

Are you beginning your walk with Jesus? It is important to locate a church that will accommodate your need to be baptized, and offer classes or groups to help you begin your journey in Christ. If you have known the Lord for years, it is important that your local church challenges you to grow and to continue to mature spiritually. Sometimes believers remain in churches that are familiar and traditional, but do not provide the kind of teaching, worship, and services that will encourage them to go further in their discipleship.

Don't remain in a church that was the will of God for you ten years ago. Don't go to a church because you are trying to please parents or friends. Sometimes seasons change and the Holy Spirit will lead you to another local church that aligns with the thing that God wants to do in your life today.

Does the Church Anchor its Services in Anointed Bible Teaching?

Holy Communion, praise and worship, children's ministries, missions programs, convenient location, and quality facilities should not be the reason you choose your local church. While all of these things have their place, the main reason you should select a church is the consistent quality, integrity, and anointing of the teaching and preaching. Everything else can grow and develop as the church grows. But the foundation of any good church is the ministry of God's Word. Nothing is more important.

Check the Doctrinal Statement (Make Sure there is One!)

Ultimately what a church believes will govern what it does. A good church should have a clear, scriptural doctrinal statement that aligns with the historic teaching of the church. Things like the doctrine of the Trinity, the deity of Jesus, the accuracy and authority of Scripture, and the need to be born again by faith alone in the finished work of Christ, are absolutely essential. If you are a believer who has experienced the gifts of the Holy Spirit, it is important that your church embraces these truths as well.

Is the Church Pursuing the Mission to Make Disciples of All Nations?

Remember that every local church is called to provide environments that enable believers to learn the doctrines and disciplines of the Christian life. A good local church will preach the gospel, baptize believers, and grow disciples. Jesus taught that the church is to "make disciples of all the nations" (Matthew 28:19). This means that a local church should be open to people from different races, nationalities, ages, socio-economic backgrounds, and neighborhoods. While a church cannot reflect diversity that isn't present in the community it serves, if it is targeting only one class of people and not accepting of others, that is a sign of immaturity. Some churches intentionally target only young people, or those of a particular race or economic ability. This is a dangerous and unscriptural practice. The early church reflected everyone—the rich and poor, Jew and Gentile, urban and rural people—that was present in the areas they served.

Is the Church Pursuing the Ten Purposes of a Local Church?

A church should also pursue the ten purposes we studied in the last chapter—the special presence of Jesus; united worship, teaching, and prayer; fellowship; good organization; recognizable authority; sacred events, such as sacraments and ordinances; exercise of spiritual gifts; community outreach and evangelism; and the receiving of tithes and offerings. Are there opportunities to serve in the church and support local outreaches and global missions?

Are the Pastor and Leadership of the Church of Good Character?

While this can be difficult to assess, in general the lead pastor of a church and the team he chooses should be men and women of good reputation. They may have all kinds of sins the Lord has delivered them from in their pasts, but their present behavior should exemplify a sincere love for Jesus and good character. How long has the church been around? Where did the pastor and his key staff receive their training for ministry and by whom are they ordained? Are the pastor and his team accountable to those who are over them? Are there leaders set in a position to help them if they are in trouble? A good church will offer the biography and history of its senior leadership. Good leaders are not afraid of questions about their history or character.

When the Lead Pastor Teaches, Does Your Heart Say, "Baaahh Baaahh?"

There is an internal mechanism in the heart of every believer that resonates when in the presence of the pastor God has called to feed them. It may sound funny, but sheep respond to the voice of their shepherd. Often when hearing your pastor teach, you will feel a sense of respect for them as you recognize the spiritual authority behind the pastor's voice. Sometimes, you will find that the pastor's message seems to be just for you. This can be a sign that the Holy Spirit is anointing this shepherd to minister to you in ways that are clearly supernatural. It can also be a confirmation that you are being called to join that local church.

Is There a Healthy Way to Enter and Exit?

A good local church will offer its guests a clear way to enter into formal relationship with their congregation, and allow those who want to exit to do so without shame, guilt, or threat of rejection. Naturally there are examples where the church leaders must remove members from its midst when their persistent, unhealthy behaviors are injuring others. In these cases, the leaders are acting in the best interest of the entire body and not endeavoring to persecute or cause injury to an offending member. As mentioned earlier, sometimes a church may be no longer moving in a direction that a member can enthusiastically support. This is not always a bad thing. It may be nothing more than the end of a season in life. Sometimes God wants to use a member in another local church. In any of these cases it is important the local church release members in good standing with a blessing. It is also important that members who exit do so without speaking evil of their former church leadership or causing division. This is never the will of God.

JOINING YOUR SPIRITUAL FAMILY

Once you have found a church that generally follows the guidelines mentioned above, and after you have prayed and have a sense of peace in your heart, immediately begin whatever membership process the church has put in place. Some churches have a single informational meeting. Others have classes or small group Bible studies to initiate new members. If you have not been water baptized since believing in Jesus for yourself, you should seek to experience this. A good membership process will include a clear set of expectations that serve to set the stage for a successful relationship with the church.

The Law of Mutual Benefit

The *law of mutual benefit* is a law that governs relationships. It teaches that the health of any relationship is determined by the mutual benefit that is derived by each party. In other words, the more mutually beneficial a relationship is, the healthier the relationship will be. The less mutually beneficial a relationship is, the less healthy it will be. It is true in nature, in physics, in love, in work, in friendship, and every other dimension of life. A marriage where one party does most of the giving, and the other party does most of the taking, will quickly erode in health and vitality. A healthy work environment is one where the employee and the employer each receive mutual benefit from the relationship. Maintaining health in any relationship requires a clear understanding up front of what each party will supply and what each party can expect from the other.

A church relationship is no different. A good local church provides powerful worship services, excellent Bible teaching, pastoral care, spiritual counseling, small group prayer and Bible studies, worship facilities, sacraments and ordinances, dedications, marriage and funeral services, ministries for families, and opportunities for believers to use their gifts to serve one another. That is a lot of benefits! It is right and appropriate for members of the church to reciprocate this care and provide mutual benefits as well. In fact, it is the only way a local church can function in health.

Jesus is Interested in Disciples—Not Consumers

> *The Lord Jesus does not ask us for anything less than giving Him our entire lives and complete surrender to His will.*

Many believers today exhibit a selfish American consumerism attitude. They think of the church like their favorite restaurant or retail store. They expect free parking, stellar customer service, the ability to come and go at will, and absolutely no obligation to buy anything, provide anything, or return with regularity. This is not only unscriptural, but it is an idolatrous way to live. In fact, it has warped the practice of many churches to focus more on appealing to the latest cultural trend than calling believers to live biblically obedient and Christ-centered lives. Following Christ involves more than a prayer and a dip in the baptismal pool. Read each of these verses carefully:

> "Whoever does not carry his own cross and come after Me cannot be My disciple" (Luke 14:27 NASB).

> "If you love your father or mother more than you love me, you are not worthy of being mine; or if you love your son or daughter more than me, you are not worthy of being mine" (Matthew 10:37 NLT).

> "If you cling to your life, you will lose it; but if you give up your life for me, you will find it" (Matthew 10:39 NLT).

Following Jesus is wonderful, but it is not without cost. The Lord Jesus does not ask us for anything less than giving Him our entire lives and complete surrender to His will. Part of that surrender includes loving and embracing His church.

YOUR RESPONSIBILITIES TO THE LOCAL CHURCH

Love the Church (Unconditionally)

> "And he has given us this command: *Those who love God must also love their Christian brothers and sisters*" (1 John 4:21 NLT).

The first and greatest commandment is to love God and love one another. This single principle is the foundation of everything in the kingdom of God. We show our love for God by loving people just as He does. He loves us fully and completely—as we are; and we must do the same. When you love people in the local church, *you are making a decision to do so unconditionally.* That means that our love for each other is not based on what others do for us or how they treat us. It is not based on how "cool" they are or the absence of sin in their life. It requires us to do the hard work of seeing others as God sees them. It is believing in their potential for change.

> "And this is His commandment: that we should believe on the name of His Son Jesus Christ and love *one another*, as He gave us commandment" (1 John 3:23).

Because churches are comprised of humans, they are imperfect places. Sometimes those imperfections can create conflicts. Sometimes those conflicts cause people to feel hurt, drift away, or leave church altogether. Sometimes people just want to get away from church and sort things out on their own. While this is understandable, *it is not scriptural*. Nowhere in the New Testament does the Scripture advocate "time off" from the body of Christ. In contrast to that, whenever problems in the church are addressed in Scripture, the Lord directs that they are to be resolved *within* the church community, not by avoiding them (Matthew 18:15-17; Galatians 6:1).

> "Beloved, let us *love one another*, for love is of God; and everyone who loves
> is born of God and knows God" (1 John 4:7).

Love requires that we forgive each other, that we support one another, and that we work together to serve our community. Scripture says we are to avoid strife in the church (2 Timothy 2:23), and maintain unity. This means we avoid gossip, slander, and speaking unkindly about people behind their backs. This is the first responsibility of every believer in the local church.

> "Always be humble and gentle. Be patient with each other, making allowance
> for each other's faults because of your love. Make every effort to keep
> yourselves united in the Spirit, binding yourselves together with peace"
> (Ephesians 4:2-3 NLT).

> "Get rid of all bitterness, rage, anger, harsh words, and slander, as well as
> all types of evil behavior. Instead, be kind to each other, tenderhearted,
> forgiving one another, just as God through Christ has forgiven you"
> (Ephesians 4:31-32 NLT).

Go to Church Weekly

> "For these laws of Moses *have been preached in Jewish synagogues* in *every*
> city on *every* Sabbath for *many* generations" (Act 15:21 NLT).

Every believer should gather weekly for local church worship and service. In the Old Testament, God commanded His people to take one day a week and dedicate it to Him. It was known as the Sabbath Day. In Leviticus, the Lord said, "Keep my Sabbath days of rest, and show reverence toward *my sanctuary*. I am the Lord" (Leviticus 19:30 NLT). He called it, "a Sabbath day of complete rest, *an official day for holy assembly*" (Leviticus 23:3a NLT). From that time forward, God's people would gather every Sabbath to worship and hear the teaching of God's Word. The entire day was devoted to the Lord and regular work was forbidden. After services, the people would eat together with their families and fellow believers, spending the day enjoying God and one another.

Jesus went to worship services every week and taught the Word.

> "Jesus and his companions went to the town of Capernaum. *When the Sabbath
> day came, he went into the synagogue* and began to teach" (Mark 1:21 NLT).

> "The next Sabbath he began teaching in the synagogue" (Mark 6:2a NLT).

"When he came to the village of Nazareth, his boyhood home, *he went as usual to the synagogue on the Sabbath* and stood up to read the Scriptures" (Luke 4:16 NLT).

"Then Jesus went to Capernaum, a town in Galilee, and taught there in the synagogue *every Sabbath day*" (Luke 4:31 NLT).

After Jesus was raised from the dead on Sunday morning, He appeared to His disciples who were gathered later in the day. Seven weeks later, the Holy Spirit was poured out as the disciples gathered for worship on Pentecost Sunday. From that time forth, the church met every week—either on Saturday or Sunday—and has continued to do so for two thousand years. The weekly gathering of believers in local churches has always been the first function of the Christian life. It has never been a question of *whether* believers should meet every week. In fact, weekly gathering has always been the heartbeat of living the Christian life in community. It is only in the past few decades that some modern Christians have suggested that this practice is unnecessary for successful Christian living. Unfortunately, they are deceived.

The Scripture makes it clear, "And let us consider one another in order to stir up love and good works, *not forsaking the assembling of ourselves together*, as is the manner of some, but exhorting one another, and so *much the more as you see the Day approaching*" (Hebrews 10:24-25).

A believer should go to church every week under normal circumstances—for worship, teaching, giving, fellowship, sacrament, witnessing, and serving one another. It is an essential part of being a disciple of Jesus, and shows honor for Him and His family.

Grow with the Church (Spiritually)

"So get rid of all evil behavior. Be done with all deceit, hypocrisy, jealousy, and all unkind speech. Like newborn babies, you must crave pure spiritual milk *so that you will grow into a full experience of salvation.* Cry out for this nourishment" (1 Peter 2:1-2 NLT).

It is the responsibility of every believer to grow up spiritually. That means we need to deal with our flesh, renew our minds, change our sinful behaviors, and take our place in the family. Everyone starts out the Christian life as a spiritual baby. We all have sins to lay aside, feelings we must overcome, and memories we need to heal. That is what the local church is for! A good local church will offer more than weekly worship and teaching services. There will be opportunities to become a disciple by joining Bible studies, classes on particular subjects, small groups, and fellowship events. Take your walk with Christ seriously and become a committed part of whatever spiritual growth or formative groups your church offers. As you meet regularly with other believers for study, prayer, fellowship, and serving, you will begin to grow up spiritually.

Additionally, it is the responsibility of every believer to develop a vibrant and intimate fellowship with God. Prayer and meditation on Scripture are disciplines that should be a daily part of your life.

DAY 3 EXERCISES

1. What single thing is the foundation of any good church?

_____

2. What four essential items should be included in a church's mission statement?
    1. _____
    2. _____
    3. _____
    4. _____

3. Explain how the *law of mutual benefit* works in the local church. What does it give to you? What can you give in return?

_____

_____

_____

_____

_____

4. What are the three responsibilities toward the church mentioned in today's reading?
    1. _____
    2. _____
    3. _____

5. What two disciplines should be a daily part of your life?
    1. _____
    2. _____

DAY 4: GIVING

Give to the Church (Generously and Faithfully)

Every member of a local church should give faithfully and generously of their finances to the Lord. I know what you're likely thinking. Hold on. Before you roll your eyes or get nervous, consider that God just might have a thing or two to say about money. The fact is, the Bible has much to say about money and our behavior towards it. And since God made both you and the material riches on this planet, what He has to say about it is one of the most important things you could ever learn. Keep an open mind and bravely read on.

> *Jesus talked about money more than He did heaven and hell combined.*

There is a Lot of Confusion about God and Money

There is much confusion and, unfortunately, controversy today around the subject of money and giving. Historically, the church has been a study in extremes. During the Middle Ages, local church ministers took vows of poverty, while higher church authorities, like bishops, enjoyed lavish lifestyles. The idea that money was evil was widely taught—and believed—by the average Christian, and those with wealth were often held in suspicion. The invention of the printing press made it possible for the common people to actually read the Word of God in their own language. As they read the Word, they saw the corruption in their present religious system, and the Reformation was born. After the Reformation in the sixteenth century, Protestant churches began to read in the Scriptures about the value of hard work, frugal saving, and financial stewardship. For the first time, church members began to start businesses, open banks, invest in and develop real estate as a part of their Christian duty to be good stewards with God's resources. Christians opened schools and universities to study for professions that would ultimately elevate the living standards of Europe and make possible the birth and rapid prosperity of America.

Then, in the nineteenth century, a movement began in Great Britain and America emphasizing personal holiness and the renouncing of materialism. As a reaction to spiritual complacency in many churches, these new churches taught that the kingdom of God was not of this world, and the pursuit of wealth was an evil that faithful believers needed to be separate from. This kind of preaching was very popular among the poor and working class people of America. Soon, a new class of Protestant churches was born in which money and wealth was once again viewed as an evil that had become the god of the unrighteous.

The final swing of the pendulum began in the late twentieth century as Spirit-filled churches and ministries began to see the promises for material prosperity in Scripture as a means to reach the world with larger churches, multi-media ministry, and highly creative (and expensive) forms of outreach. Some preachers and ministries began to emphasize personal prosperity and unlimited wealth as a sign of God's love and personal blessing. The biblical truths of stewardship and prosperity became eclipsed by extremism, and increasingly bizarre, teachings and fund-raising practices that preyed on the blind faith of sincere and desperate believers, the uneducated, and the poor.

God Has a Lot to Say about Money and its Role in Your Life

As a result of all this, when the subject of money comes up in church, many people tune out. Worse yet, some people are so skeptical of the motives of Christian teaching about finances that they turn off their hearts and minds altogether. The unfortunate thing about this is that the Bible's true teaching on poverty, stewardship, and prosperity is beautifully balanced. It actually has the power to transform your life and the experience of the local church. What is important to remember is that *the truth* will *always* set us free. This includes the truth about money and generous giving.

The fact is that God's Word is filled with promises, warnings, and guidelines that give the believer all the wisdom needed to be an excellent steward of material riches. Nearly twenty-five percent of the Proverbs give direct instructions on money and material stewardship. They show how a biblical person may prosper while simultaneously avoiding the pitfalls of poverty and materialism.

There are few truths that will set you free in life like the *balanced* teaching of God's Word on the proper stewardship of money, generous giving, and abundant receiving.

Jesus Talked About Money—a Lot

Here are some facts:

- Jesus talked about money more than He did heaven and hell combined.
- Jesus talked about money more than anything else except the kingdom of God.
- Twenty-five out of thirty-nine parables (over half) involve money, assets, or material stewardship.
- One of every seven verses in the gospel of Luke refers to money or material assets.

Jesus' teaching included many warnings about the abuse, misuse, and deceitful nature of material things. He also advocated using money for good, caring for your family, and generous giving for the purposes of God's kingdom.

Jesus Challenged His Disciples to Give Generously and Receive Bountifully

Jesus told His parables to the leaders of His future church, and was unashamed to challenge His followers to give generously, regularly, and sacrificially. Jesus said this:

> "Give, and you will receive. Your gift will return to you in full—pressed down, shaken together to make room for more, running over, and poured into your lap. The amount you give will determine the amount you get back" (Luke 6:38 NLT).

When challenging a wealthy, young Jewish politician Jesus said,

"One thing you lack: Go your way, sell whatever you have and *give to the poor*, and you will have treasure in heaven; and come, take up the cross, and *follow Me*" (Mark 10:21).

This promise of heavenly treasure was not good enough for this materialistic and powerful man. So he walked away from the opportunity to follow Jesus. Unfortunately, his materialism kept him from getting the rest of the story. Jesus was not trying to impoverish him materially, but deliver him from the *deception of materialism*. The Lord was testing him to see whether or not he loved God more than his money. Jesus was not planning to keep him perpetually poor. In fact, the Lord was planning to both save his soul, *and* prosper him materially! Jesus went on to explain to His disciples,

"Assuredly, I say to you, there is no one who has left house or brothers or sisters or father or mother or wife or children or lands, for My sake and the gospel's, who shall not *receive a hundredfold now in this time*—houses and brothers and sisters and mothers and children and lands, with persecutions—and in the age to come, eternal life" (Mark 10:29-30).

From these passages, we see that Jesus expects his followers to be generous in their material giving so He can be radically gracious in material blessing!

> *Nearly every time God instructs us to give, He promises to give back to us. This is not an occasional or obscure teaching of Scripture. It is all over the Old and New Testaments.*

When the Bible Tells Us to Give, God Promises to Give Back

It is true that we should not give to the Lord like we are playing a heavenly slot machine. It is totally selfish to give to others solely so that we can get something back. The highest reason for generous giving is love. We give because we love God, we love His church, we love to help others, and we love His commandments. If we never received anything back in this life or eternity, we should still be radically generous just because it pleases Jesus—our generous Lord and Savior.

At the same time, we cannot ignore the fact that nearly every time God instructs us to give, He promises to give back to us. This is not an occasional or obscure teaching of Scripture. It is all over the Old and New Testaments. God has promised to multiply our financial giving—back into our lives—in order to bless us personally and to enable us for further generosity. Read each of the following Scriptures out loud. As you do, consider the incredible promise that the Lord has made to those who give.

"Honor the Lord with your possessions, and with the firstfruits of all your increase; so *your barns will be filled with plenty, and your vats will overflow with new wine*" (Proverbs 3:9-10).

"The wicked borrow and never repay, but *the godly are generous givers*. Those the Lord blesses will possess the land" (Psalm 37:21-22 NLT).

"*Give freely* and *become more wealthy*; be stingy and lose everything. The *generous will prosper*; those who refresh others will themselves be refreshed" (Proverbs 11:24-25 NLT).

"'*Bring all the tithes* into the storehouse so there will be enough food in my Temple. If you do,' says the Lord of Heaven's Armies, 'I will open the windows of heaven for you. I will pour out *a blessing so great you won't have enough room to take it in*! Try it! Put me to the test! *Your crops will be abundant*, for I will guard them from insects and disease. Your grapes will not fall from the vine before they are ripe,' says the Lord of Heaven's Armies" (Malachi 3:10-11 NLT).

You yourselves also know..after I left Macedonia, no church shared with me in the matter of giving and receiving but you alone…But I have received everything in full, and have an abundance; I am amply supplied, having received…what you have sent, a fragrant aroma, an acceptable sacrifice, well-pleasing to God. *And my God shall supply all your needs according to His riches in glory in Christ Jesus"* (Philippians 4:15, 18, 19 NASB).

"So I thought I should…make sure the gift you promised is ready. But I want it to be a willing gift, not one given grudgingly. Remember this—a farmer who plants only a few seeds will get a small crop. But the one who plants *generously will get a generous crop*.…For God is the one who provides seed for the farmer and then bread to eat. In the same way, he will provide *and increase your resources* and then produce a great *harvest of generosity* in you. Yes, you will be *enriched in every way* so that you can *always be generous*. And when we take your gifts to those who need them, they will thank God" (2 Corinthians 9:5-6, 10-11 NLT).

There Are Different Kinds of Giving Taught in the Bible

There are three general categories of financial giving advocated in the Old and New Testaments. Each has its place in serving God's purposes for the church. They are tithes, offerings, and alms.

1. Tithes
Tithes are the first tenth of your income. You cannot tithe five percent or fifteen percent. It is only and always ten percent. It is to be offered to the local church whenever income is received. It is to be given first, not last. It is to be given regularly as an act of worship. It is not something you try. It is not something you do when you feel led. It is a principle of honor that you set aside on your own and bring to support the work of the church faithfully.

2. Alms
Alms are gifts to the poor or gifts to meet charitable needs. Alms are given as a person feels inspired by their own hearts. There is no specific percentage. Alms are given over and above the tithe. They are post-tithe offerings. You may give alms through the local church, to people you know who are in need, or to ministries that are serving the poor and destitute. God commands us to give alms regularly.

3. Offerings

Offerings are gifts that are given over and above the tithe that do not fall into the category of alms. Offerings fall into two categories—project offerings and general offerings. Project offerings include onetime or ongoing pledges to building projects, missions and outreach, or other designated programs. General offerings are everything else an individual feels prompted to sow into the church, other ministries, or the lives of fellow believers. God expects His people to give to projects in their local churches, missions, and the people around them, as His Spirit directs.

TITHING: THE FIRST PRINCIPLE OF GIVING

This is often the most controversial category of giving because is it the clearest, and therefore most difficult to avoid. The word *tithe* means "tenth," or ten percent. The Bible teaches that God's children are in a covenant with Him as stewards (or managers) of the earth. Out of love for God and His work on earth, God instructs us to give the first tenth of our income back to Him in acknowledgment that He is the owner of everything we possess. Contrary to the thinking of some, the tithe was a *covenant principle of grace* long before it was added to Jewish law.

Tithing is by Grace through Faith, Not by the Law

Abraham is known in Scripture as the father of all who believe—among both Israel and the church. This means that in Abraham we have an example of faith and a pattern for living that is a foundation for the church.

> "And now that you belong to Christ, you are the true children of Abraham. You are his heirs, and God's promise to Abraham belongs to you" (Galatians 3:29 NLT).

> "So the promise is received by faith. It is given as a free gift. And we are all certain to receive it, whether or not we live according to the law of Moses, if we have faith like Abraham's. *For Abraham is the father of all who believe*" (Romans 4:16 NLT; see also Romans 11:17.)

In Genesis 14, Abraham returned from a great battle with the wealth and riches of His victory. As he passed through the hill country of Judea, he came to a small mountain city known as Salem, or "peace." As Abraham passed by, he was met by a very mysterious figure who somehow had anticipated his coming. His name was *Melchizedek*. He was both the King of Salem and "the Priest of the Most High God." The Hebrew name, *Melchizedek* means "King of Righteousness." What is so unusual about this man is that he was a priest of God nearly five hundred years before Moses, the Law, and the Jewish priesthood existed! Every other priest in Scripture was born a priest under the law of Moses. This mysterious king-priest was later described as being "without father, without mother…having neither beginning of days nor end of life, but *made like the Son of God"* (Hebrews 7:3).

When Melchizedek met Abraham, he brought him a very curious gift: *bread and wine.* Years later the book of Hebrews tells us plainly what you may have already guessed: Melchizedek was a type of Jesus Christ. Jesus is our King and High Priest. He offered us His body and blood and we remember His sacrifice in Holy Communion. Abraham was undone by his visit with the Christ-like figure of Melchizedek and responded by giving him the first tithe.

> "Then Melchizedek king of Salem brought out bread and wine; he was the priest of God Most High. And he blessed him and said: 'Blessed be Abram of God Most High, Possessor of heaven and earth; and blessed be God Most High, who has delivered your enemies into your hand.' And he [Abraham] gave him *a tithe* of all" (Genesis 14:18-20).

Jesus, Our High Priest, Receives Our Tithes

Today, Jesus is our High Priest and King. His priesthood is not from the law of Moses, but "according to the order of Melchizedek" (Hebrews 7:11). Later Israel was commanded to pay tithes of all they possessed under the Law. But tithing began under the covenant of grace when Abraham gave the first tithe to Melchizedek. The Scripture also says, "Here mortal men receive tithes, but there he receives them, *of whom it is witnessed that he lives*" (Hebrews 7:8). This is speaking of Jesus. He was in Melchizedek receiving tithes from Abraham. And He lives today and receives tithes from His church under the covenant of grace.

Tithes Are Brought to the House of God

Tithing was taught by Abraham to his children. His grandson, Jacob, reaffirmed the practice of tithing after he had been visited by angels in a vision as he slept. In the vision, he saw angels ascending and descending on a ladder *that connected heaven to earth*. When he awoke, he took the rock he had used as a pillow and set it up as a physical marker of the place where God had met him. He called the place the "house of God."

> "Then Jacob prayed and vowed, 'If God will indeed be with me and protect me on this journey, and if he will provide me with food and clothing, and if I return safely to my father's home, then the Lord will certainly be my God. And this memorial pillar I have set up *will become a place for worshiping God*, and I will *present to God a tenth of everything he gives me*'" (Genesis 28:20-22 NLT).

In this story, we see the pattern for tithing that was later followed by Israel, and today for the New Testament church. Tithing is brought to the house of God. It is brought to the place on earth where God speaks to His people when they gather to worship Him. The Old Testament house of God were the tabernacles of Moses, then David, and later the temple. What each of these places had in common was that God's people gathered there under spiritual leadership to worship, be taught, give tithes, and serve one another. The Lord specifically told Israel that they were to bring the tithes to the house of God (Malachi 3:10-11).

The question is this: What is the New Testament house of God? Thankfully, we have a clear answer in Scripture:

> "But if I am delayed, I write so that you may know how you ought to conduct yourself in *the house of God, which is the church of the living God*, the pillar and ground of the truth" (1 Timothy 3:15).

"But Christ as a Son over *His own house, whose house we are* if we hold fast the confidence and the rejoicing of the hope firm to the end" (Hebrews 3:6).

"You also, as living stones, are being built up *a spiritual house*, a holy priesthood, to offer up spiritual sacrifices acceptable to God through Jesus Christ" (1 Peter 2:5).

The church spoken of in 1 Timothy 3:15 was the local church of Ephesus where Timothy was pastor. Today the local church is the house of God. While each believer is a "temple" of God's presence because of the indwelling of the Holy Spirit, when we gather together in the local assembly we become a special dwelling place for the presence of God. That is why we bring our tithes to our local church today.

Jesus Endorsed Tithing

Once when Jesus was correcting the Pharisees, He addressed their tendency to do the right things on the outside while having the wrong motives on the inside. He said, "What sorrow awaits you Pharisees! For you are careful *to tithe even the tiniest income* from your herb gardens, but you ignore justice and the love of God. *You should tithe, yes,* but do not neglect *the more important things"* (Luke 11:42 NLT). Jesus affirmed the practice of tithing, while teaching that it is the motives of the heart that make it meaningful.

The Early Church Practiced Tithing

The oldest church document that exists today describing the practices of the first Christians is a little manual called *The Didache*, or simply *The Teaching*. It gives instructions on how believers should live, worship, baptize, receive communion, and conduct church meetings. It is a glimpse into the life of the very first Christians and what their church gatherings were like. Notice the high value placed on giving tithes (or firstfruits) as well as offerings and alms for the poor:

"To everyone that asketh thee give, and ask not back; for to all the father desires to give of his own gracious gifts. Blessed is he that giveth according to the commandment, for he is guiltless. (lines 8,9,Chapter 1)Thou shalt not hesitate to give, nor when giving shalt thou murmur …Thou shalt not turn away the needy, but shall share all things with thy brother" (lines 6,7, Chapter 4) "*Every first-fruit,* then, of the products of wine-press and threshing-floor, of oxen and of sheep, thou shalt take and give to the prophets (preaching pastors), for they are (like) your high priests. But if ye have no prophet (pastor), give it to the poor. If thou makest a baking of bread, *take the first of it* and give to the prophets; and *of money (silver) and clothing and every possession, take the first*, as seems right to thee, and give according to the commandment."[23]

Tithing is the Primary Way the Mission of the Local Church is Funded

Paul wrote the church at Corinth and taught them about their obligation to support the preaching of the gospel through the local church.

---

23. *The Didache*, chapter 13, lines 3-5, Public Domain.

> "Don't you realize that those who work in the temple get their meals from the offerings [tithes] brought to the temple? And those who serve at the altar get a share of the sacrificial offerings. *In the same way, the Lord ordered* that those who preach the Good News *should be supported* by those who benefit from it"
> (1 Corinthians 9:13-14 NLT).

This is teaching that just as the Jewish temple and its ministers were supported by the tithes of the people, *in the same way* the local church members should support the work of the church by their tithes. It is an exact endorsement of tithing in the New Testament church according to the Old Testament pattern.

The Tithe is the Lord's—If You Keep It, You are Stealing

We often speak of "paying" our tithes like we would pay a bill. But the fact is, our tithes were never ours to begin with. "The tithe…is the Lord's" (Leviticus 27:30). We actually bring our tithes. When we tithe, we are acknowledging that everything we have is His to begin with. That is why the most famous passage on tithing begins with a rebuke to His people for robbing God by keeping His tithe! "Will a man rob God? Yet ye have robbed me. But ye say, Wherein have we robbed thee? In tithes and offerings" (Malachi 3:8 KJV).

Tithing is an Act of Love and Honor

God promises to reward faithful tithing. Yet we are always to remember that we offer our tithes and offerings to Him in love and honor—not as a legal obligation or to earn His favor. Israel tithed to become righteous under the Law. We tithe because we are righteous under grace. It is an act of honor we offer by faith. The moment we forget this, giving becomes little more than a ritual. One of the reasons believers don't tithe today is because they are struggling to pay bills, debts, and care for families. Often when we first hear about the principle of the tithe, it is frightening. Sometimes we begin to bring our tithes in faith, but the pressures of life cause our faith to falter. It is important to remember that our salvation is not based upon our giving. We give because we are saved. If you truly desire to honor God, you should give as generously as you can by faith. Here are some ways to get started:

How to Give

1. Begin where you are. Make a decision to begin giving today. Don't wait until you are able to give a certain amount. Don't diminish the importance of having a starting point.

2. The next time you receive income, set aside your tithe or offering first. God wants to be first. That means before you pay anything else, separate out your giving to the Lord. Don't use it for anything else! Make a decision to give to God right off the top of everything that comes in. The principle of giving to Him first is even more important than the actual amount you give. Make sure you do it faithfully every time.

3. Stretch to your level of faith. The tithe (ten percent) is the best place to start. If you choose to start beneath that level, make certain that you are giving at your maximum level of faith. Commit to arrange your life and finances in such a way that you can begin tithing as soon as possible. If you are already tithing ten percent, add an offering to every gift. If you have

faith to tithe off your net income, begin there. When your faith increases to where you can tithe off your gross income, stretch to that level.

4. After you have mastered faithful tithing, give regularly to the building fund or vision of your local church. A growing church is always in need of upgrading, enhancing, or adding facilities to promote the Lord's work. In Scripture, there are numerous detailed examples of building projects that God directed His people to undertake. Without exception, these projects were funded by special offerings over and above the regular tithes. When you give sacrificially to your church vision, you are giving to your own future and the future of your community.

5. Give to the poor and undeserving. If your church has a mission to needy people in your community or elsewhere in the world, give whenever you can. This kind of giving is always honored by the Lord.

6. Give to world missions. If your local church has mission projects or missionaries it supports, ask the Lord for opportunities to give. If you pray for the seed to sow, watch the Lord bring it into your life. His heart beats for world missions and growing churches and Christians who support such works.

7. Sow into the lives of fellow believers. The New Testament tells of how the Holy Spirit moved so powerfully in the early church that Christians in the local church began to help one another with their financial needs. If you have a need in your life, sow a seed into someone else's life. God will make possible for you what you make possible for others!

8. Give offerings and special gifts to your pastor(s) and those who feed you the Word of God. The Scripture teaches "Those who are taught the word of God should provide for their teachers, sharing all good things with them. Don't be misled—you cannot mock the justice of God. You will always harvest what you plant" (Galatians 6:6-7 NLT). God's ministers are His servants. Remember them on their birthdays, on holidays, and for special events. As you are so led, give to help them take vacations, get rest, and build their marriages and families. If you are generous with His ministers, He will be generous with you!

9. If you are married, make sure to communicate with your spouse about your decision to tithe. Naturally, you cannot tithe or give your spouse's income for them. God only expects you to give the firstfruits of all *your* increase or that which is in your control (Proverbs 3:9).

10. Take every opportunity to learn about financial management and stewardship. Get your financial house in order. The better you take care of your finances—no matter how little you may have—the more you will have to live, and give!

Taking your place in the local church is a choice that you alone can make. It is important for you to know that if you are a follower of Jesus Christ, He expects you to find, join, attend, love, grow with, and give generously to a good local church. When you support the local church, you are supporting the heartbeat of God on the earth. Jesus loves His family. He has one for you. It is time to take your place. Once you have done so, He can begin to activate within you the special abilities He has given you. The Lord wants you to be more than a member, a student, a worshipper, and a giver. He wants you to be a *servant*.

DAY 4 EXERCISES

1. What are the three different kinds of giving taught in the Bible? Describe each one.

   1. _____

   _____

   2. _____

   _____

   3_____

   _____

2. What is the most important aspect of tithing?

   _____

   _____

   _____

3. According to the teaching of Jesus, what makes a tithe meaningful when given?

   _____

   _____

   _____

4. When we bring our tithe to God, what are we acknowledging?

   _____

   _____

   _____

CHAPTER TEN

TRANSFORMING OUR WORLD

CHAPTER TEN
Transforming Our World

DAY 1: DESIGNED TO SERVE

You Have a Purpose

You are not an accident. You were designed on purpose, with a purpose, and for a purpose. That isn't just a play on words. Our Father has created us, saved us, and is in the process of transforming us according to a *plan* and for a specific reason. God never does anything *accidentally*. He doesn't figure things out as He goes along. He figured you out long before you were able to figure yourself out. God is intentional. The Scripture says that we have been "predestined according to the purpose of Him who works all things according to the counsel of His will" (Ephesians 1:11).

> "May He grant you according to your heart's desire, a*nd fulfill all your purpose*" (Psalm 20:4).

> "You can make many plans, but the Lord's *purpose* will prevail" (Proverbs 19:21 NLT).

> "When he came and had seen the grace of God, he was glad, and encouraged them all that with *purpose of heart* they should continue with the Lord" (Acts 11:23).

You are not an accident. You were designed on purpose, with a purpose, and for a purpose.

Imagine you are walking through a wild forest in a remote part of the world, when suddenly you see a shiny object in the distance. As you approach the mysterious thing, you begin to notice its shape. It has two wheels and bright red painted fenders. Its sleek shape contains a complicated metallic mechanism just beneath a soft leather seat. A large silver bowl sits just in front of and beneath two broad handlebars.

Now imagine you had never seen or heard of a motorcycle before. Without any frame of reference, several things could be immediately discerned. First, this object does not "fit" in this place where it has been found. Secondly, you would quickly conclude from its precise detail, beautiful lines, and intricate design, that it could not have come about *on its own*, or somehow formed *accidentally*. The existence of this *machine* mandates the existence of a *maker*. Such a *design* requires a *designer*.

Now you may have no idea what exactly this object does, why it is in the forest, or how it got there, but you *would* know immediately some things about the person who designed it. You would know he or she appreciates beauty. You would immediately discern that they were creative and artistic. You would know they were intelligent. You would know they were *purposeful*.

From these observations alone you might assume some things about the object itself. You would know such an object had value and worth—particularly to the designer. A painting by Picasso is of far greater value than that of an exact replica made by an unknown artist, simply because of the hand that touched the canvas. The designer gives value to the design. Finally you would know that this strange object existed for a *purpose*. But without something that gave you insight into the mind of the maker, you would have no way of knowing why it exists, where it belongs, or how it works. You might dismantle it and use its seat as a pillow, its tank as a water pot, steering column as a two-handled hoe. Ignorance of the maker guarantees misuse of the thing which was made.

In the same way, your very existence on this planet demands that you have a purpose. You are not an accident. The conditions of your arrival on this planet do not dictate your worth or determine the reason for your design. Regardless of your net worth, annual salary, number of friends, or national home, your identity and purpose for existence cannot be divined by the circumstances surrounding your life. You are a beautiful, amazing, intentional creation of God. You were designed for a reason. You have a purpose. You may feel lost in this life, but there is One who knows why you are here, the features and unique abilities you possess, and how you were designed to "work."

> "I cry out to God Most High, to *God who will fulfill his purpose for me*"
> (Psalm 57:2 NLT).

In this final chapter of our study on the transformed life, we are going to learn about the journey of discovering and fulfilling God's purpose for your life. It is only when we begin to live our lives in harmony with the purpose for which we were designed that this stage of our transformation is completed. God intended something *for you* when He put you on the earth. He began something *in you* on the day you were born again. And He is revealing something *through you* as you take your place as a disciple of Jesus Christ in the local church.

YOU WERE CREATED AND DESIGNED TO SERVE

You Were Purposefully Designed

Each one of us is a multi-talented, multi-gifted, purposeful creation of the Most High God. The Bible teaches that God was masterfully designing everything about us from the beginning. Read this passage out loud to yourself. Think about each word and concept as you read.

> "O Lord, you have examined my heart and know everything about me....You made all the delicate, inner parts of my body and *knit me together* in my mother's womb. Thank you for making me *so wonderfully complex*! Your workmanship is marvelous—how well I know it....You saw me before I was born. Every day of my life was recorded in your book. Every moment was laid out before a single day had passed. How precious are your thoughts about me, O God. They cannot be numbered!" (Psalm 139:1, 13-14, 16-17 NLT).

The Lord was intricately involved in our creation. He made us with a plan. He created us to fulfill a purpose on earth. From inside our mother's womb, He put within each of us the personality, gifts, talents, and mental capacities necessary to fulfill the purposes for which we were made. Because of the presence of sin, each of us have also been deeply impacted and "broken." It is only when we are born again that we begin our journey of transformation that results in our being restored to our original design.

> *The conditions of your arrival on this planet do not dictate your worth or determine the reason for your design.*

You Are Infinitely Valuable

You and I are incredibly valuable to God. The world may not recognize your true worth, but the God who formed you sure does. Jesus, when teaching about our value to God, said,

> "What is the price of two sparrows—one copper coin? But not a single sparrow can fall to the ground without your Father knowing it. And the very hairs on your head are all numbered. So don't be afraid; *you are more valuable to God* than a whole flock of sparrows" (Matthew 10:29-31 NLT).

The ultimate statement of your value to God is the cross of Jesus Christ. Once, when selling a home, my real estate agent reminded me of a very important fact—nothing is worth any more than what someone is willing to pay for it. You know the value of something by the price that was paid to obtain it. When God sent Jesus to the cross to shed His blood for our sin, God was setting our global market value for all time. Could there be anything more valuable or precious than the blood of God the Son? "Knowing that you were not redeemed with corruptible things, like silver or gold…but *with the precious blood of Christ*, as of a lamb without blemish and without spot" (1 Peter 1:18-19). You are a part of the "church of God which He purchased with His own blood" (Acts 20:28b). No price could be greater! The life of the Son of God is of infinite worth. Therefore, your value is infinite. Take a moment and say this out loud: "I was purchased by God with the blood of Jesus Christ. Therefore, I am of infinite value."

You've Been Restored to God's Image and Purpose

> "Blessed be the God and Father of our Lord Jesus Christ, who according to His great mercy *has caused us to be born again to a living hope*…to obtain an inheritance which is imperishable and undefiled and will not fade away" (1 Peter 1:3-4 NASB).

When you received Jesus Christ as your Savior and your spirit was reborn, God began the work of restoring His image in you. Paul said that we "put on the *new self*, which in the likeness of God has been created" (Ephesians 4:24 NASB).

Our spirits have been "renewed in knowledge according to the image of Him who created him" (Colossians 3:10). This new spiritual nature now enables us to recover the original purposes of God for our lives. Our inner transformation begins the process of our outer transformation.

DAY 1 EXERCISES

1. Your very existence on this planet demands that you have a purpose. Why?

_____

_____

_____

2. God intended something _____ when He put you on the earth.

3. God began something _____ on the day you were born again.

4. God is revealing something _____ as you take your place as a disciple of Jesus Christ in the local church.

5. What is the ultimate statement of our value to God?

_____

_____

_____

6. What begins our process of outer transformation?

_____

_____

_____

DAY 2: THE SECRET TO DISCOVERING YOUR PURPOSE

Redeemed for His Glory

The first purpose of God in our lives is to glorify and honor Him. Because we have been purchased by Him, we are now owned by Him. "Or do you not know that your body is the temple of the Holy Spirit who is in you…and you are not your own? For you were bought at a price; *therefore glorify God* in your *body* and in your spirit, *which are God's*" (1 Corinthians 6:19-20). It is our duty to use our lives in ways that bring glory to Him. That means that our desires, our plans, our purposes, and our pursuits need to change and align with the true purposes for which He has made us.

Reborn to Your Purpose

Very often we spend our time, talents, and energies serving our own purposes. But ultimately, we were not put on the earth to live our lives outside of His purposes! Notice that being born again requires us to rethink who we are serving and how we are using our lives.

> "For we ourselves were also once foolish, disobedient, deceived, *serving various lusts and pleasures,* living in malice and envy, hateful and hating one another" (Titus 3:3).

The life of the unsaved person is devoted to serving their own deceptions, lusts, and pleasures. It is a life that is self-focused. Our world today is sometimes known as the "me" generation. It is all about our wants, our needs, our happiness, and a constant competition to achieve more for ourselves at the expense of others. Becoming a believer changes all that.

> "But when the kindness of God our Savior and His love for mankind appeared,
> He saved us…by the washing of regeneration and renewing by the Holy Spirit…
> so that those who have believed God will be careful to engage in good deeds"
> (Titus 3:4-5, 8 NASB).

Now that we are in Christ, our focus turns to pleasing God. Our gifts and goals become reevaluated, and often our time becomes repurposed around our new value system. We are changed; and now we want to use our bodies, our gifts, and lives to do *good works* for others.

> *When your actions align with your true spiritual purposes, you will always experience a feeling of joy and inner peace. It is one of the ways you discover your gifts and find your purpose in life.*

Re-Created for Good Works

> "For we are His workmanship, created in Christ Jesus for good works, which God prepared beforehand so that we would walk in them" (Ephesians 2:10 NASB).

Did you know that there are particular good works and purposes that God has prepared for you to perform? When you were born again, your spirit was re-formed and equipped to the specific works that God has planned for your future. The Lord has prepared works that are yours alone to accomplish. These are not the achievements and purposes of the Lord for just anyone. They are the particular works that you were literally created in Christ to do. Some believers never consider the things that God had planned for them to do with their lives. They finish school, work in careers, raise families, pursue their hobbies and interests, and sometimes live and die without ever really doing what they were designed by God to do.

Most believers know this in their hearts. They often sense that their successes are somewhat empty—as if in the middle of it all, they are missing their true purpose. Of all the things we could study, pursue, and develop in our lives, there is nothing more important than discovering your spiritual purpose in life, and using the abilities God has given you.

When Your Daily Actions Align with Your Gifts and Purpose, You Will Have Inner Peace!

One of the passions of my life is leading church members on high-impact, short-term mission trips to developing and impoverished nations. There is nothing quite like seeing the impact that these adventures make in the lives of believers as they see international poverty and expansive suffering for the first time. The real joy is watching how their lives change as they put their spiritual and natural gifts to work to make a real difference in the lives and experiences of others. Nothing motivates me like helping people discover their gifts, connecting them to their purpose, and helping them reach their potential.

On one trip to Africa, I was able to bring a young woman who had grown up in our church from infancy. She loved God, and had become successful in the nursing profession. All her life she had felt an urge to visit one of our missions in Africa. Finally, at the prodding of the Holy Spirit and the suggestion of her fiancé, she took some time off work and joined our mission. Naturally, she was overwhelmed by the needs she encountered and quickly began working with our medical team to treat the sick. One morning, a young homeless boy in tattered clothes wandered into our clinic, tightly clasping his arm to his chest. He looked bewildered and almost walked back out to the streets when our young missionary saw him and began to minister to his needs. He hadn't eaten or had anything to drink in some time. After offering the boy some water, we learned his story. He had been beaten by his alcoholic father. After breaking his arm, his father threw him out into the streets. The young nurse from our church made it her mission to treat and reset the boy's mangled arm, get him a bath and new clothes, and within twenty-four hours, we found him an adoptive family. The "before" and "after" pictures of this little boy are worth a thousand words.

But perhaps the greatest part of the story came several nights later as I was meeting with the team for the last time before returning to the United States. This beautiful young professional nurse, beaming with the joy of the Lord, proclaimed "For the first time in my life, I feel like I have finally found the reason I am here. I have my purpose in life!" She was never the same again.

When your actions align with your true spiritual purposes, you will always experience a feeling of joy and inner peace. It is one of the ways you discover your gifts and find your purpose in life.

YOU HAVE GIFTS THAT ALIGN WITH YOUR PURPOSE

We are all multi-gifted. Every person on this planet has been given something in their bodies and souls that are designed to guide them to their purpose in life. We call these abilities talents, traits, or *gifts*. Understanding the different kinds of gifts that God has given and how to use them is one of the most important things you must figure out in life.

NATURAL GIFTS

Natural gifts are special abilities given by God to everyone that enable them to find success in their natural lives. They are part of God's creative act in graciously providing for the human race—whether they acknowledge Him or not. They reside in the soul (mind, intellect, imagination, emotions, and will) and the physical body. Natural gifts or skills are abilities that we are naturally proficient in. Let's look at some characteristics of natural gifts.

1. Natural Gifts Are Given to All People at Birth

God has graciously gifted every human with certain natural gifts that correspond with their place in the natural world. They may not discover some of their natural talents until many years after they have grown, but they were present in seed form in their bodies and minds at birth.

2. Natural Gifts Tend to Fall into One of These Categories

Intellectual gifts—abilities that reside in the mind. This may include the sciences, education, and problem solving.

Relational gifts—talents with people or social gifts. Gifts in psychology, coaching, communication and interactive skills, and building bridges with people and cultures, may be present.

Mechanical gifts—having competencies with building, repairing, engineering, understanding simple and complex mechanisms, and a knowledge of how things function. This also includes people with physical strength and abilities.

Artistic gifts—skills that use various means to express feeling, beauty, and creativity. This includes actors, authors, painters, dancers, musicians, designers, entertainers, and artists of all sorts.

Athletic gifts—skills that give one great proficiency in physical competition and achievement.

Leadership gifts—referring to competencies that inspire others to follow a vision, plan, or idea to achieve a desired goal. These may be found in every area of life.

Economic/Commercial gifts—special abilities to make and multiply wealth, manage assets, or handle affairs of business.

Service gifts—abilities to get behind others and make them successful. These gifts are most satisfied when they are enabling someone else to achieve something.

Innovative gifts—these are the inventors, or the people who have the capacity to see a need and discover new ways to meet it. True innovators are rare, and often need others with gifts unlike theirs to complement their own skill sets and help bring their vision to pass.

3. Natural Gifts Are the Key to Material Success

The key to becoming successful in your natural life is to discover and develop your natural gifts. God gives them to everyone so they may become productive members of society and provide materially for themselves and their families. Your financial success is typically tied to discovering your natural gifts and developing them into brilliance. Do what you are naturally good at and you will always have something to do.

4. Sometimes a Person's Natural Gifts and Their Personal Interests Are Different

However, you will never be as successful pursuing interests you are only *moderately* gifted in or not *gifted* in at all. You may love baseball, and you may become pretty good at it. But unless it is an innate, or natural, gifting, chances are you will not find personal success pursuing it.

5. We Need to Embrace Our Natural Gifts and Indulge Our Hobbies and Interests

There are many talent competitions on television in which extremely untalented or moderately gifted people compete only to be devastated to discover the only person who enjoys their talent is themselves and their mother. Find your real gifts. Make them shine. Use them to make a living. Indulge your personal passions and interests without placing yourself in the position of having to make a living out of them.

6. Sometimes We Discover Our Gifts by Accident

They start out as experiences or hobbies, and we quickly discover that we are naturally talented at something we were previously clueless about. There might be an athlete hiding under that extra twenty pounds. A successful author, artist, or blogger might be lurking beneath that passion to read. A potential business owner could be tucked away in those pie recipes you pull out every holiday to make for all your friends. Keep trying new things. You may discover natural gifts at any age—and everyone has more than one.

7. God Uses Our Natural Gifts to Help Build and Develop the Church

Although our natural gifts are primarily to help us fulfill our natural purposes and provide for our material success in life, every natural skill can be used by the Lord to help the local church too! Churches need skilled business people to advise and assist in financial stewardship. The church needs builders, contractors, artists, and athletes. Those with natural skills at serving, leading, and working with different kinds of people all have a responsibility to offer their natural gifts in service to Jesus and His church. While some may be paid for their skills, every believer should seek to not be a burden on the church, using their natural gifts to earn a living in the world and offering to help the others in the church with their talents as they are able *without charge.*

SPIRITUAL GIFTS

"Now, dear brothers and sisters, regarding your question about the special abilities [spiritual gifts] the Spirit gives us. I don't want you to misunderstand this" (1 Corinthians 12:1 NLT).

Spiritual gifts are special abilities given by God to His children to enable them to find success and fulfill their purpose in the local church. They reside in the believer's born-again spirit. Spiritual gifts are part of God's way of building community and love within the local church. Let's look at some characteristics.

1. The Greek Word Translated "Gift" is *Charisma*

It comes from the root word *charis* which means "grace." A spiritual gift is a special measure of God's grace that enables a believer to do something he or she could not otherwise do. Spiritual gifts are talents that reside within the believer at all times. They are potentially available to be used when the need arises for them. They can also operate in any believer on occasion as the Holy Spirit wills. While no believer has every spiritual gift, every believer has at least one spiritual gift that will be a part of their spiritual "inventory" for life.

2. Every Believer Received at Least One Spiritual Gift the Moment They Were Saved

"As *each one has received* a gift [*charisma*], minister it to one another, as good stewards of the manifold grace of God" (1 Peter 4:10).

There is no such thing as a believer who does not possess a spiritual gift. If you are born again, you have at least one—and probably more than one!

3. God Chooses What Your Spiritual Gift or Gifts Will Be

"It is the one and only Spirit who distributes all these gifts. He *alone decides which gift each person should have*" (1 Corinthians 12:11 NLT).

Because they are given by the Holy Spirit by grace, God distributes spiritual gifts according to His own pleasure and perfect plan. In other words, you and I do not get to choose our gifts. It is not like going to the local buffet and picking out the things you prefer. You may admire a spiritual gift and eagerly desire it, but the Lord chooses whether or not you will receive it. The important thing is to appreciate all the gifts, because if we don't have one particular gift when we need it, *someone else will!*

4. The Spiritual Gifts Fall into Three General Types

1. Gifts that *say*
These are special abilities given by the Holy Spirit to speak by His inspiration.

2. Gifts that *do*
These are special abilities to perform or do something by the Holy Spirit.

3. Gifts that *see*

These are special abilities given by the Spirit to *know* or *see* something you would not otherwise see or know. These gifts are very special and function under the direction of the Spirit.

5. The New Testament Specifically Mentions Sixteen Spiritual Gifts or *Charismas*

"There are different kinds of spiritual gifts, but the same Spirit is the source of them all" (1 Corinthians 12:4 NLT).

The Holy Spirit is in charge of distributing the spiritual gifts. They are found primarily in two lists found in Romans 12 and 1 Corinthians 12. In this chapter, our purpose is to introduce the biblical teaching of spiritual gifting, not to study each gift individually. What is important to realize is that these gifts are given by the Holy Spirit and that they operate in the church in different ways. Sometimes they are given to the believer and remain as *resident gifts* that may be used when either the need arises or the Spirit inspires us. Other gifts in these lists are more spectacular in nature and manifest through the believer according to the will of God. In this second case, the believer must rely more heavily upon the Holy Spirit to initiate and supply the manifestation.

The Functional Gifts (Romans 12:6-8)

1. Prophecy
2. Teaching
3. Exhortation
4. Leadership with Diligence
5. Serving
6. Giving with Liberality
7. Mercy with Cheerfulness

The Manifestation Gifts (1 Corinthians 12:8-10)

1. Prophecy (listed in both passages)
2. Different Kinds of Tongues
3. Interpretation of Different Kinds of Tongues
4. Word of Wisdom
5. Word of Knowledge
6. Discerning of Spirits
7. Special Faith (1 Corinthians 13:2)
8. Workings of Miracles
9. Gifts of Healing

Plus One

The only other ability specifically mentioned as a *charisma* in the New Testament is the gift of *celibacy* (1 Corinthians 7:7 NLT; Matthew 19:10-12). It takes a special grace and ability from God to remain happily single and sexually inactive. (All single Christians need to believe for God to give them this gift until they find their spouse!)

6. Spiritual Gifts Are Not the Same as Natural Gifts or Personality Traits

Some people think that because they are a professional teacher in the public school that God has called them to be a spiritual teacher in the local church. This is not the case. While a natural teaching gift can be used in service to the church, the spiritual *charisma* of teaching is a supernatural ability that comes from the Spirit's life within the believer. Others have assumed that spiritual gifts are just another way of discussing our personal tendencies and dispositions. For instance, some have taught that if someone has the gift of mercy, they are naturally soft-spoken, not personally assertive, and easy to take advantage of because they are always emotional and sensitive to everyone's feelings. This describes a personality trait like gentleness, but not a spiritual gift. The spiritual gift of mercy is not a set of emotional dispositions, but spiritually motivated actions governed by mercy.

7. Spiritual Gifts Are Never Taken Away Once They Have Been Given

"For God's gifts and his call can never be withdrawn" (Romans 11:29 NLT).

Every believer will be responsible to God for both the natural and spiritual gifts they have been given. God will never take them away regardless of your faithfulness to Jesus. We all will have to give an account of what we did with the gifts and opportunities Jesus gave us in life. He will never take your gifts away.

8. Spiritual Gifts Can Be Neglected

"Do not neglect the gift *that is in you*, which was given to you" (1 Timothy 4:14a).

Sometimes through ignorance, personal failure, or the distractions of life, we can neglect the spiritual gifts that have been given to us. If we do not attend churches that believe that every member has a spiritual gift or do not teach you how to recognize and use them, our gifts can become dormant. In the passage above, Paul was writing to a local church pastor named Timothy. From this passage, we can see that even spiritual leaders, pastors, and ministers can get so tied up with the duties of their daily work that they neglect their own spiritual gifts.

9. Spiritual Gifts Can Be Stirred up by Faith, Even if They Have Become Dormant

"Therefore I remind you *to stir up the gift of God which is in you*" (2 Timothy 1:6).

The New Living Translation says, "*fan into flames* the spiritual gift God gave you when I laid my hands on you" (2 Timothy 1:6). When we don't use our spiritual gifts to serve others in the church, they begin to become indistinct to us. Like a fire that has died down to slowly burning embers, it can look like our spiritual "fire" and power is just a distant memory. When this happens, it is not God's responsibility to stir up our gift. We are not instructed to ask the pastor or some other believer to stir us up. We are to stir up ourselves.

The way we stir our gifts *is by faith*. In the previous verse Paul said, "When I call to remembrance the genuine faith that…I am persuaded is in you…I remind you to stir up the gift" (2 Timothy 1:5-6). Begin to confess that you have received a gift. Declare that it can never be taken away (Romans 11:29). Say, "In the name of Jesus Christ, I stir up the gift that is in me by faith! Holy

Spirit, use me to help others. Let Your gifts burn brightly within me once again." Powerful things happen when we speak God's purpose by faith.

10. Your Spiritual Gifts Are for Others in the Local Church

> "A spiritual gift is given to each of us *so we can help each other.*...This
> makes for harmony among the members, so that *all the members care for
> each other*....All of you together are Christ's body, *and each of you is a part
> of it*" (1 Corinthians 12:7, 25, 27 NLT).

In every place the New Testament teaches about spiritual gifts, it makes one thing very clear: Your spiritual gifts do not exist for your benefit, but for the benefit of others in the local church. Once I was listening to a well-known Christian teacher complain about how believers are so inwardly focused. "God did not give the gifts of the Spirit to the church to be used in the church," he proclaimed. "God put the gifts of the Spirit in the church to be used on the world!" While I understood the point that the minister was trying to make, he couldn't have been more scripturally incorrect. The fact is this: Every time the gifts of the Spirit are presented, they are clearly indicated as gifts that are to be primarily used by the local church, in the local church, and for the benefit of the local church body. Every single time.

Certainly spiritual gifts can operate through believers as they minister to their non-believing friends and neighbors, but this is not their primary purpose. The gifts of the Spirit are in us so that we can help each other. They are specifically designed for use in the local church. Peter said this,

> "Most important of all, continue to show deep love *for each other*...God has
> given each of you a gift from his great variety of spiritual gifts. Use them well
> *to serve one another*" (1 Peter 4:8, 10).

DAY 2 EXERCISES

1. List the nine categories of natural gifts, then list those you possess that fit each category.

   1._____
   2._____
   3._____
   4._____
   5._____
   6._____
   7._____
   8._____
   9._____

2. How can you use your natural gifts to build and develop the local church?

   _____
   _____
   _____
   _____

3. Why did God give us natural gifts?

   _____
   _____

4. What is the difference between natural gifts and spiritual gifts?

   _____
   _____
   _____

5. Read over the spiritual gifts listed in this section again. Scripture tells us to "Desire spiritual gifts" (1 Corinthians 14:1). What is the purpose of spiritual gifts?

   _____
   _____

6. What are the three general types of spiritual gifts?

   1._____
   2._____
   3._____

7. Looking at the list of spiritual gifts in this chapter, what are some spiritual gifts you believe you may have? List at least three in order of strength.

   1._____
   2._____
   3._____

DAY 3: FIND YOUR GIFTS THROUGH SERVICE

You will not experience the transformed life by simply attending church services, giving financially, and receiving from the good works of others. Many churches today are filled with people who love Jesus, yet attend the church as *consumers.* In order for the local church to grow and thrive, every member needs to take their place in *serving.* Paul said,

> "Now these are the gifts Christ gave *to the church:* the apostles, the prophets, the evangelists, and the pastors and teachers. Their responsibility is *to equip God's people to do his work and build up the church*, the body of Christ" (Ephesians 4:11-12 NLT).

The work of the local church leaders is to equip believers to serve one another. When we joyfully and willingly serve others in the church, we begin to discover our gifting and fulfill our purpose.

> "As each one has received a gift, minister it to one another, as good stewards of the manifold grace of God. If anyone speaks, let him speak as the oracles of God. If anyone ministers, let him do it as with the ability which God supplies, that in all things God may be glorified through Jesus Christ, to whom belong the glory and the dominion forever and ever. Amen" (1 Peter 4:10-11).

Getting off the Bench and into the Game

Some people see being part of the church much like attending a local football game. The believers fill the stadium and watch the pastor(s), elders, and church leaders play the game. The pastor is viewed much like the quarterback. He makes the calls, runs the plays, and directs the team. When the pastor preaches a particularly great message, it is like throwing a great pass. Everyone cheers. When the game is over, everyone leaves the stadium with little more than an emotional experience. The spectators haven't really gained any particular skill. They certainly aren't any healthier. *All the work was done by the team.* Someone once said that a football game is 30,000 people, desperately needing exercise, watching 11 people, desperately needing rest, make a success out of their lives. The Lord's plan for the church service is very different from this idea.

In a biblical model of the local church, the members are not in the stands; they are *on the field.* They are the players. The pastor of the church is like the head coach. The elders, deacons, and church leaders are like assistant coaches—offensive and defensive—and there are also special teams, coordinators, and trainers. The stands are filled with the lost and seeking world. When a person is "drafted" into the kingdom, they join the team. It's the job of the coaches and staff to prepare the team to play according to their unique talents, abilities, and skills. The problem today is that most believers are content with sitting on the bench. They will never discover their purpose and fulfill their destiny until they get off the bench and *into the game*!

> "From whom the whole body, joined and knit together by what *every joint supplies*, according to the effective working by which *every part does its share*, causes growth of the body for the edifying of itself in love" (Ephesians 4:16).

> *Most of the time we discover our gifts and find our purpose as we take action to serve wherever we are needed.*

The Church Grows When the Body Serves

It is only when *every joint supplies* what it was designed to supply and *every part does its share* that the local church can grow. In Scripture, Paul's favorite illustration for the local church is that of a human body made up of various parts. Each part is designed to do something. In our bodies, if one part does not supply what it was designed to supply, we typically end up at the doctor's office. Imbalance or absence of supply in the physical body is the definition of sickness, injury, or physical handicap. The key is that each part has a place. Each part has a particular function. If each part does not give its supply and do its share, the body will not grow in a healthy manner. Notice this same passage in the New Living Translation,

> "He makes the whole body fit together perfectly. As each part does its own special work, it helps the other parts grow, so that the whole body is healthy and growing and full of love" (Ephesians 4:16 NLT).

Your Gifts Help You Find Your Place

Let's review for a moment. There are good works that God has planned for you to perform (Ephesians 2:10). You have been designed by God to perform these works. God has equipped you with natural and spiritual gifts to guide you into your place and fulfill your purpose. All of these things are realized as we serve one another within the visible body of Christ, which is the local church. The question most of us must answer, then, is how do I discover my gifts and find my places of service in the local church?

Gifts Are Discovered by Action, Not by Prayer and Study Alone

Studying the Scripture and praying are very important components in our spiritual development. Study helps us learn about gifts, purpose, and the importance of serving. Prayer opens our heart to the Lord and makes us spiritually sensitive to the Holy Spirit's leadings. But most of the time, we discover our gifts and find our purpose as we take action to serve wherever we are needed. Most believers will do a variety of things in the local church before they find their "sweet spot."

When I first began serving the Lord as a teenager, I had no idea what spiritual gifts were—much less which gifts the Lord had given *me*. But I loved Jesus and I loved His church. When the pastor announced a workday to clean the church building, I showed up. When there was a need in the children's ministry for a helper to keep the kids from climbing out of the windows (figuratively), I met the need. There was not a formal process for becoming a member in our church at the time, much less a program to develop church volunteers. I just had a love for Jesus and a desire to do whatever was needed. A few years later, the youth leader of our local church asked me to lead a team of young people in "street witnessing," which is the equivalent of confronting people with their need for Jesus as they endeavor to walk in and out of stores or visit the local library and post office.

I didn't feel particularly *gifted* at anything I was asked to do, and I was only moderately useful at some of the areas in which I served. Manual labor and handing out crackers to preschoolers was not my forté. But as I served wherever I was needed, I began to notice certain things about myself. When I went street witnessing, for instance, I was never successful in leading a single person to Christ. But every time I tried to share Jesus with someone who was already saved, we ended up in a conversation about the Bible. I'd spend more time teaching my teammates about God's Word than actually talking to seekers about salvation. Sometimes when I was only assigned to pass out crackers and monitor bathroom breaks in kid's church, I'd end up at the front of class giving the object lesson or filling in for the puppet shows. In almost every case, I found myself naturally teaching—even when I had no intention to do so. Later in Bible college, I studied the gifts of the Spirit and realized I had the gift of teaching.

Serving Jesus Will Always Require You to Do Things Outside Your "Gifting Zone"

Every one of the spiritual gifts the Lord has placed in my life I discovered by accident—as I was serving the Lord doing whatever needed to be done. This is why it is more important to take action in serving now than it is to wait until you figure out what all your gifts are and wait for "openings" to begin using them. My work as a pastor still has a lot of requirements that I have very little natural or spiritual gifting to perform. I thank God every day for the great team of dedicated men and women who work with me to help me and cover my weaknesses! There will always be things I should do that are outside my gift zone, but are still important for me to do on some level. I do some of the things I *have* to do so I can do all of the things I was *born* to do!

DAY 3 EXERCISES

1. If Christianity were a football stadium, what part of the stadium should we be in?

_____

2. If you are not sure what to do in the church or how you are gifted, what should you do?

_____
_____
_____
_____

3. Gifts are discovered as we _____.

4. Write 1 Peter 4:8-11 below.

_____
_____
_____
_____
_____
_____
_____
_____
_____
_____
_____

DAY 4: TRUTHS ABOUT SERVICE

TEN IMPORTANT TRUTHS ABOUT SERVING THE BODY OF CHRIST

1. Serving is More than Volunteering

The term *volunteer* is a very good word. We use it to describe hall monitors in public schools, Earth Day workers, and blood donors. Our world needs good volunteers. You have likely been asked to volunteer dozens of times in your life, with varying degrees of satisfaction. I like the word *volunteer*, but I don't think it's the right word to use in the church. A volunteer is known as someone who offers to perform work for an organization without getting paid. This emphasizes the idea of doing something for nothing. Volunteers commonly have the attitude, "They better appreciate that I am doing this for free." Volunteers come when they can, work as long as they want, and leave when they please. This is understandable, since they are doing something for nothing.

The church of Jesus Christ does not need volunteers. When we as believers use our time, talents, and treasure to perform good works for the body of Christ, we are not just volunteering. We are *serving*.

> *A servant owes his master his life. We work in the world for pay. We serve in the church for love.*

On the night before He was crucified, Jesus met with His disciples one last time. After entering the room where their final meal together would be shared, it was obvious that someone was late. It was the custom of the time to have a *servant of the lowest rank* wash the feet of the guests *as they entered* a dining area. On this occasion, they had all been seated without the servant performing this customary task. Jesus, noticing the servant's absence, quietly rose from the table, filled a basin with water, and suddenly began washing and drying His disciples' feet. This was a job that was *far beneath* the One who created the very feet He was washing. It was so shocking that Peter resisted the experience at first.

After Jesus finished, He said, "Do you know what I have done to you? You call Me Teacher and Lord…for so I am. If I then, your Lord and Teacher, *have washed your feet*, you also ought to wash *one another's feet*. For I have given you an example, that you should do as I have done to you….If you know these things, blessed are you if you do them" (John 13:12-15, 17).

When we work in the church, we are not doing something for nothing. We are acting as servants of our Lord Jesus Christ. Our pay has already been received. We have been chosen by God, born again, washed from our sins, and given eternal life. We are not doing our church a favor. Our church is doing us a great honor by allowing us to take a place serving the body of Christ. Jesus washed your whole life with His precious blood. How do you repay Him? By washing His feet. The local church is the body of Christ. When you serve one another in the local church you are washing the feet of Jesus.

A servant owes his master his life. We work in the world for pay. We serve in the church for love. Don't ever volunteer for your church again. Become a servant of Jesus Christ, then do whatever tasks His body asks or needs you to do.

2. Take the Initiative to Begin Serving

Don't wait for someone to recruit you. If you don't have a leader in charge of developing and placing volunteers, approach various leaders, elders, and pastors and ask how you can help them. Find out what needs to be done in the church. Make yourself available to your small group leader, facilities director, music department, or ushering team. Do whatever they ask you to do. Nothing is beneath you—no matter how long you've known Christ or how much experience you've had in the past.

3. Practice Formal and Informal Serving

Most churches have formal systems to train and fill positions. If there are classes to take or membership requirements to meet before you can serve formally in your church, then begin them as soon as possible. A well-organized church will often want to train their members to prepare them for spiritual service. Don't complain about these requirements. If there are ways you can begin to help that are available immediately, but are not highly visible, jump in and start helping.

> "Whatever your hand finds to do, do it with [all] your might; for there is no work...in the grave where you are going" (Ecclesiastes 9:10).

Informal serving is doing whatever your hand finds to do, and doing it well! You don't have to finish a class or wait for a formal serving position in your church to begin. If you see trash on the ground, pick it up! If you notice someone hurting and in need of prayer, give them a call or take them out for coffee. If you see a visitor, greet them and make them feel loved. Offer to drive a single mother to church. Check up on a teenager you haven't seen in church for a while. Give your life away in service for the members of the body of Christ. All believers should seek both formal and informal avenues for serving the local church. Serving is a way of life. Begin today!

4. Servants Do Not Expose the Weaknesses of Others

> "Hatred stirs up strife, but love covers all sins" (Proverbs 10:12).

Serving with others can be challenging, especially when they are not as organized as you would like, or the leader seems unprepared. Very often God will place you in positions of service along with someone who agitates you. God isn't being mean. He uses these experiences to mature both of you! The Bible says that "As iron sharpens iron, so a man sharpens the countenance of his friend" (Proverbs 27:17). It is one of the best things in the world for your personal growth to serve under or alongside someone who rubs you the wrong way. This is sometimes the only way to "rub" the impatience, intolerance, critical judgments, and pride out of your flesh!

Sometimes the Lord will allow you to see the exposed weaknesses (or nakedness) of others. To be naked is to be exposed to shame or injury. When this occurs, God expects you to cover your brother or sister's nakedness, not expose it. This doesn't mean we are dishonest or hide illegal or immoral behaviors that endanger others, but it does mean that sometimes our fellow servants have weak spots that they need others to "cover."

The Prophet Noah was a great man. He was so honorable before the Lord that God chose him to save the human race from the flood of God's judgment. He was an astounding leader. But the Bible records that he was not perfect. Once, when Noah drank too much wine, he lay naked in a drunken stupor, exposing himself in his tent. When Noah's son entered the tent and saw his father's sin, he laughed mockingly, left the tent, and told his brothers. His other two sons, in a spirit of honor, picked up a robe and entered the tent walking slowly backwards, and covered their father. This act was greatly blessed by God, while the act of dishonor by the first son brought a curse upon his life (Genesis 9:22-25).

5. Be Excellent in Serving

"Do you see a man who excels in his work? He will stand before kings; he will not stand before unknown men" (Proverbs 22:29).

When you accept a role of serving in your church, give God your very best efforts. Read any materials you are asked to read. Show up on time and give your best. If you are going to be on vacation, or have an illness, call your leader or designated team member in advance so they can arrange to fill your spot. Don't promise you will do something and then leave it undone. If you tell someone you will call them, do it in a timely fashion. Leave when the work is done. Constantly look for ways to improve your serving capacities and gifts. Read good books about "customer service." Talk to others who you admire in serving ministries. Make it your goal to be the best you can be.

"Serve the Lord with gladness; come before His presence with singing" (Psalm 100:2).

God's church deserves your very best. Sometimes we grow weary from the pressures of life. Often the enemy will stir up family strife or problems just before we come to church and serve. But no matter what you may be going through personally, when you come to serve, make a decision to leave it in the parking lot. As you get out of your car, tap the doorframe of your car and say, "Lord, I leave everything here. I cast all of my cares upon You (1 Peter 5:7). I ask You to take my burdens, my sins, my mistakes, and all my negative emotions. I am serving Your body today. Take care of my problems as I take care of Your church. Help me to honor You as I serve You today." Watch the Lord work on your behalf as you offer your life in service to Him.

6. Learn to Receive Correction

Most of us don't like to be corrected. We like to think that we have it all together. But the only way to grow is to receive correction. The Bible says,

"He who hates correction *is stupid"* (Proverbs 12:1b).

"Poverty and shame will come to him who disdains correction, but he who regards a *rebuke* will be *honored"* (Proverbs 13:18).

"He who receives correction is prudent" (Proverbs 15:5b).

Those who lead will sometimes need to correct you. It's a part of the way God helps us to grow. Sometimes we may feel offended because of the way others correct us. Occasionally, we may be wrongfully corrected. When this occurs, it's a test for you. Avoid getting in the flesh. Take time to process what has happened. Think about what might have been right about the correction—even if the way you were corrected was offensive. The Bible says "A fool is quick-tempered, but a wise person stays calm when insulted" (Proverbs 12:16 NLT).

7. Address Conflicts Privately, Truthfully, Lovingly, and Honorably

I know that's a mouthful, but each word of the above statement is very important. When conflicts arise with others in the body of Christ, God expects us to deal with them—not bury them. There are guidelines in Scripture to properly handling conflicts that we need to follow.

> *When we nurse unresolved conflicts and allow them to fester, they cause a loss of joy, undermine our confidence in one another, and ultimately resurface in unhealthy and destructive ways.*

First of all, when conflicts arise, we need to keep our mouths shut. Most of the time, whatever we say in strong emotion is said unwisely. Pray before doing anything. Ask the Lord to give you wisdom. Secondly, go to the proper person in private. No one wants to be confronted or corrected in front of others. Jesus said that offenses are to be handled first in a one-on-one private meeting.

Thirdly, we need to balance the two important values of truth and love. Ephesians 4:15 tells us to practice "speaking the truth in love" to each other as we serve in the church. That means we cannot be so focused on being loving that we obscure the facts. Nor should we be so confrontational that the person we are dealing with feels unsupported and attacked. Finally we need to do all things in an honorable way. We need to honor God, others, ourselves, and the church body as a whole. Paul gives us a good prescription for confronting problems.

> "Brethren, if a man be overtaken in a fault, ye which are spiritual, restore such an one in the spirit of meekness; considering thyself, lest thou also be tempted"
> (Galatians 6:1 KJV).

8. Leave with Integrity and Honor

If you feel God is leading you to another area of service, or need time off for personal matters, give plenty of notice and help train your replacement. Give God your best and you will be greatly blessed. The way you leave a thing will determine how you enter the next thing. Never just "fade away" from your place in the local church. A person of integrity will be thoughtful and gracious in transition, always seeking to honor those he or she serves.

9. Don't Wait to Start Serving

There will rarely be a perfectly convenient time in your life to begin serving the local church. Life will see to it that natural responsibilities will fill your schedule. You and I must make time to serve the Lord. Now what I am going to say may sound intense, but stay with me on this.

There is very little in life that is more important than loving Jesus, loving your family, and loving your church. If God has given you spiritual and natural gifts that He will someday hold you accountable for, then what kinds of things in life could be more important than making room in your schedule to use them? There is never a convenient time to start attending church faithfully. There is never a convenient time to start obeying God with your tithes. Prayer and Bible study are almost never things that you have time for *before you begin to practice them.* Yet all of these things are absolutely essential to your personal growth and spiritual development.

10. Make Connections through Serving

When we serve the body, we need to open our hearts to one another. Don't just show up and perform the tasks. Get to know those with whom you are serving. Take some time with each other outside of church. Share meals together. Pray together. Learn and grow together. Remember that the local church is your spiritual family. When you serve with others, the Lord will make you sensitive to their needs and vice versa. Support one another. This honors God and strengthens the church family.

DAY 4 EXERCISES

1. This section explored ten truths about serving. List them here and note what you feel is most important about each.

   1._____
   2._____
   3._____
   4._____
   5._____
   6._____
   7._____
   8._____
   9._____
   10._____

2. What is the difference between volunteering and serving?

   _____
   _____

3. Why does God choose to put us in positions of service with people who may aggravate us?

   _____
   _____
   _____

4. The only way to grow is to _____.

5. What is the first thing we need to do when conflict arises?

   _____
   _____

CONCLUSION

FINDING YOUR PURPOSE: SERVING OUR WORLD

I was blessed to discover my purpose early in life. When I was sixteen years old, I had an encounter with God that changed the direction of my life. Having been raised in church, I was keenly aware of the importance of serving. My parents both worked diligently to provide for our family. We always attended weekly services and served in the church doing whatever the pastor and leaders needed to be done. Although I was born again at the age of nine, I was in a state of teenage rebellion—biding my time until I could graduate from high school and pursue a career as an actor. I resented all the time we had spent in church. I was tired of the selfless way our home was always open to others and how my parents had structured our lives around serving the body and sharing Jesus with everyone they knew. In my heart, I truly loved Jesus, but I was being pulled away by the world, my flesh, and the lies of the Devil.

On Halloween night 1980, I was leaving my house for a night of carefully premeditated "hell-raising" with some friends from school. As I was slipping out the door at sunset, my mom caught me leaving and gave me one of two choices: either I could stay home and help pass out candy and Bible tracts (little pamphlets about Jesus), or I could go to the "harvest party" our church youth group had planned. After a few minutes of futile teenage ranting, I reluctantly got in the car with my dad to go to the church party. I was not into it *at all*. The event took place in a big barn out in the country. For the entire evening, I was defiant and resistant to what I thought was a lame and pointless Christian activity.

After an hour or so of games, we were all rounded up for the big event of the night—an hour of preaching by a guest evangelist. Sitting as close to the exit as I could possibly get, I determined to sneak out as soon as the opportunity arose. The man who stood to speak that night immediately caught my attention. He spoke with authority and a passion that stirred something deep inside me. He announced that God had spoken to him that very day, and instructed him to preach about the call of God to the ministry. "This message is only for a few that are here tonight. You have had other plans for your life. You have been counting the days until you can escape from your home and live for yourself. But God told me to tell you tonight that He has called you to give your life serving Him." For the next hour I sat and listened as the preacher talked about the price that Jesus requires of those who enter full-time ministry. He said that if God calls you to the ministry, you have to be willing to give your life to the service of His church. He said that most believers are called to be faithful church members, working in the world to support their families. But some are called to give more. "And," he continued, "the Lord told me that some of you are here tonight."

At that moment, something happened inside my spirit. I felt a massive shift occur deep in my chest. Suddenly, it was as if the roof of the barn disappeared. As tears of struggle, resistance, and surrender coursed down my face, I saw in my spirit a massive hand descend out of the roof of that barn and a pointed finger bump me in the chest. And I heard these words resound through my soul, "I have called YOU to My ministry!" At that moment, everything changed. In a moment, my short sixteen years of life flashed before my mind and suddenly everything I had felt since I was a child made sense. I had always seen myself *on a stage communicating and influencing people*. As a little boy, I would jump up on a rock and begin talking as if the whole world was listening. I had always thought I was supposed to be *an actor*. But instantly I knew that my purpose in life was to stand before people and preach God's Word.

Before I could mentally resist this experience, I found myself jumping to my feet and walking forward toward the preacher. The grace of God pulled me forward. It was as if I had no choice in the matter. I would either surrender the purpose of God for my life, or live the rest of my life in total rebellion to Him. That night He changed my heart by showing me my purpose. Over thirty years have passed since I discovered my purpose. Pursuing it has required everything I've had. I've given my youth, my voice, my mind, and my life's work to following that Voice and building His church. I have made a thousand mistakes. I have failed Him too many times to count. It has been incredibly hard. It has been all-consuming, and at times I have felt *completely consumed*. But I wouldn't have had it any other way. It has been a wonderful honor and great adventure to be a servant of the church of Jesus Christ. Following Jesus' purposes for me has transformed my life. They are still transforming me.

David Livingstone, the famous missionary and African explorer, once said, "If a commission by an earthly king is considered an honor, how can a commission by a heavenly King be considered a sacrifice?"[24] There is a King in heaven. He is the Creator of all things and the One who put you on this planet. He has designed you with a purpose. You will not find peace in your life until you surrender to this King. He loves you. He is calling you to His purpose. He sent His Son to find you, redeem you, and transform your life. Don't settle for anything less.

> *You are not an accident. You were designed on purpose, with a purpose, and for a purpose.*

---

24. Quote by David Livingstone, Public Domain.

FINDING MY PURPOSE

1. Write a "Life Sentence." If you could state your driving purpose in life in a single sentence, what would it be? Often the statement begins with "My purpose is..." Take out a note pad and begin completing that sentence. Write as many sentences as you can as fast as you can without taking time to think too much about your answers. Keep writing until you write something that rings an emotional "bell" inside you. You may cry or experience some type of emotional recognition when you finally write something that is close to your life's definite major purpose(s). Once you identify it, write your major purpose here.

_____

_____

_____

2. Time Machine. Imagine that you are on your deathbed and you know you will be passing away (painlessly) within twelve hours. As you reflect upon the life you lived, what do you need to have done to feel peace about the life you are leaving behind? What do you want to have accomplished and achieved—academically, vocationally, personally, athletically, etc...?

_____

_____

_____

- You're still in your future, what things would you want to have done for others? This would include things you would like to have given away and volunteered; as well as ways you would want to have helped or blessed family, friends, the people of God and His church?

_____

_____

_____

- What places or situations do you want to have seen or visited in your lifetime? Be specific.

_____

_____

_____

- What do you want to have earned, saved, or set aside for your children, church, or others, materially?

_____

_____

_____

- What do you want to have learned or studied in your lifetime?

_____

_____

_____

- What skills, habits, talents, or disciplines do you want to have mastered?

_____
_____
_____
_____

- What do you want to have achieved personally? This relates to your struggles in character development, your relationships with others, and your spiritual growth?

_____
_____

- Ask yourself, "What do I truly need to have done, experienced, or become in order to be ready to die happy?"

_____
_____
_____
_____

3. Prepare for the Big Meeting. Read Romans 14:12 and 2 Corinthians 5:10. In this exercise, imagine that you have left the earth; at last, you are standing toe-to-toe with Jesus Christ for your big meeting. In this meeting, you and Jesus are going to discuss your life, including the weaknesses you neglected, the opportunities you missed, as well as the accomplishments you achieved for His glory. What do you want to talk to Jesus about? What do you want to be able to say you did with your body while you were on the earth? What do you think He will want to talk with you about? Make a list of the topics you believe will be most important to Jesus in that meeting. What do you think will not be very important? List each. After you have done this, go back and look at your lists.

_____
_____
_____
_____
_____
_____

- Ask yourself this question, "How much of my life and/or time am I spending on the things that will be on the big meeting's 'agenda'"?

- Finally go back and review all the exercises in this section. The lists, paragraphs, and statements you have created are a roadmap for the transformation of your life. Unless God directs you otherwise, beginning today, and for the rest of your life, you need to work every day on making your life reflect the things you just wrote about. As life passes, you may add to this list; you may also edit it or qualify some of the items you have written. That's fine. Life is fluid and may be bent at any time in the direction of God's newly revealed plan for your life.

ABOUT THE AUTHOR

John R. Carter is committed to helping people reach their potential in life through spiritual transformation. Known for his engaging and practical teaching style, he is the senior pastor of Abundant Life Christian Center, a culturally diverse church located in Syracuse, NY. He is the founder and president of Mercy Works, a charitable organization that creatively meets the practical needs of distressed urban communities. John and his wife, Lisa, have three sons—Jordan, Joshua, and Caleb.

Find out more at www.transformedlifenow.com

MORE PRODUCTS BY JOHN R. CARTER

Taking Emotional Responsibility

Emotions—what do you do with them? Follow them or deny them? Express them or suppress them? One thing is clear. Emotions are part of who we are. They are a gift from God.

In this six-part series, *Taking Emotional Responsibility*, Pastor John Carter reveals how our emotions were designed to motivate us into God's best for our life. Learn how to manage and process your emotions responsibly and in a way that causes you to walk in victory and lead a productive life, rather than a destructive one. Take charge over your emotions today so they don't take charge over you!

Vision Velocity

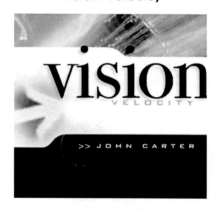

Our God is a God of Vision! He never creates anyone or anything, without first considering the final outcome. If you are a child of God, you too should have vision. In order to move forward in creating your vision, you must first consider the best path to follow.

In this eight part series, *Vision Velocity*, Pastor John Carter walks you through the steps you must take to define and develop your vision in order to reach your highest potential in life. If you are ready to move up to a higher place, then get this series and get ready to set your course to create a final outcome that will surely bring success!

Find these and other products by John R. Carter at www.alcclife.org/store

5 Fold Media, LLC is a Christ-centered media company. Our desire is to produce lasting fruit in writing, music, art, and creative gifts.

"To Establish and Reveal"
For more information visit:
www.5foldmedia.com

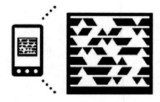

Use your mobile device to scan the tag above and visit our website.
Get the free app: http://gettag.mobi

Like 5 Fold Media on Facebook, follow us on Twitter!